OUT OF
THE BEST
BOOKS

OUT OF THE BEST BOOKS

AN ANTHOLOGY OF LITERATURE

VOLUME 5: COMMUNITY RESPONSIBILITY

Bruce B. Clark and Robert K. Thomas

1969

Published by Deseret Book Company, Salt Lake City, Utah

Library of Congress No. 68-56386

Copyright 1969
by
DESERET BOOK COMPANY

LITHOGRAPHED BY

IN THE UNITED STATES OF AMERICA

To all the Relief Society sisters,
who have been so loyal to the Cultural Refinement program
during the past six years

Preface

The Cultural Refinement program of lessons using *Out of the Best Books* as a basic text has now functioned for five years in the Relief Society organization of the Church. Volume 5, to be used during 1969-70, will complete the sixth year of what was planned from the beginning as a six-year program. Volume 1, used in 1964-65 and 1965-66, stressed the individual and human values as seen through literature. Volumes 2 and 3, used in 1966-67 and 1967-68, widened the horizon, drawing for enrichment materials upon the related arts in addition to literature, and emphasizing ideals and problems in marriage, parenthood, and family relationships. Now the closing two years of the program, Volume 4 for 1968-69 and Volume 5 for 1969-70, widen the scope still further, stressing our activities and responsibilities in community life and the world in which we live.

As pointed out a year ago, no individual or family can exist in isolation. In many significant ways a person's first responsibility is to himself and to his family, but we also need to function meaningfully with other people—as friends and neighbors, as church workers, and as citizens of the community, the nation, and the world. Moreover, in all of these things we need to find a happy balance between work, recreation, relaxation, spirituality, and cultural fulfillment. Therefore, each lesson in the Cultural Refinement program for this year will focus upon community involvement that is meaningful, wholesome, and well balanced.

When I was first approached seven years ago and invited to help develop a strengthened, enriched literature program for the Relief Society, I felt that two things should be stressed: first, that the women of the Relief Society should individually read the selections of literature and then in a group discuss them rather than have lectures, however good these might be, on works that most of the women had not read; and second, that the focus in discussing the literature should be upon the rich insights that literature can give into the problems, values, and ideals of living, because such an approach would be more valid and valuable than any other for a study of literature within the Church.

In the Preface to Volume 3 in 1967 I tried to summarize our goals in these volumes as follows: "The emphasis is upon the works of literature themselves rather than upon authors' lives or historical background although pertinent biographical and historical facts are given as needed for interpretation. This emphasis on the work itself is intended to encourage stimulating discussion and exchange of ideas with all the insight into life and life's values that selections from the world's great literature can yield. Also, continuing concern is given to harmonizing literature with the Gospel, permitting a rich correlation between the ideals of our cultural heritage and the ideals of our religion. . . . At its best, literature is concerned with building faith and championing spiritual values—and with opposing and exposing selfishness, materialism, shallowness, and all things harmful to human personality or destructive in human relationships. . . . As we approach another volume it is also good to remind ourselves that reading a work of literature is a beginning and not an end. It opens doors rather than closes them. When we finish reading a selection we should be left thinking, not with all questions answered, but with sufficient insight that we are just a little better prepared to meet life's challenges and achieve life's eternal goals. . . . As we participate in the cultural enrichment program of the Church, we should remember that the program will be fully successful only if we carry it into our homes, sharing the wonder and wisdom and beauty of good literature and art, as well as their delights, with our families. . . . The principal idea behind this series of books is that the best way to study literature is to read it—that the work of literature itself is more important than anything that can be said about it, including all that we have said in our analytical discussions. So, readers, don't let anything stand between you and your personal experience with the literature itself."

Now as we move into the final year of our five volumes and six-year program, Brother Thomas and I join in expressing our appreciation that we have been privileged to write these books and lessons. For us it has been an extraordinary experience through the past six years. How successful we have been in developing a rich cultural program for the families of the Church, only the readers of these volumes can know. We hope we have been successful in opening doors to works of literature that have enriched your lives. If this has been so, and particularly if you or your associates have had any especially meaningful experiences through these volumes, we invite you to write us at Brigham Young University and tell us of your responses and experiences. Once again we thank you, the Relief Society, and the Church for the privilege of preparing these books for you.

Bruce B. Clark
June, 1969

A Note about the Authors:

Bruce B. Clark, who has written the preface and sections 2, 4, and 6 of this fifth volume, has been a teacher at Brigham Young University since 1950, where he served from 1960 to 1965 as Chairman of the English Department and currently is Professor of English and Dean of the College of Humanities. Widely known as a teacher and educational administrator, he has been listed since 1962 in *Who's Who in America*. Within the L.D.S. Church he has held many positions, including service as a bishop twice and as a high councilor four times.

Robert K. Thomas, who has written sections 1, 3, 5, and 7 of this volume, has been at Brigham Young University since 1951, where he too is a Professor of English and has had a distinguished career as a teacher and administrator. For several years he served as Director of the B.Y.U. Honors Program, then in 1967 became Assistant Academic Vice-President, and in 1968 was appointed Academic Vice-President at Brigham Young University. He too has been a bishop and high councilor in the L.D.S. Church and is currently serving as a counselor in the B.Y.U. Eighth Stake presidency.

Acknowledgments

Selections under copyright are reprinted by permission and courtesy of publishers indicated below:

The Atlantic Monthly: for "Indispensable Opposition" by Walter Lippmann, by The Atlantic Monthly Company, Boston, Mass. Reprinted with permission.

Mortimer J. Adler and Institute for Philosophical Research: for "What Makes a Great Book," reprinted from *Great Ideas from the Great Books*, by Mortimer J. Adler. Copyright 1961, 1963 by Mortimer J. Adler.

Brandt & Brandt: for "The Devil and Daniel Webster" by Stephen Vincent Benet, from *The Selected Works of Stephen Vincent Benet*, published by Holt, Rinehart and Winston, Inc. Copyright 1936 by Stephen Vincent Benet. Copyright renewed (c) 1965 by Thomas C. Benet, Rachel Benet Lewis, Stephanie B. Mahin.

The John Day Company, Inc., Publishers: for "The Importance of Loafing" by Lin Yutang, reprinted from *The Importance of Living* by Lin Yutang. Copyright 1937 by The John Day Company, Inc.

Doubleday & Company: for "Great Possessions" by David Grayson, from *Great Possessions*. Copyright 1917 by Doubleday & Company, Inc. Reprinted by permission of the publisher.

Dr. Dale D. Drain: for "What Is Liberty?" by Woodrow Wilson.

Edward D. Fales, Jr.: for "Can You Get Along with Your In-Laws" by Edward D. Fales.

Harper & Row, Publishers, Incorporated: for "Mark Twain's Family Letters," ed. Dixon Wecter, from *The Love Letters of Mark Twain*. Copyright 1947, 1946 by The Mark Twain Company. Reprinted by permission of Harper & Row, Publishers.

Holt, Rinehart and Winston, Inc.: for "After Apple-Picking" by Robert Frost, from *Complete Poems of Robert Frost*. Copyright 1930, 1939 by Holt, Rinehart and Winston, Inc. Copyright (c) 1958 by Robert Frost. Copyright (c) 1967 by Lesley Frost Ballantine.

Holt, Rinehart and Winston, Inc.: for "Oven Bird" and "Stopping by the Woods on a Snowy Evening" by Robert Frost. From *Complete Poems of Robert Frost.* Copyright 1916, 1923 by Holt, Rinehart and Winston, Inc. Copyright 1944, 1951 by Robert Frost. Reprinted by permission of Holt, Rinehart and Winston, Inc.

Little, Brown and Company: for "A Wreath for Miss Totten" by Hortense Calisher, from *In the Absence of Angels.* Copyright 1951 by Hortense Calisher.

The Macmillan Company: for "The Secret Heart" by Robert P. Tristram Coffin, from *Strange Holiness.* Copyright 1935 by the Macmillan Company, renewed 1963 by Margaret Coffin Halvosa.

Jean E. Mizer: for "Cipher in the Snow," reprinted by permission of the author and the National Education Association from the *N.E.A. Journal* for November 1964, Volume LIII, pp. 8-10.

The Overstreets: for "Keeping Mentally Alive" by H. A. Overstreet.

Random House, Inc., and Alfred A. Knopf, Inc.: for "The Life of Ma Parker" by Katherine Mansfield, reprinted from *The Short Stories of Katherine Mansfield.* Copyright 1922 by Alfred A. Knopf, Inc., and renewed 1948 by John M. Murry.

Random House, Inc. & Alfred A. Knopf, Inc.; for "Neighbor Rosicky" by Willa Cather, from *Obscure Destinies,* published by Random House, Inc. & Alfred A. Knopf, Inc.

Charles Scribner's Sons: for "Haircut" by Ring Lardner, reprinted from *The Love Nest and Other Stories* by Ring Lardner. Copyright 1925 by Ellis A. Lardner; renewal copyright 1953.

Science: for "Mother of Comptons" by Milton M. S. Mayer, from *Scientific Monthly* for November 1938, Volume 47, pp. 458-461.

Jesse Stuart: for "Another April" by Jesse Stuart.

Mrs. James Thurber (Helen Thurber): for "The Secret Life of Walter Mitty" by James Thurber, reprinted from *My World—and Welcome to It,* published by Harcourt, Brace and World. Originally printed in *The New Yorker.* Copyright (c) 1942 by James Thurber.

The Viking Press, Inc.: for "First Lesson" by Irwin Edman, reprinted from *Philosopher's Quest* by Irwin Edman. Copyright 1947 by Irwin Edman.

TABLE OF CONTENTS

Page

Section 1: The Meaning of Freedom, by Robert K. Thomas — 1
   Introductory Comments — 3
   From "The Hind and the Panther" by John Dryden — 5
      Comment on "The Hind and the Panther" — 5
   "The Indispensable Opposition" Walter Lippmann — 6
      Comment on "The Indispensable Opposition" — 8
   "What Is Liberty?" by Woodrow Wilson — 9
      Comment on "What Is Liberty?" — 10
   "Independence" by Henry David Thoreau — 12
      Comment on "Independence" — 12
   "The Slave" by James Oppenheim — 14
      Comment on "The Slave" — 14
   "The Bride Comes to Yellow Sky" by Stephen Crane — 16
      Comment on "The Bride Comes to Yellow Sky" — 25

Section 2: The Role of Education, by Bruce B. Clark — 29
   "The Girl in White" illustration — 31
   Introductory Comments — 33
      Comment on "What Makes a Great Book?" — 37
   "What Makes a Great Book?" by Mortimer J. Adler — 37

Comment on "Cipher in the Snow"	39
"Cipher in the Snow" by Jean E. Mizer	39
Comment on "Professor Agassiz and 'A Great Teacher's Method'"	42
"A Great Teacher's Method" by Samuel H. Scudder	42
Comment on "Socrates and the Dialogues of Plato"	46
From "Plato's 'Symposium'"	47
From "Book X of Plato's 'Republic'"	49
Comment on Edman's "First Lesson"	53
"First Lesson" by Irwin Edman	54
Selections from the Writings of the Author	59
Seven Qualities of an Educated Person	59
The Faces of Anger	60
Excerpts from "The Challenge of Teaching"	62
Comment on "The Fish, the Man, and the Spirit"	68
From "The Fish, the Man, and the Spirit" by Leigh Hunt	68
Comment on "He Ate and Drank the Precious Words"	70
"He Ate and Drank the Precious Words" by Emily Dickinson	70
Section 3: The Problem of Communication, by Robert K. Thomas	71
"Advice to a Young Artist" illustration	73
Introductory Comments	75
"The Secret Heart" by Robert P. Tristram Coffin	77
Discussion of "The Secret Heart"	77
"Another April" by Jesse Stuart	79
Discussion of "Another April"	85

"From the Autocrat of the Breakfast Table"
by Oliver Wendell Holmes ----------------------- 87
    Discussion of "The Autocrat of the Breakfast Table" ----- 88
"Can You Get Along With Your In-Laws?"
    by Edward D. Fales, Jr. ------------------------- 89
        Young Wives Helped ----------------------- 89
        Advice for Daughters-in-Law ------------------- 90
        Advice for Parents-in-Law --------------------- 90
        Finances Cause Headaches --------------------- 91
    Discussion of "Can You Get Along With
        Your In-Laws?" ---------------------------- 92
Mark Twain's Family Letters------------------------- 93
"Neighbor Rosicky" by Willa Cather ------------------- 101
    Discussion of "Neighbor Rosicky" ------------------- 126

Section 4: The Place of Entertainment, by Bruce B. Clark ------ 129
Introductory Comments ---------------------------- 131
"The Devil and Daniel Webster" by Stephen Vincent Benet -- 134
    Discussion of "The Devil and Daniel Webster" --------- 145
"Haircut" by Ring Lardner -------------------------- 148
    Discussion of "Haircut"-------------------------- 157
"Baker's Blue-Jay Yarn" by Mark Twain----------------- 160
    Discussion of "Baker's Blue-jay Yarn"---------------- 164
Charles Lamb and the Informal Essay ------------------ 166
    From "Poor Relations -------------------------- 168
    From "A Chapter on Ears" ----------------------- 168
Section 5: The Necessity of Service, by Robert K. Thomas------- 169
"The Blind Girl" illustration ------------------------- 171

Introduction ----------------------------------- 173
"Song of Myself" by Walt Whitman ------------------ 176
    Discussion of "Song of Myself" -------------------- 179
"To Fight Aloud" by Emily Dickinson ------------------ 181
    Discussion of "To Fight Aloud" -------------------- 181
"A Wreath for Miss Totten" by Hortense Calisher -------- 183
    Discussion of "A Wreath for Miss Totten" ----------- 191
"Concord Hymn" by Ralph Waldo Emerson -------------- 193
    Discussion of "Concord Hymn" -------------------- 193
"An Airman's Letter," Anonymous --------------------- 195
    Discussion of "An Airman's Letter" ---------------- 197
"Mother of Comptons" by Milton S. Mayer -------------- 198
    Discussion of "Mother of Comptons" --------------- 202
"The Story of Jephthah's Daughter" -------------------- 204
    Discussion of "The Story of Jephthah's Daughter" ------- 206

Section 6: The Power of Work and the Use of Leisure,
by Bruce B. Clark ----------------------------------- 207
"Sunday Afternoon on the Island of La Grande Jatte" ------- 211
Introductory Comments ------------------------------ 213
From the "Essays of Thomas Carlyle" ------------------ 215
    Discussion of Excerpts from the "Essays of
        Thomas Carlyle" ------------------------- 218
From "The Importance of Loafing" by Lin Yutang --------- 220
    Discussion of "The Importance of Loafing" ---------- 224
"After Apple-Picking" by Robert Frost ------------------ 226

Discussion of "After Apple-Picking" ---------------- 227
"Life of Ma Parker" by Katherine Mansfield -------------- 229
    Discussion of "Life of Ma Parker" ------------------ 234
"The Secret Life of Walter Mitty" by James Thurber ------- 236
    Discussion of "The Secret Life of Walter Mitty" -------- 240
From "The Roots of Honor" by John Ruskin ------------ 242
    Discussion of "The Roots of Honor" ---------------- 243

Section 7: The Thrill and Reward of Participation,
    by Robert K. Thomas ------------------------------ 245
Introduction --- 247
"The Oven Bird" by Robert Frost -------------------- 250
    Discussion of "The Oven Bird" -------------------- 250
"Life" by George Herbert --------------------------- 252
    Discussion of "Life" ----------------------------- 252
"Keeping Mentally Alive" by H. A. Overstreet ------------ 254
    Discussion of "Keeping Mentally Alive" -------------- 258
From "Great Possessions" by David Grayson ------------- 260
    Discussion of "Great Possessions" ------------------ 264
"Stopping by Woods on a Snowy Evening" by Robert Frost -- 266
    Discussion of "Stopping by Woods on a Snowy Evening" - 266
"The Canterbury Pilgrims" by Nathaniel Hawthorne -------- 268
    Discussion of "The Canterbury Pilgrims" ------------ 275

SECTION ONE

The Meaning of Freedom

by Robert K. Thomas

THE MEANING OF FREEDOM

"My soul standeth fast in that liberty in the which God hath made us free."—Book of Mormon (Al. 61:9.)

Introductory Comments

So much has been written and spoken about freedom that we must be at some pains to define what we are trying to express when we plead for liberty or rail against bondage. At its most basic level, man's freedom to choose, his "agency," is fundamental to all that he does. We are told in 2 Nephi 2:26 that the redemption of Christ makes men "free forever, knowing good from evil, to act for themselves and not be acted upon. . . ." It is this liberty that the New Testament enjoins us to "stand fast" in.

John Dryden, the English poet and dramatist, asks us to remember the heavenly source of our freedom in some well-known lines from "The Hind and the Panther." Written nearly three hundred years ago, this poem still speaks with quiet insistence to a continuing problem: the necessity for man to establish his relationships with others on a basis worthy of the God-like image in which he is made.

In his essay "The Indispensable Opposition," Walter Lippmann presents convincing contemporary arguments for what is a cardinal principle in the church. When Lehi explains to his son Jacob why there "must needs be . . . an opposition in all things" (2 Nephi 2:11) we are quite prepared for Mr. Lippmann's plea that other points of view are necessary and not merely a matter of our tolerance. It simply is not possible to understand a concept unless we can define it in terms of an opposite.

Woodrow Wilson, the twenty-eighth President of the United States, shifts our attention from definition of individual liberty to a concern for social freedom. In his short statement we focus on the adjustment which we must make individually if the "machinery" of society is to function smoothly and efficiently.

Poems by Henry David Thoreau and James Oppenheim recall us to awareness of how crucial inner peace and personal integrity are in giving meaning to liberty, and Stephen Crane's "The Bride Comes to Yellow Sky" lets us participate in a situation which illuminates the fundamental part that self-control plays in a developing sense of freedom. The "liberty in which God has made us free" is never the liberty of indulgence, and it cannot be guaranteed by governmental force. Only to the extent that we can subject ourselves to the truth can the truth make us free.

From the Hind and the Panther
by John Dryden

Of all the tyrannies of human kind
The worst is that which persecutes the mind.
Let us but weigh at what offence we strike;
'Tis but because we cannot think alike.
In punishing of this we overthrow
The laws of nations and of nature too.
Beasts are the subjects of tyrannic sway,
Where still the stronger on the weaker prey;
Man only of a softer mould is made,
Not for his fellows' ruin but their aid:
Created kind, beneficent and free,
The noble image of the Deity.

Comment on
"The Hind and the Panther"

John Dryden (1631-1700) was one of the most versatile of English poets. He seemed to be at home in dramatic, satiric, narrative, and didactic poetry. He was also one of the greatest of English translators and one of the most accomplished writers of English prose. At the time of his death, he was the undisputed king of English letters.

In 1686, during the first year of the reign of James II, Dryden was converted to Roman Catholicism, and "The Hind and the Panther," his most famous religious poem, is a defense of his new faith. The Hind apparently represents the Roman Catholic Church, while the Panther stands for the Church of England. The lines we quote above are from Part I of this long account of persecution and religious intolerance.

It seems to Dryden to be particularly ironic that pagan sects were often more merciful to those that disagreed with them than Christian churches. Unless we are free from the prejudice which would force others to agree with us, we are probably not prepared to persuade others that our vision of the Truth is superior.

The Indispensable Opposition

by Walter Lippmann

Were they pressed hard enough, most men would probably confess that political freedom—that is to say, the right to speak freely and to act in opposition—is a noble ideal rather than a practical necessity. As the case for freedom is generally put today, the argument lends itself to this feeling. It is made to appear that, whereas each man claims his freedom as a matter of right, the freedom he accords to other men is a matter of toleration. Thus, the defense of freedom of opinion tends to rest not on its substantial, beneficial, and indispensable consequences, but on a somewhat eccentric, a rather vaguely benevolent, attachment to an abstraction.

It is all very well to say with Voltaire, "I wholly disapprove of what you say, but will defend to the death your right to say it," but as a matter of fact most men will not defend to the death the rights of other men: if they disapprove sufficiently what other men say, they will somehow suppress those men if they can.

So, if this is the best that can be said for liberty of opinion, that a man must tolerate his opponents because everyone has a "right" to say what he pleases, then we shall find that liberty of opinion is a luxury, safe only in pleasant times when men can be tolerant because they are not deeply and vitally concerned.

Yet, actually, as a matter of historic fact, there is a much stronger foundation for the great constitutional right of freedom of speech, and as a matter of practical human experience there is a much more compelling reason for cultivating the habits of free men.

We take, it seems to me, a naively self-righteous view when we argue as if the right of our opponents to speak were something that we protect because we are magnanimous, noble, and unselfish. The compelling reason why, if liberty of opinion did not exist, we should have to invent it, why it will eventually have to be restored in all civilized countries where it is now suppressed, is that we must protect the right of our opponents to speak because we must hear what they have to say.

We miss the whole point when we imagine that we tolerate the freedom of our political opponents as we tolerate a howling baby next door, as we put up with the blasts from our neighbor's radio because we are too peaceable to heave a brick through the window. If this were all there is to freedom of opinion, that we are too good-natured or too timid to do anything about our opponents and critics except to let them talk, it would be difficult to say whether we are tolerant because we are magnanimous or because we are lazy, because we have strong principles or because we lack serious convictions, whether we have the hospitality of an inquiring mind or the indifference of an empty mind. And so, if we truly wish to understand why freedom is necessary in a civilized society, we must begin by realizing that, because freedom of discussion improves our own opinions, the liberties of other men are our own vital necessity.

We are much closer to the essence of the matter, not when we quote Voltaire, but when we go to the doctor and pay him to ask us the most embarrassing questions and to prescribe the most disagreeable diet. When we pay the doctor to exercise complete freedom of speech about the cause and cure of our stomachache, we do not look upon ourselves as tolerant and magnanimous, and worthy to be admired by ourselves. We have enough common sense to know that if we threaten to put the doctor in jail because we do not like the diagnosis and the prescription it will be unpleasant for the doctor, to be sure, but equally unpleasant for our own stomachache. That is why even the most ferocious dictator would rather be treated by a doctor who was free to think and speak the truth than by his own Minister of Propaganda. For there is a point, the point at which things really matter, where the freedom of others is no longer a question of their right but of our own need.

The point at which we recognize this need is much higher in some men than in others. The totalitarian rulers think they do not need the freedom of an opposition: they exile, imprison, or shoot their opponents. We have concluded on the basis of practical experience, which goes back to Magna Carta and beyond, that we need the opposition. We pay the opposition salaries out of the public treasury.

In so far as the usual apology for freedom of speech ignores this experience, it becomes abstract and eccentric rather than concrete and human. The emphasis is generally put on the right to speak, as if all that mattered were that the doctor should be free to go out into the park and explain to the vacant air why I have a stomachache. Surely that is a miserable caricature of the great civic right which men have bled and died for. What really matters is that the doctor should tell me what ails me, that I should listen to him; that if I do not like what he says I should be free to call in another doctor; and that then the first doctor should have to listen to the second doctor; and that out of all the speaking and listening, the give-and-take of opinions, the truth should be arrived at.

This is the creative principle of freedom of speech, not that it is a system for the tolerating of error, but that it is a system for finding the truth. It may not produce the truth, or the whole truth all the time, or often, or in some cases ever. But if the truth can be found, there is no other system which will normally and habitually find so much truth. Until we have thoroughly understood this principle, we shall not know why we must value our liberty, or how we can protect and develop it.

Comment on "The Indispensable Opposition"

Walter Lippmann (1899 -   ) was a member of the famous Class of 1910 at Harvard University. Since his graduation, he has had a distinguished career as a journalist, editor, and author. Mr. Lippmann's widely ranging interests in the fields of politics, diplomacy, morality, and freedom have borne fruit in many articles, essays, and books. Probably his most influential work is *A Preface to Morals,* first published in 1929. The essay from which this excerpt was taken appeared in *The Atlantic Monthly* for August, 1939.

For members of the Church, Mr. Lippmann's insistence on the *necessity* of opposition strikes an immediately responsive chord. In the second chapter of 2 Nephi we find the following verse:

> For it must needs be, that there is an opposition in all things. If not so, my first-born in the wilderness, righteousness could not be brought to pass, neither wickedness, neither holiness nor misery, neither good nor bad. Wherefore, all things must needs be a compound in one: . . . (2 Ne. 2:11)

The context in which this verse is found makes it clear that man must exercise his God-given agency in order that the purposes of the Lord might be totally fulfilled. If Mr. Lippmann's case lacks the sanction provided for it by the Book of Mormon, it demonstrates his instinct for the Truth.

The illustration used in this selection—the doctor who must tell us what we do not want to hear—is a particularly apt one. Not only does this reflect general experience, it strikes through all the sham and pretense with which we have insulated ourselves and touches a concern so basic that it is shared by all men.

Reading Mr. Lippmann's essay in the light shed upon it by 2 Nephi, we become aware of the creative part that can be played by opposition. We can come to an appreciation of righteousness by noting its opposite, and we can learn the value of liberty by experiencing bondage. Yet most negative experiences cost more than we can afford to pay. If we can only learn from the plight of others, we can avoid the painful detours along the road to political and spiritual salvation which need to be understood, but which need not be experienced.

What Is Liberty?

by Woodrow Wilson

I have long had an image in my mind of what constitutes liberty. Suppose that I were building a great piece of powerful machinery, and suppose that I should so awkwardly and unskillfully assemble the parts of it that every time one part tried to move it would be interfered with by the others, and the whole thing would buckle up and be checked. Liberty for the several parts would consist in the best possible assembling and adjustment of them all, would it not? If you want the great piston of the engine to run with absolute freedom, give it absolutely perfect alignment and adjustment with the other parts of the engine, so that it is free, not because it is let alone or isolated, but because it has been associated most skillfully and carefully with the other parts of the great structure.

What is liberty? You say of the locomotive that it runs free. What do you mean? You mean that its parts are so assembled and adjusted that friction is reduced to a minimum, and that it has perfect adjustment. We say of a boat skimming the water with light foot, "How free she runs," when we mean, how perfectly she is adjusted to the force of the wind, how perfectly she obeys the great breath out of the heavens that fills her sails. Throw her head up into the wind and see how she will halt and stagger, how every sheet will shiver and her whole frame be shaken, how instantly she is "in irons," in the expressive phrase of the sea. She is free only when you have let her fall off again and have recovered once more her nice adjustment to the forces she must obey and cannot defy.

Human freedom consists in perfect adjustments of human interests and human activities and human energies.

Comment on "What is Liberty?"

Woodrow Wilson (1856-1929), the son of a Presbyterian preacher, was born in Virginia and spent his boyhood and youth in various places in the post-Civil War South, where his father was a pastor. He completed his college work at Princeton University and then studied law at the University of Virginia. For a short time he practiced law but then entered Johns Hopkins University from which he received a PhD in 1886. He taught for a few years, and then he became successively President of Princeton, Governor of New Jersey and, in 1913, President of the United States.

His theory of democracy, which he set forth during his first presidential campaign, was published in *The New Freedom*. The selection we have reprinted is taken from this well-known work.

Where Walter Lippmann illustrated his concept of freedom by citing a person-to-person relationship between patient and physician, President Wilson uses the image of the complicated piece of machinery in which all parts must work in perfectly balanced, reciprocally adjusted harmony. His conclusion is that "human freedom consists in perfect adjustments of human interests and human activities and human energies."

The picture here presented is an attractive one. There *is* something thrilling in cooperative, harmonious interplay. If we have any uneasiness in contemplating a finely tuned machine as a symbol of liberty, it comes from our reluctance to accept an analogy in which human beings are reduced to repetitive cogs in any machine, no matter how impressive.

This analogy seems to allow little chance for growth. A piston must be content to remain a piston. Any argument which talks of the "good of the whole" must, somehow, convince each part that its role in the machine is not only important but inevitable and unchanging.

Independence

by Henry David Thoreau

My life more civil is and free
Than any civil polity

Ye Princes, keep your realms
    and circumscribed power,
Not wide as are my dreams,
    Nor rich as is this hour.

What can ye give which I have not?
What can ye take which I have got?
    Can ye defend the dangerless?
    Can ye inherit nakedness?

To all true wants Time's ear is deaf,
Penurious States lend no relief
    Out of their pelf:
    But a free soul—thank God—
    Can help itself.

    Be sure your fate
Doth keep apart its state,—
Not linked with any band,
Even the noblest in the land,—

In tented fields with cloth of gold
    No place doth hold.
But is more chivalrous than they are,
    and sigheth for a nobler war;

A finer strain its trumpet rings,
A brighter gleam its armour flings,

The life that I aspire to live,
    No man proposeth me;
No trade upon the street
Wears its emblazonry.

Comment on "Independence"

While Henry David Thoreau (1817-1862) has been cited in earlier volumes (see pp. 227-28 in volume 3 particularly), he is not usually remembered as a poet. The sinewy strength of his prose is replaced by cryptic assertion in his few poems. Yet, occasionally, a Thoreau poem is memorable for both concept and phrasing.

Such a poem is "Independence." If Thoreau seems just a bit truculent here, such a stance may be appropriate for a poem that is so strong a statement on self-reliance. Even the rhyme scheme refuses to follow an expected pattern. It would be a mistake, however, to see in this poem only self-assertion. One needs to know that Thoreau's belief in reliance on self is just another way of expressing his confidence in personal revelation. None of the group (usually called Transcendentalists) of which Thoreau was a part felt that God was likely to speak through man-made institutions. Trusting one's own deepest feelings and instinct, they believed, was as direct an access to God as man was capable of receiving.

Note that the opening line of this poem explicitly rejects the state as the source of true liberty. The honors of men are next described as limiting, not freedom-giving. Finally any "band"—even the noblest—is rejected. Many readers feel that Thoreau's point becomes a little overstated here. After all, Thoreau himself was a loving son and brother, and a family is, among other things, a social group. But the implicit theme of this poem—that others can't provide and preserve your freedom—is worth remembering.

The Slave

by James Oppenheim

They set the slave free, striking off his chains;
Then he was as much of a slave as ever.

    He was still chained to servility,
    He was still manacled to indolence and sloth,
    He was still bound by fear and superstition,
    By ignorance, suspicion, and savagery.
    His slavery was not in the chains,
    But in himself.

    They can only set free men free,
    And there is no need of that:
    Free men set themselves free.

Comment on "The Slave"

James Oppenheim (1882-1939) was an American short story writer, novelist, journalist, and poet. Born in St. Paul, Minnesota, he studied at Columbia University. From 1909 to 1924 he saw the publication of six volumes of his poetry. "The Slave" is from *Songs for a New Age.*

The form of this poem helps dramatize it. The informative, almost narrative opening lines are quickly countered by the repeated phrases in the succeeding lines. "He was still" becomes a hammer blow by which links in his chains are forged. The final line of the second stanza is as abrupt as it is cruelly matter of fact. The final three lines are flat assertions that appropriately extend the poet's beginning statement that external bands are not the real badge of slavery.

The appeal of this poem is to man's responsibility for and control of his own destiny. The mild paradox of the concluding stanza, with its implicit recognition of the power of positive thinking, and with its echo of the scriptural "As a man thinketh in his heart, so is he," rallies and focuses our effort. Perhaps the danger here is that we can delude ourselves into believing that wholly man-made freedom is really possible. The internal bands which the poet names—servility, sloth, fear, superstition, ignorance, suspicion and savagery—are severed by beliefs which counter them. This is the freedom which only deep religious faith can bring. That a man must strive to prepare for this faith is certain, but he should never forget that faith is finally a gift from God.

The Bride Comes to Yellow Sky

by Stephen Crane

The great Pullman was whirling onward with such dignity of motion that a glance from the window seemed simply to prove that the plains of Texas were pouring eastward. Vast flats of green grass, dull-hued spaces of mesquite and cactus, little groups of frame houses, woods of light and tender trees, all were sweeping into the east, sweeping over the horizon, a precipice.

A newly married pair had boarded this coach at San Antonio. The man's face was reddened from many days in the wind and sun, and a direct result of his new black clothes was that his brick-coloured hands were constantly performing in a most conscious fashion. From time to time he looked down respectfully at his attire. He sat with a hand on each knee, like a man waiting in a barber's shop. The glances he devoted to other passengers were furtive and shy.

The bride was not pretty, nor was she very young. She wore a dress of blue cashmere, with small reservations of velvet here and there, and with steel buttons abounding. She continually twisted her head to regard her puff sleeves, very stiff, straight, and high. They embarrassed her. It was quite apparent that she had cooked, and that she expected to cook, dutifully. The blushes caused by the careless scrutiny of some passengers as she had entered the car were strange to see upon this plain, under-class countenance, which was drawn in placid, almost emotionless lines.

They were evidently very happy. "Ever been in a parlour-car before?" he asked, smiling with delight.

"No," she answered; "I never was. It's fine, ain't it?"

"Great! And then after a while we'll go forward to the diner, and get a big lay-out. Finest meal in the world. Charge a dollar."

"Oh, do they?" cried the bride. "Charge a dollar? Why, that's too much—for us—ain't it, Jack?"

"Not this trip, anyhow," he answered bravely. "We're going to go the whole thing."

Later he explained to her about the trains. "You see, it's a thousand miles from one end of Texas to the other; and this train runs right across it, and never stops but four times." He had the pride of an owner. He pointed out to her the dazzling fittings of the coach; and in truth her eyes opened wider as she contemplated the sea-green figured velvet, the shining brass, silver, and glass, the wood that gleamed as darkly brilliant as the surface of a pool of oil. At one end a bronze figure sturdily held a support for a separated chamber, and at convenient places on the ceiling were frescos in olive and silver.

To the minds of the pair, their surroundings reflected the glory of their marriage that morning in San Antonio; this was the environment of their estate, and the man's face in particular beamed with an elation that made him appear ridiculous to the Negro porter. This individual at times surveyed them from afar with an amused and superior grin. On other occasions he bullied them with skill in ways that did not make it exactly plain to them that they were being bullied. He subtly used all the manners of the most unconquerable kind of snobbery. He oppressed them; but of this oppression they had small knowledge, and they speedily forgot that infrequently a number of travellers covered them with stares of derisive enjoyment. Historically there was supposed to be something infinitely humorous in their situation.

"We are due in Yellow Sky at 3:42," he said, looking tenderly into her eyes.

"Oh, are we?" she said, as if she had not been aware of it. To evince surprise at her husband's statement was part of her wifely amiability. She took from a pocket a little silver watch; and as she held it before her, and stared at it with a frown of attention, the new husband's face shone.

"I bought it in San Anton' from a friend of mine," he told her gleefully.

"It's seventeen minutes past twelve," she said, looking up at him with a kind of shy and clumsy coquetry. A passenger, noting this play, grew excessively sardonic, and winked at himself in one of the numerous mirrors.

At last they went to the dining-car. Two rows of Negro waiters, in glowing white suits, surveyed their entrance with the interest, and also the equanimity, of men who had been forewarned.

The pair fell to the lot of a waiter who happened to feel pleasure in steering them through their meal. He viewed them with the manner of a fatherly pilot, his countenance radiant with benevolence. The patronage, entwined with the ordinary deference, was not plain to them. And yet, as they returned to their coach, they showed in their faces a sense of escape.

To the left, miles down a long purple slope, was a little ribbon of mist where moved the keening Rio Grande. The train was approaching it at an angle, and the apex was Yellow Sky. Presently it was apparent that, as the distance from Yellow Sky grew shorter, the husband became commensurately restless. His brick-red hands were more insistent in their prominence. Occasionally he was even rather absent-minded and far-away when the bride leaned forward and addressed him.

As a matter of truth, Jack Potter was beginning to find the shadow of a deed weigh upon him like a leaden slab. He, the town marshal of Yellow Sky, a man known, liked, and feared in his corner, a prominent person, had gone to San Antonio to meet a girl he believed he loved, and there, after the usual prayers, had actually induced her to marry him, without consulting Yellow Sky for any part of the transaction. He was now bringing his bride before an innocent and unsuspecting community.

Of course people in Yellow Sky married as it pleased them, in accordance with a general custom; but such was Potter's thought of his duty to his friends or of their idea of his duty, or of an unspoken form which does not control men in these matters, that he felt he was heinous.

He had committed an extraordinary crime. Face to face with this girl in San Antonio, and spurred by his sharp impulse, he had gone headlong over all the social hedges. At San Antonio he was like a man hidden in the dark. A knife to sever any friendly duty, any form, was easy to his hand in that remote city. But the hour of Yellow Sky—the hour of daylight was approaching.

He knew full well that his marriage was an important thing in his town. It could only be exceeded by the burning of the new hotel. His friends could not forgive him. Frequently he had reflected on the advisability of telling them by telegraph, but a new cowardice had been upon him. He feared to do it. And now the train was hurrying him toward a scene of amazement, glee, and reproach. He glanced out of the window at the line of haze swinging slowly in toward the train.

Yellow Sky had a kind of brass band, which played painfully, to the delight of the populace. He laughed without heart as he thought of it. If the citizens could dream of his prospective arrival with his bride, they would parade the band at the station and escort them, amid cheers and laughing congratulations, to his adobe home.

He resolved that he would use all the devices of speed and plainscraft in making the journey from the station to his house. Once within the safe citadel, he could issue some sort of vocal bulletin, and then not go among the citizens until they had time to wear off a little of their enthusiasm.

The bride looked anxiously at him. "What's worrying you, Jack?"

He laughed again. "I'm not worrying, girl; I'm only thinking of Yellow Sky."

She flushed in comprehension.

A sense of mutual guilt invaded their minds and developed a finer tenderness. They looked at each other with eyes softly aglow. But Potter often laughed the same nervous laugh; the flush upon the bride's face seemed quite permanent.

The traitor to the feelings of Yellow Sky narrowly watched the speeding landscape. "We're nearly there," he said.

Presently the porter came and announced the proximity of Potter's home. He held a brush in his hand, and, with all his airy superiority gone, he brushed Potter's new clothes as the latter slowly turned this way and that way. Potter fumbled out a coin and gave it to the porter, as he had seen others do. It was a heavy and muscle-bound business, as that of a man shoeing his first horse.

The porter took their bag, and as the train began to slow they moved forward to the hooded platform of the car. Presently the two engines and their long string of coaches rushed into the station of Yellow Sky.

"They have to take water here," said Potter, from a constricted throat and in a mournful cadence, as one announcing death. Before the train stopped his eye had swept the length of the platform, and he was glad and astonished to see there was none upon it but the station-agent, who, with a slightly hurried and anxious air, was walking toward the water-tanks.

When the train had halted, the porter alighted first, and placed in position a little temporary step.

"Come on, girl," said Potter, hoarsely. As he helped her down they each laughed on a false note. He took the bag from the Negro, and bade his wife cling to his arm. As they slunk rapidly away, his hang-dog glance perceived that they were unloading the two trunks, and also that the station-agent, far ahead near the baggage-car, had turned and was running toward him, making gestures. He laughed, and groaned as he laughed, when he noted the first effect of his marital bliss upon Yellow Sky. He gripped his wife's arm firmly to his side, and they fled. Behind them the porter stood, chuckling fatuously.

II

The California express on the Southern Railway was due at Yellow Sky in twenty-one minutes. There were six men at the bar of the Weary Gentleman saloon. One was a drummer who talked a great deal and rapidly, three were Texans who did not care to talk at that time; and two were Mexican sheep-herders, who did not talk as a general practice in the Weary Gentleman saloon. The barkeeper's dog lay on the board walk that crossed in front of the door. His head was on his paw, and he glanced drowsily here and there with the constant vigilance of a dog that is kicked on occasion. Across the sandy street were some vivid green grass-plots, so wonderful in appearance, amid the sands that burned near them in a blazing sun, that they caused a doubt in the mind.

They exactly resembled the grass mats used to represent lawns on the stage. At the cooler end of the railway station, a man without a coat sat in a tilted chair and smoked his pipe. The freshcut bank of the Rio Grande circled near the town, and there could be seen beyond it a great plum-coloured plain of mesquite.

Save for the busy drummer and his companions in the saloon, Yellow Sky was dozing. The new-comer leaned gracefully upon the bar, and recited many tales with the confidence of a bard who has come upon a new field.

"—and at the moment that the old man fell downstairs with the bureau in his arms, the old woman was coming up with two scuttles of coal, and of course—"

The drummer's tale was interrupted by a young man who suddenly appeared in the open door. He cried: "Scratchy Wilson's drunk, and has turned loose with both hands." The two Mexicans at once set down their glasses and faded out of the rear entrance of the saloon.

The drummer, innocent and jocular, answered, "All right, old man. S'pose he has? Come in and have a drink, anyhow."

But the information had made such an obvious cleft in every skull in the room that the drummer was obliged to see its importance. All had become instantly solemn. "Say," said he, mystified, "what is this?" His three companions made the introductory gesture of eloquent speech, but the young man at the door forestalled them.

"It means, my friend," he answered, as he came into the saloon, "that for the next two hours this town won't be a health resort."

The barkeeper went to the door, and locked and barred it; reaching out of the window, he pulled in heavy wooden shutters, and barred them. Immediately a solemn, chapel-like gloom was upon the place. The drummer was looking from one to another.

"But say," he cried, "what is this, anyhow? You don't mean there is going to be a gun-fight?"

"Don't know whether there'll be a fight or not," answered one man, grimly; "but there'll be some shootin'—some good shootin'."

The young man who had warned them waved his hand. "Oh, there'll be a fight fast enough, if anyone wants it. Anybody can get a fight out there in the street. There's a fight just waiting."

The drummer seemed to be swayed between the interest of a foreigner and a perception of personal danger.

"What did you say his name was?" he asked.

"Scratchy Wilson," they answered in chorus.

"And will he kill anybody? What are you going to do? Does this happen often? Does he rampage around like this once a week or so? Can he break in that door?"

"No; he can't break down that door," replied the barkeeper. "He's tried it three times. But when he comes you'd better lay down on the floor, stranger. He's dead sure to shoot at it, and a bullet may come through."

Thereafter the drummer kept a strict eye upon the door. The time had not yet been called for him to hug the floor, but, as a minor precaution, he sidled near to the wall. "Will he kill anybody?" he said again.

The men laughed low and scornfully at the question.

"He's out to shoot, and he's out for trouble. Don't see any good in experimentin' with him."

"But what do you do in a case like this? What do you do?"

A man responded: "Why, he and Jack Potter—"

"But," in chorus the other men interrupted, "Jack Potter's in San Antonio."

"Well, who is he? What's he got to do with it?"

"Oh, he's the town marshal. He goes out and fights Scratchy when he gets on one of these tears."

"Wow!" said the drummer, mopping his brow. "Nice job he's got."

The voices had toned away to mere whisperings. The drummer wished to ask further questions, which were born of an increasing anxiety and bewilderment; but when he attempted them, the men merely looked at him in irritation and motioned him to remain silent. A tense waiting hush was upon them. In the deep shadows of the room their eyes shone as they listened for sounds from the street. One man made three gestures at the barkeeper; and the latter, moving like a ghost, handed him a glass and a bottle. The man poured a full glass of whisky, and set down the bottle noiselessly. He gulped the whisky in a swallow, and turned again toward the door in immovable silence. The drummer saw that the barkeeper, without a sound, had taken a Winchester from beneath the bar. Later he saw this individual beckoning to him, so he tiptoed across the room.

"You better come with me back of the bar."

"No thanks," said the drummer, perspiring; "I'd rather be where I can make a break for the back door."

Whereupon the man of bottles made a kindly but peremptory gesture. The drummer obeyed it, and, finding himself seated on a box with his head below the level of the bar, balm was laid upon his soul at sight of various zinc and copper fittings that bore a resemblance to armor-plate. The barkeeper took a seat comfortably upon an adjacent box.

"You see," he whispered, "this here Scratchy Wilson is a wonder with a gun—a perfect wonder; and when he goes on the war-trail, we hunt our holes—naturally. He's about the last one of the old gang that used to hang out along the river here. He's a terror when he's drunk. When he's sober he's all right—kind of simple—wouldn't hurt a fly—nicest fellow in town. But when he's drunk—whoo!"

There were periods of stillness. "I wish Jack Potter was back from San Anton'," said the barkeeper. "He shot Wilson up once—in the leg—and he would sail in and pull out the kinks in this thing."

Presently they heard from a distance the sound of a shot, followed by three wild yowls. It instantly removed a bond from the men in the darkened saloon. There was a shuffling of feet. They looked at each other. "Here he comes," they said.

III

A man in a maroon-coloured flannel shirt, which had been purchased for purposes of decoration, and made principally by some Jewish women on the East Side of New York, rounded a corner and walked into the middle of the main street of Yellow Sky. In either hand the man held a long, heavy, blue-black revolver. Often he yelled, and these cries rang through the semblance of a deserted village, shrilly flying over the roofs in a volume that seemed to have no relation to the ordinary vocal strength of a man. It was as if the surrounding stillness formed the arch of a tomb over him. These cries of ferocious challenge rang against walls of silence. And his boots had red tops with gilded imprints, of the kind beloved in winter by little sledding boys on the hillsides of New England.

The man's face flamed in a rage begot of whisky. His eyes, rolling, and yet keen for ambush, hunted the still doorways and windows. He walked with the creeping movement of the midnight cat. As it occurred to him, he roared menacing information. The long revolvers in his hands were as easy as straws; they were moved with an electric swiftness. The little fingers of each hand played sometimes in a musician's way. Plain from the low collar of the shirt, the cords of his neck straightened and sank, straightened and sank, as passion moved him. The only sounds were his terrible invitations. The calm adobes preserved their demeanour at the passing of this small thing in the middle of the street.

There was no offer of fight—no offer of fight. The man called to the sky. There were no attractions. He bellowed and fumed and swayed his revolvers here and everywhere.

The dog of the barkeeper of the Weary Gentleman saloon had not appreciated the advance of events. He yet lay dozing in front of his master's door. At sight of the dog, the man paused and raised his revolver humorously. At sight of the man, the dog sprang up and walked diagonally

The Meaning of Freedom 23

away, with a sullen head, and growling. The man yelled and the dog broke into a gallop. As it was about to enter an alley, there was a loud noise, a whistling, and something spat the ground directly before it. The dog screamed, and wheeling in terror, galloped headlong in a new direction. Again there was a noise, a whistling, and sand was kicked viciously before it. Fear-stricken, the dog turned and flurried like an animal in a pen. The man stood laughing, his weapons at his hips.

Ultimately the man was attracted by the closed door of the Weary Gentleman saloon. He went to it and, hammering with a revolver, demanded drink.

The door remaining imperturbable, he picked a bit of paper from the walk, and nailed it to the framework with a knife. He then turned his back contemptuously upon this popular resort and, walking to the opposite side of the street and spinning there on his heel quickly and lithely, fired at the bit of paper. He missed it by a half-inch. He swore at himself, and went away. Later he comfortably fusilladed the windows of his most intimate friend. The man was playing with this town; it was a toy for him.

But still there was no offer of fight. The name of Jack Potter, his ancient antagonist, entered his mind, and he concluded that it would be a glad thing if he should go to Potter's house, and by bombardment induce him to come out and fight. He moved in the direction of his desire, chanting Apache scalp-music.

When he arrived at it, Potter's house presented the same still front as had the other adobes. Taking up a strategic position, the man howled a challenge. But this house regarded him as might a great stone god. It gave no sign. After a decent wait, the man howled further challenges, mingling with them wonderful epithets.

Presently there came the spectacle of a man churning himself into the deepest rage over the immobility of a house. He fumed at it as the winter wind attacks a prairie cabin in the North. To the distance there should have gone the sound of a tumult like the fighting of two hundred Mexicans. As necessity bade him, he paused for breath or to reload his revolvers.

IV

Potter and his bride walked sheepishly and with speed. Sometimes they laughed together shamefacedly and low.

"Next corner, dear," he said finally.

They put forth the efforts of a pair walking bowed against a strong wind. Potter was about to raise a finger to point the first appearance of the new home when, as they circled the corner, they came face to face with a man in a maroon-coloured shirt, who was feverishly pushing cartridges into a large revolver. Upon the instant the man dropped his revolver to the ground and, like lightning, whipped another from its holster. The second weapon was aimed at the bridegroom's chest.

There was a silence. Potter's mouth seemed to be merely a grave for his tongue. He exhibited an instinct to at once loosen his arm from the woman's grip, and he dropped the bag to the sand. As for the bride, her face had gone as yellow as old cloth. She was a slave to hideous rites, gazing at the apparitional snake.

The two men faced each other at a distance of three paces. He of the revolver smiled with a new and quiet ferocity.

"Tried to sneak up on me," he said. "Tried to sneak up on me!" His eyes grew more baleful. As Potter made a slight movement, the man thrust his revolver venomously forward. "No, don't you do it, Jack Potter. Don't you move a finger toward a gun just yet. Don't you move an eyelash. The time has come for me to settle with you, and I'm going to do it my own way, and loaf along with no interferin'. So if you don't want a gun bent on you, just mind what I tell you."

Potter looked at his enemy. "I ain't got a gun on me, Scratchy," he said. "Honest, I ain't." He was stiffening and steadying, but yet somewhere at the back of his mind a vision of the Pullman floated: the sea-green figures velvet, the shining brass, silver, and glass, the wood that gleamed as darkly brilliant as the surface of a pool of oil—all the glory of the marriage, the environment of the new estate. "You know I fight when it comes to fighting, Scratchy Wilson; but I ain't got a gun on me. You'll have to do all the shootin' yourself."

His enemy's face went livid. He stepped forward, and lashed his weapon to and fro before Potter's chest. "Don't you tell me you ain't got no gun on you, you whelp. Don't tell me no lie like that. There ain't a man in Texas ever seen you without no gun. Don't take me for no kid." His eyes blazed with light, and his throat worked like a pump.

"I ain't takin' you for no kid," answered Potter. His heels had not moved an inch backward. "I'm taking' you for a fool. I tell you I ain't got a gun, and I ain't. If you're goin' to shoot me up, you better begin now; you'll never get a chance like this again."

So much enforced reasoning had told on Wilson's rage; he was calmer. "If you ain't got a gun, why ain't you got a gun?" he sneered. "Been to Sunday-school?"

"I ain't got a gun because I've just come from San Anton' with my wife. I'm married," said Potter. "And if I'd thought there was going to be any galoots like you prowling around when I brought my wife home, I'd had a gun, and don't you forget it."

"Married!" said Scratchy, not at all comprehending.

"Yes, married, I'm married," said Potter, distinctly.

"Married?" said Scratchy. Seemingly for the first time, he saw the drooping, drowning woman at the other man's side. "No!" he said. He was like a creature allowed a glimpse of another world. He moved a pace backward, and his arm, with the revolver, dropped to his side. "Is this the lady?" he asked.

"Yes, this is the lady," answered Potter.

There was another period of silence.

"Well," said Wilson at last, slowly, "I s'pose it's all off now."

"It's all off if you say so, Scratchy. You know I didn't make the trouble." Potter lifted his valise.

"Well, I 'low it's off, Jack," said Wilson. He was looking at the ground. "Married!" He was not a student of chivalry; it was merely that in the presence of this foreign condition he was a simple child of the earlier plains. He picked up his starboard revolver, and, placing both weapons in their holsters, he went away. His feet made funnel-shaped tracks in the heavy sand.

Comment on
"The Bride Comes to Yellow Sky"

The fourteenth child in a minister's family, Stephen Crane (1871-1900) spent a restless youth in a series of small towns in New York and New Jersey. In and out of college, he was a free-lance reporter in New York City by the time he was twenty-one. Two years later he was in the Far West and Mexico collecting short story and sketch material. Although it was not written until later, "The Bride Comes to Yellow Sky" is an obvious result of Crane's western year.

Many critics feel that "The Bride" is the best short story Crane wrote during his brief career. Crane himself felt that this was a "daisy" of a story, and two generations of readers agree. The author's eye for details and his deft phrasing of them is stunningly evident. From the opening paragraph, in which the movement of a train is memorably described, to the closing sentence with its suggestion of weary defeat, Crane's style is arrestingly effective. This story is also put together skillfully in building toward its ironic climax: The sheriff, whose business it is to carry a gun, is caught without one, yet he still triumphs. Scratchy Wilson, who has a gun and is prepared to use it, finds himself disarmed by no gun at all. The frontier code by which both Scratchy and the Sheriff have lived is no match for the way of life which the Sheriff is now assuming. Scratchy comprehends this only dimly; he is allowed but "a glimpse of another world," but that brief vision is overwhelming. It is classic confrontation between the freedom of indulgence and the freedom of discipline.

Although the town expects the Sheriff to "fight Scratchy Wilson" when this derelict from an earlier day becomes belligerent—and the Sheriff has heretofore indulged the town, Scratchy and himself in so doing—his marriage changes everything. Both bride and groom are a bit embarrassed by what they have done, and they are apprehensive about their reception in Yellow Sky. Those who see or guess their discomfort exploit it to the full, and the newly married pair are so self-conscious that they attract attention. Neither is young nor particularly attractive, but there is something transcendent in their new state, and neither the derision of fellow passengers on the train nor the drunken rage of Scratchy Wilson can totally counter their elation.

The Sheriff's bride may be uneasy about her new clothes —and she is terrified of Scratchy—yet as she clings to her husband's arm she is a more potent weapon than any he has had before; she stands for a world unknown to the gunman menacing her husband. In marrying, Jack Potter has freed himself from the meaningless game he has been playing. If Scratchy has been trapped in a degrading cycle of sober passivity and drunken belligerence, the Sheriff has been no less in bondage to the town's mechanical expectations. The addition of a wife and the manifest obligations of his married state give the Sheriff a dimension that Scratchy cannot share and which the town will have to accept. As a single man, the Sheriff played a role; as a husband he will hold a job.

One of the most interesting ideas in this unusual story

is that freedom is expanded, not curtailed, by the assumption of responsibility. We have no reason to believe that Jack Potter will be less effective as a Sheriff now that he is married, but the order which he must now maintain will no longer be the counter-play by which the town is entertained.

Under the press of responsibility we are tempted to equate freedom with lack of obligations. As children, however, our instinct was sure. We wanted to leave the circumscribed sphere of childhood for an adult world as soon as possible. If we lose some of a child's careless zest in growing up, we trade it gladly for the expanded position of provider, helpmate, father, mother. As Lehi reminds us, a garden of Eden universe is static. In the range of our choices lies our earthly freedom, and in proper choice there is eternal liberty.

SECTION TWO

The Role of Education

by Bruce B. Clark

"THE GIRL IN WHITE"

By Julian Alden Weir (1852-1919) American
Brigham Young University Collection, Provo, Utah

Commentary by
Floyd E. Brienholt, Chairman, Department of Art
Brigham Young University

"Whom do we need more, or who should be more profoundly honored, than a man of complete integrity?" This is the first sentence of the foreword of the *Life and Letters of J. Alden Weir*, compiled by Dorothy W. Young.

Every sincere painting by an accomplished artist is essentially a self-portrait, a portrait of his complete personality. Just as we seem to be drawn to some people more than to others, so are we drawn to some works of art. While reading about the life of this man and studying his paintings, one becomes acutely aware of the truism that his art and personality are compounded and inseparable. "And by . . . their works you shall know them." (D&C 18:38.) If the above statement is true, then a description of the artist would resemble a description of his work.

Study "The Girl in White" and see if you can see how the artist identified himself with his work as you read the following statements about the man taken from the comments of Duncan Phillips, a friend who knew him well:

1. He has the capacity to make us feel that ordinary human experiences are desirable and delightful, that the world is full of places and people worth knowing.
2. He was a man of charm, nobility, and taste.
3. He sought to tell the truth of the matter.
4. There was no sham nor pretense.
5. "He could see distinction in an apparently ordinary model, and make us see what he had seemed to like and admire."

A close study of "The Girl in White," then, provides a rewarding educational experience in that one learns about the personality and tastes of the artist. To the more casual observer, however, the picture represents an educational experience on another level—the experience of a lovely child involved in the beauty and wonders of nature.

J. Alden Weir enjoyed the beautiful in life. It became an integral part of him. He also found a technique peculiar to him by which he could pass *this* on to us in the form of his paintings; a technique which harmonized with his personality and his special way of seeing. Such men of integrity and character play an important role in our education. As John Ruskin says, "The object of true education is to make people not merely do the right things but enjoy them."

THE ROLE OF EDUCATION

The object of true education is to make people not merely do the right things but enjoy them. —John Ruskin

Introductory Comments

Throughout the entire history of our Church there has been an emphasis upon education. From the very beginning, schools were established at all levels, and church members were encouraged to cultivate not only gospel knowledge and the skills of learning but also the cultural arts. The goal has always been to build in the hearts of Latter-day Saints an informed faith, an enlightened testimony. Rather than being hostile to knowledge and the arts, the Church has encouraged and sponsored them. Hence the rich program of cultural activities emphasizing drama, dance, music, literature, public speaking, etc., in the auxiliary organizations as well as the vast network of schools, seminaries, institutes, and colleges provided by the Church.

Nor are these just modern developments. Any study of the pioneer days of the Church will reveal that in spite of the struggle for food and clothing and homes, priority was given to schools, theaters, and music halls, along with chapels and temples, for the pioneers understood that the mind and the spirit need food for growth just as vitally as the physical body does. Their westward-bound wagons were loaded with books and musical instruments as well as spinning wheels and blacksmith forges. Many of the pioneers were self-educated, but most of them *were* nevertheless educated, even to the point of consciously cultivating skill in elocution, rhetoric, and penmanship.

This is our pioneer heritage! No wonder we look back with admiration and a glow of pride, not only for their great spiritual and physical courage as they triumphed over human persecution and the hostile, barren desert lands, but also for their love of the beautiful and the intellectually uplifting. ". . . seek ye diligently and teach one another words of wisdom; yea, seek ye out of the best books words of wisdom; seek learning, even by study, and also by faith." (D&C 88:118.) Thus the Lord gave counsel through the Prophet Joseph Smith as the gospel was being restored, urging us above all else to study the scriptures, but also to study other things.

What other things? Earlier in Section 88 of the Doctrine and Covenants the Lord instructed us that we are to "teach one another . . . in all things that pertain unto the kingdom of God," including, in his words, "things both in heaven and in the earth, and under the earth; things which have been, things which are, things which must shortly come to pass; things which are at home, things which are abroad; the wars and the perplexities of the nations, and the judgments which are on the land; and a knowledge also of countries and of kingdoms." (D&C 88:77-79.) A little later in Section 90 he advised us to "become acquainted with all good books, and with languages, tongues, and people." (D&C 90:15.) Still later, in Section 93, we are counseled to "obtain a knowledge of history, and of countries, and of kingdoms, of laws of God and man, and all this for the salvation of Zion." (D&C 93:53.) We are even promised that "whatever principle of intelligence we attain unto in this life, it will rise with us in the resurrection," for "if a person gains more knowledge and intelligence in this life through his diligence and obedience than another, he will have so much the advantage in the world to come." (D&C 130:18-19.)

Not only Joseph Smith as he was inspired of the Lord but also Brigham Young stressed the need for learning. Listen to the words of President Young:

> All the knowledge, wisdom, power, and glory that have been bestowed upon the nations of the earth, from the days of Adam till now, must be gathered home to Zion.
>
> Every art and science known and studied by the children of men is comprised within the Gospel.

The Role of Education

See that your children are properly educated in the rudiments of their mother tongue, and then let them proceed to higher branches of learning; let them become more informed in every department of true and useful learning than their fathers are. When they have become well acquainted with their language, let them study other languages, and make themselves fully acquainted with the manners, customs, laws, governments and literature of other nations, peoples, and tongues. Let them also learn all the truth pertaining to the arts and sciences, and how to apply the same to their temporal wants. Let them study things that are upon the earth, that are in the earth, and that are in the heavens.

We have the privilege of enjoying the spirit of revelation and the knowledge which comes from above, and in addition to this, every branch of education known in the world should be taught among and acquired by us.

We should be a people of profound learning pertaining to the things of the world. We should be familiar with the various languages, for we wish to send missionaries to the different nations and to the islands of the sea. . . . We also wish them to understand the geography, habits, customs, and laws of nations and kingdoms.

I would advise you to read books that are worth reading; read reliable history, and search wisdom out of the best books you can procure. "Shall I sit down and read the Bible, the Book of Mormon, and the Book of Covenants all the time?" says one. Yes, if you please, and when you have done, you may be nothing but a sectarian after all. It is your duty to study to know everything upon the face of the earth in addition to reading those books. We should not only study good, and its effects upon our race, but also evil, and its consequences.[1]

As in the past, so now, those we sustain as our living prophets encourage us to develop our talents and widen our intellectual and cultural horizons, as evidenced not only by their encouragement to education but also by the breadth of their own reading. All of us know how abundantly President McKay and the other General Authorities enrich their talks and writings with passages drawn from the great literature of the world. Listen also as President McKay counsels us to harmonize learning with character:

---
[1]These statements by Brigham Young are quoted from *Discourses of Brigham Young*, selected and arranged by John A. Widtsoe (Salt Lake City: Deseret Book Company, 1943), pp. 245, 246, 252, 252, 254-55, and 256-57.

Wisdom is the right application of knowledge; and true education—the education for which the Church stands—is the application of knowledge to the development of a noble and a Godlike character. . . . True education seeks to make men and women not only good mathematicians, proficient linguists, profound scientists, or brilliant literary lights, but also honest men combined with virtue, temperance, and brotherly love—men and women who prize truth, justice, wisdom, benevolence, and self-control as the choicest acquisitions of a successful life.[2]

Our first responsibility as members of the Church is to study the scriptures and the words of the modern prophets for the fullness of the gospel that they contain. But beyond these we are invited to explore the best writings of the world for the supplemental knowledge and insight that these can give. At their best both religion and literature are concerned with building faith and affirming spiritual values and with opposing and exposing evil, worldliness, superficiality, and all things base and false.

In the material that now follows we shall explore some stimulating thoughts on education as these are presented in poetry, philosophy, stories, and essays. Several of the finest selections on teaching are, unfortunately, too long to include here—works such as Lionel Trilling's great short story "Of This Time, Of That Place" and William Gibson's moving play *The Miracle Worker,* which dramatizes how Anne Sullivan brought to the blind and deaf Helen Keller the miracle of language. Although lack of space prevents our printing these, what we do have space to print should be stimulating to all readers. And always we have before us the example of the world's greatest teacher, Christ himself,[3] who exemplified in both his life and his words the statement by Thomas Henry Huxley that the ultimate goal of education is "to learn what is true in order to do what is right."

---

[2]From Preface to booklet on *L.D.S. Church Schools,* 1968.

[3]See my comments on Christ as a great teacher in Vol. III, p. 200, of *Out of the Best Books.* For other important selections on education and great teaching in earlier volumes of this series, see "A Grammarian's Funeral" by Robert Browning, I, 73-79; "The Bear" by William Faulkner, I, 179-197; "My Little Boy" by Carl Ewald, II, 8-23; "The Educated Gentleman" by John Henry Newman, II, 196-199; "People and Ants" by Peter Balgha, IV, 22-27; and "Learning the River" by Mark Twain, IV, 194-208.

Comment on "What Makes a Great Book?"

At the beginning of Volume I of *Out of the Best Books*, when we were just starting the Cultural Refinement program with which we have now been working for the past five years, we printed the following little essay by Mortimer Adler. Because it is such an excellent statement on the power of great books to enlarge and elevate the mind, we have decided to re-print it in this section on education.

Mortimer J. Adler (1902-   ) is a distinguished American college professor, philosopher, and literary critic. This little essay by him is now widely recognized as a classic statement on the challenge and reward of reading at its best.

What Makes a Great Book?

by Mortimer J. Adler

Great books are those that contain the best materials on which the human mind can work in order to gain insight, understanding, and wisdom. Each of them, in its own way, raises the recurrent basic questions which men must face. Because these questions never are completely solved, these books are the sources and monuments of a continuing intellectual tradition.

Carl Van Doren once referred to great books as "the books that never have to be written again." They are the rare, perfect achievements of sustained excellence. Their beauty and clarity show that they are masterpieces of the fine as well as of the liberal arts. Such books justifiably are called great whether they are books of science, poetry, theology, mathematics, or politics.

The richness of great books shows itself in the many levels of meaning they contain. They lend themselves to a variety of interpretations. This does not mean that they are ambiguous or that their integrity is compromised. The different interpretations complement one another and allow the reader to discover the unity of the work from a variety of perspectives. We need not read other books more than once to get all that they have to say. But we can always go deeper into great books. As sources of enlightenment, they are inexhaustible.

The interest in many good books that are written is limited to a definite period of history. They do not exhibit the universal appeal that results from dealing with the fundamental questions which confront men in all times and places and in a way that men in all times and places can understand. Great books, on the contrary, transcend the provincial limits of their origin. They remain as world literature. The ones we are sure are great are the ones men everywhere turn to again and again through the centuries.

In view of this, it is often said that great books must pass the test of time. This is quite true. But it is not the passage of time that makes the books great. They were great when they were written. An enduring interest in a book merely confirms its greatness. We may consider some contemporary books great, but we cannot be sure. Their excellence still remains to be proved before the tribunal of the ages.

Mark Twain once remarked that "The great books are the books that everyone wishes he *had* read, but no one *wants* to read." People wish they had read them because they are the indispensable material of a liberal education. They shy away from reading them because these books require thought. And thinking is hard. It is probably one of the most painful things that human beings are called upon to do.

The great books are not easy to read. No one should expect to understand them very well on a first reading, nor even to master them fully after many readings. I have often said that they are the books which are over everyone's head all of the time. That is why they must be read and reread. That is also why they are good for us. Only the things which are over our head can lift us up.

Like all the other good things in life, what the great books have to offer is hard to get. But it is precisely because great books are difficult that they are more readable and more worth reading than other books. It is precisely because they raise problems which they do not finally answer that they can provoke us to think, inquire, and discuss. It is precisely because their difficulty challenges our skill in reading that they can help us to improve that skill. It is precisely because they often challenge our accepted prejudices and our established opinions that they can help us to develop our critical faculties.

Comment on "Cipher in the Snow"

This dramatic real-life story was written by Jean E. Mizer, who is, or at least was in 1964, a teacher and counselor in Wood River High School, Hailey, Idaho. The story received the first-place award of $1000 in the National Education Association's 1964 Teachers' Writing Contest and was published in the *NEA Journal* for November 1964. According to the author, the story is true but the names and location have been changed.

Because the story speaks its dramatic message so simply yet powerfully, no discussion seems needful except perhaps three little comments: (1) As most readers probably know, *cipher* is another name for *zero*. (2) If the need to reach the lonely, insecure child is urgent in public school teaching, surely it is no less urgent in our teaching within the Church. (3) Is it true, as this story suggests, that the child who needs help and encouragement most is often least likely to ask for that help and encouragement?

Cipher in the Snow

by Jean E. Mizer

It started with tragedy on a biting cold February morning. I was driving behind the Milford Corners bus as I did most snowy mornings on my way to school. It veered and stopped short at the hotel, which it had no business doing, and I was annoyed as I had to come to an unexpected stop. A boy lurched out of the bus, reeled, stumbled, and collapsed on the snowbank at the curb. The bus driver and I reached him at the same moment. His thin, hollow face was white even against the snow.

"He's dead," the driver whispered.

It didn't register for a minute. I glanced quickly at the scared young faces staring down at us from the school bus. "A doctor! Quick! I'll phone from the hotel. . . ."

"No use. I tell you he's dead." The driver looked down at the boy's still form. "He never even said he felt bad," he muttered, "just tapped me on the shoulder and said, real quiet, 'I'm sorry. I have to get off at the hotel.' That's all. Polite and apologizing like."

At school, the giggling, shuffling morning noise quieted as the news went down the halls. I passed a huddle of girls. "Who was it? Who dropped dead on the way to school?" I heard one of them half-whisper.

"Don't know his name; some kid from Milford Corners," was the reply.

It was like that in the faculty room and the principal's office. "I'd appreciate your going out to tell the parents," the principal told me. "They haven't a phone and, anyway, somebody from school should go there in person. I'll cover your classes."

"Why me?" I asked. "Wouldn't it be better if you did it?"

"I didn't know the boy," the principal admitted levelly. "And in last year's sophomore personalities column I note that you were listed as his favorite teacher."

I drove through the snow and cold down the bad canyon road to the Evans place and thought about the boy, Cliff Evans. His favorite teacher! I thought. He hasn't spoken two words to me in two years! I could see him in my mind's eye all right, sitting back there in the last seat in my afternoon literature class. He came in the room by himself and left by himself. "Cliff Evans," I muttered to myself, "a boy who never talked." I thought a minute. "A boy who never smiled. I never saw him smile once."

The big ranch kitchen was clean and warm. I blurted out my news somehow. Mrs. Evans reached blindly toward a chair. "He never said anything about bein' ailing."

His step-father snorted. "He ain't said nothin' about anything since I moved in here."

Mrs. Evans pushed a pan to the back of the stove and began to untie her apron. "Now hold on," her husband snapped. "I got to have breakfast before I go to town. Nothin' we can do now anyway. If Cliff hadn't been so dumb, he'd have told us he didn't feel good."

After school I sat in the office and stared bleakly at the records spread out before me. I was to close the file and write the obituary for the school paper. The almost bare sheets mocked the effort. Cliff Evans, white, never legally adopted by step-father, five young half-brothers and sisters. These meager strands of information and the list of D grades were all the records had to offer.

Cliff Evans had silently come in the school door in the mornings and gone out the school door in the evenings, and that was all. He had never belonged to a club. He had never played on a team. He had never held an office. As far as I could tell, he had never done one happy, noisy kid thing. He had never been anybody at all.

How do you go about making a boy into a zero? The grade-school records showed me. The first and second grade teachers' annotations read "sweet, shy child"; "timid but eager." The third grade note had

The Role of Education

opened the attack. Some teacher had written in a good, firm hand, "Cliff won't talk. Uncooperative. Slow learner." The other academic sheep had followed with "dull"; "slow-witted"; "low I.Q." They became correct. The boy's I.Q. score in the ninth grade was listed at 83. But his I.Q. in the third grade had been 106. The score didn't go under 100 until the seventh grade. Even shy, timid, sweet children have resilience. It takes time to break them.

I stomped to the typewriter and wrote a savage report pointing out what education had done to Cliff Evans. I slapped a copy on the principal's desk and another in the sad, dog-eared file. I banged the typewriter and slammed the file and crashed the door shut, but I didn't feel much better. A little boy kept walking after me, a little boy with a peaked, pale face; a skinny body in faded jeans; and big eyes that had looked and searched for a long time and then had become veiled.

I could guess how many times he'd been chosen last to play sides in a game, how many whispered child conversations had excluded him, how many times he hadn't been asked. I could see and hear the faces and voices that said over and over, "You're dumb. You're dumb. You're a nothing, Cliff Evans."

A child is a believing creature. Cliff undoubtedly believed them. Suddenly it seemed clear to me: When finally there was nothing left at all for Cliff Evans, he collapsed on a snowbank and went away. The doctor might list "heart failure" as the cause of death, but that wouldn't change my mind.

We couldn't find ten students in the school who had known Cliff well enough to attend the funeral as his friends. So the studentbody officers and a committee from the junior class went as a group to the church, being politely sad. I attended the services with them, and sat through it with a lump of cold lead in my chest and a big resolve growing through me.

I've never forgotten Cliff Evans nor that resolve. He has been my challenge year after year, class after class. I look up and down the rows carefully each September at the unfamiliar faces. I look for veiled eyes or bodies scrouged into a seat in an alien world. "Look, kids," I say silently, "I may not do anything else for you this year, but not one of you is going to come out of here a nobody. I'll work or fight to the bitter end doing battle with society and the school board, but I won't have one of you coming out of here thinking himself a zero."

Most of the time—not always, but most of the time—I've succeeded.

Comment on Professor Agassiz and "A Great Teacher's Method"

In his brilliant little book the *ABC of Reading,* Ezra Pound says: "No man is equipped for modern thinking until he has understood the anecdote of Agassiz and the fish." Louis Agassiz (1807-1873) was a world-renowned scientist and educator who, after training in Switzerland and Germany, came to the U. S. and achieved international acclaim as a teacher of geology and biology at Harvard University. The story Pound tells about Agassiz and the fish is not exactly the same as the one reprinted below, but the point is the same. Professor Agassiz taught his students to look at simple objects and study their minutest details until the simple was seen to be exceedingly complex—and then finally simple again. Sometimes, as Pound suggests, the fish, or whatever else was being observed, was in an advanced state of decomposition before Professor Agassiz permitted his student to stop looking at it, but by that time the student not only knew the fish—really knew it—but also knew a good deal about the great principle of learning through observation.

After reading the following account by Samuel Scudder,[4] consider these questions: (1) Why didn't Professor Agassiz simply hand Scudder a list of things to observe and questions to answer? Wouldn't this have saved the student a great deal of time? (2) Is it often better teaching to compel students to find things out for themselves through their own observing and thinking than it is to just give them the information and the answers to questions?

A Great Teacher's Method

by Samuel H. Scudder

It was more than fifteen years ago that I entered the laboratory of Professor Agassiz, and told him I had enrolled my name in the Scientific

---

[4]Samuel H. Scudder (1837-1911), author of this imaginative essay about Professor Agassiz, learned his lesson well and became himself an entomologist and teacher of eminent reputation.

The Role of Education

School as a student of natural history. He asked me a few questions about my object in coming, my antecedents generally, the mode in which I afterwards proposed to use the knowledge I might acquire, and, finally, whether I wished to study any special branch. To the latter I replied that, while I wished to be well grounded in all departments of zoology, I purposed to devote myself specially to insects.

"When do you wish to begin?" he asked.

"Now," I replied.

This seemed to please him, and with an energetic "Very well!" he reached from the shelf a huge jar of specimens in yellow alcohol.

"Take this fish," said he, "and look at it; we call it a haemulon; by and by I will ask what you have seen."

With that he left me, but in a moment returned with explicit instructions as to the care of the object entrusted to me.

"No man is fit to be a naturalist," said he, "who does not know how to take care of specimens."

I was to keep the fish before me in a tin tray, and occasionally moisten the surface with alcohol from the jar, always taking care to replace the stopper tightly. Those were not the days of ground-glass stoppers and elegantly shaped exhibition jars; all the old students will recall the huge neckless glass bottles with their leaky, wax besmeared corks, half eaten by insects, and begrimed with cellar dust. Entomology was a cleaner science than ichthyology, but the example of the Professor, who had unhesitatingly plunged to the bottom of the jar to produce the fish, was infectious; and though this alcohol had a "very ancient and fishlike smell," I really dared not show any aversion within these sacred precincts, and treated the alcohol as though it were pure water. Still I was conscious of a passing feeling of disappointment, for gazing at a fish did not commend itself to an ardent entomologist. My friends at home, too, were annoyed when they discovered that no amount of eau-de-Cologne would drown the perfume which haunted me like a shadow.

In ten minutes I had seen all that could be seen in that fish, and started in search of the Professor—who had, however, left the Museum; and when I returned, after lingering over some of the odd animals stored in the upper apartment, my specimen was dry all over. I dashed the fluid over the fish as if to resuscitate the beast from a fainting-fit, and looked with anxiety for a return of the normal sloppy appearance. This little excitement over, nothing was to be done but to return to a steadfast gaze at my mute companion. Half an hour passed—an hour—another hour; the fish began to look loathsome. I turned it over and around; looked it in the face—ghastly; from behind, beneath, above, sideways, at a three-quarters' view—just as ghastly. I was in despair; at an early hour I concluded that lunch was necessary; so, with infinite relief, the fish was carefully replaced in the jar, and for an hour I was free.

On my return, I learned that Professor Agassiz had been at the Museum, but had gone, and would not return for several hours. My fellow-students were too busy to be disturbed by continued conversation. Slowly I drew forth that hideous fish, and with a feeling of desperation again looked at it. I might not use a magnifying-glass; instruments of all kinds were interdicted. My two hands, my two eyes, and the fish; it seemed a most limited field. I pushed my finger down its throat to feel how sharp the teeth were. I began to count the scales in the different rows, until I was convinced that that was nonsense. At last a happy thought struck me—I would draw the fish; and now with surprise I began to discover new features in the creature. Just then the Professor returned.

"That is right," said he; "a pencil is one of the best of eyes. I am glad to notice, too, that you keep your specimen wet, and your bottle corked."

With these encouraging words, he added:

"Well, what is it like?"

He listened attentively to my brief rehearsal of the structure of parts whose names were still unknown to me: the fringed gill-arches and movable operculum; the pores of the head, fleshy lips and lidless eyes; the lateral line, the spinous fins and forked tail; the compressed and arched body. When I had finished, he waited as if expecting more, and then, with an air of disappointment:

"You have not looked very carefully; why," he continued more earnestly, "you haven't even seen one of the most conspicuous features of the animal, which is as plainly before your eyes as the fish itself; look again, look again!" and he left me to my misery.

I was piqued; I was mortified. Still more of that wretched fish! But now I set myself to my task with a will, and discovered one new thing after another, until I saw how just the Professor's criticism had been. The afternoon passed quickly; and when, toward its close, the Professor inquired:

"Do you see it yet?"

"No," I replied, "I am certain I do not, but I see how little I saw before."

"That is next best," said he, earnestly, "but I won't hear you now; put away your fish and go home; perhaps you will be ready with a better answer in the morning. I will examine you before you look at the fish."

This was disconcerting. Not only must I think of my fish all night, studying, without the object before me, what this unknown but most visible feature might be; but also, without reviewing my discoveries, I must give an exact account of them the next day. I had a bad memory; so I walked home by Charles River in a distracted state, with my two perplexities.

The cordial greeting from the Professor the next morning was re-

The Role of Education

assuring; here was a man who seemed to be quite as anxious as I that I should see for myself what he saw.

"Do you perhaps mean," I asked, "that the fish has symmetrical sides with paired organs?"

His thoroughly pleased "Of course! of course!" repaid the wakeful hours of the previous night. After he had discoursed most happily and enthusiastically—as he always did—upon the importance of this point, I ventured to ask what I should do next.

"Oh, look at your fish!" he said, and left me again to my own devices. In a little more than an hour he returned, and heard my new catalogue.

"That is good, that is good!" he repeated; "but that is not all; go on"; and so for three long days he placed that fish before my eyes, forbidding me to look at anything else, or to use any artificial aid. "Look, look, look," was his repeated injunction.

This was the best entomological lesson I ever had—a lesson whose influence has extended to the details of every subsequent study; a legacy the Professor had left to me, as he has left it to many others, of inestimable value, which we could not buy, with which we cannot part.

A year afterward, some of us were amusing ourselves with chalking outlandish beasts on the Museum blackboard. We drew prancing starfishes; frogs in mortal combat; hydra-headed worms; stately crawfishes, standing on their tails, bearing aloft umbrellas; and grotesque fishes with gaping mouths and staring eyes. The Professor came in shortly after, and was as amused as any at our experiments. He looked at the fishes.

"Haemulons, everyone of them," he said; "Mr. Scudder drew them."

True; and to this day, if I attempt a fish, I can draw nothing but haemulons.

The fourth day, a second fish of the same group was placed beside the first, and I was bidden to point out the resemblances and differences between the two; another and another followed, until the entire family lay before me, and a whole legion of jars covered the table and surrounding shelves; the odor had become a pleasant perfume; and even now, the sight of an old, six-inch, worm-eaten cork brings fragrant memories.

The whole group of haemulons was thus brought in review; and, whether engaged upon the dissection of the internal organs, the preparation and examination of the bony framework, or the description of the various parts, Agassiz's training in the method of observing facts and their orderly arrangement was ever accompanied by the urgent exhortation not to be content with them.

"Facts are stupid things," he would say, "until brought into connection with some general law."

At the end of eight months, it was almost with reluctance that I left these friends and turned to insects; but what I had gained by this outside experience has been of greater value than years of later investigation in my favorite groups.

Comment on Socrates and the Dialogues of Plato

In Volume IV we studied the death of Socrates and admired the courage, integrity, self-discipline, and obedience to principle of that great philosopher of ancient Greece. Now we examine the technique of his teaching, for he was surely one of the great teachers of all time. His most famous pupil was Plato, who in turn was the teacher of Aristotle—and these three form the most impressive trio of philosophers the world has yet known.

As Robert Thomas wrote in Volume IV, "So far as scholars have been able to discover, Socrates (about 469-399 B.C.) was a citizen of ancient Athens who made it his business to discuss the great issues of the day with his fellow Athenians. By vocation a stonemason, Socrates himself apparently wrote nothing. What we know about him comes mainly from the writings of his pupil Plato (about 427-347 B.C.), who was a philosophical writer of the first rank. It is difficult, if not impossible, to distinguish between what Socrates actually said and what Plato puts in his mouth. If this is historically important, it makes little difference to us today. The dialogues are as fresh and provocative now as they have ever been, and they still speak clearly to man's basic problems."

Socrates used to call himself "the midwife of men's thoughts." Cicero, the famous Roman scholar, said of Socrates that he "brought down philosophy from the heavens to the earth." Socrates' main method of teaching, at least if we accept the Plato dialogues as accurate, was to ask stimulating, probing, leading questions that maneuvered whatever person he was talking to deeper and deeper into thought and ever farther along the road of truth until together they finally arrived at the fundamental answers Socrates intended.

It has often been said that the ideal teaching situation would be Socrates (great teacher) on one end of a log with Mark Hopkins (brilliant student) on the other end. Although teaching generally cannot be this individual between teacher and student, we all know that one of the finest techniques

The Role of Education 47

for good teaching is still asking the right questions, for this compels the student to think and to become personally involved in the process of learning.

The principal dialogues of Plato, in all of which Socrates is the main speaker, are the *Apology, Republic* (his masterpiece), *Laws, Symposium, Phaedrus, Phaedo,* and *Crito.* The two brief excerpts we have chosen to print here are, first, from the *Symposium,* in which Socrates interrogates Agathon about love; and second, from Book X of the *Republic,* in which Socrates talks with Glaucon about the immortality of the human soul. Earlier, in the *Phaedo,* Socrates had already argued lengthily in defense of human immortality. Now he here presents one more brief argument.

Our chief purpose in printing these excerpts from Plato's dialogues is not for the significance of the comments on love and immortality, however important these may be, but rather for the illustration of a time-proven educational technique—the question-and-answer method of exploring ideas and stimulating thought. All who would teach can learn from these skillful examples.

Thoughts and questions for discussion: As presented by Plato, Socrates is endlessly brilliant in his probing comments and questions, skillfully maneuvering whatever person he is talking to into situations where he is compelled to agree with Socrates and reach the conclusions Socrates desires. Although Socrates is portrayed as both brilliant and profound, the one to whom he is talking sometimes appears not too bright and little better than a manipulated stooge. If Socrates actually talked to people this way, is it understandable that his probing questions would sometimes arouse hostility and anger in spite of his own high idealism and dedicated search for truth?

From Plato's "Symposium"

"And now," said Socrates, "I will ask about Love: Is Love of something or of nothing?"

"Of something, surely," Agathon replied.

"Keep in mind what this is, and tell me what I want to know—whether Love desires that of which love is."

"Yes, surely."

"And does he possess, or does he not possess, that which he loves and desires?"

"Probably not, I should say."

"Nay," replied Socrates, "I would have you consider whether 'necessarily' is not rather the word. The inference that he who desires something is in want of something, and that he who desires nothing is in want of nothing, is in my judgment, Agathon, absolutely and necessarily true. What do you think?"

"I agree with you," said Agathon.

"Very good. Would he who is great, desire to be great, or he who is strong, desire to be strong?"

"That would be inconsistent with our previous admissions."

"True. For he who is anything cannot want to be that which he is?"

"Very true."

"And yet," added Socrates, "if a man being strong desired to be strong, or being swift desired to be swift, or being healthy desired to be healthy, in that case he might be thought to desire something which he already has or is. I give the example in order that we may avoid misconception. For the possessors of these qualities, Agathon, must be supposed to have their respective advantages at the time, whether they choose or not; and who can desire that which he has? Therefore, when a person says, I am well and wish to be well, or I am rich and wish to be rich, and I desire simply to have what I have—to him we shall reply: You, my friend, having wealth and health and strength, want to have the continuance of them; for at this moment, whether you choose or no, you have them. And when you say, I desire that which I have and nothing else, is not your meaning that you want to have what you now have in the future? He must agree with us—must he not?"

"He must," replied Agathon.

"Then," said Socrates, "he desires that what he has at present may be preserved to him in the future, which is equivalent to saying that he desires something which is nonexistent to him, and which as yet he has not got."

"Very true," he said.

"Then he and everyone who desires, desires that which he has not already, and which is future and not present, and which he has not, and is not, and of which he is in want; these are the sort of things which love and desire seek?"

"Very true," he said.

"Then now," said Socrates, "let us recapitulate the argument.

The Role of Education 49

First, is not love of something, and of something too which is wanting to a man?"

"Yes," he replied.

"Remember further what you said in your speech, or if you do not remember I will remind you: you said that the love of the beautiful set in order the empire of the gods, for that of deformed things there is no love—did you not say something of that kind?"

"Yes," said Agathon.

"Yes, my friend, and the remark was a just one. And if this is true, Love is the love of beauty and not of deformity?"

He assented.

"And the admission has been already made that Love is of something which a man wants and has not?"

"True," he said.

"Then Love wants and has not beauty?"

"Certainly," he replied.

"And would you call that beautiful which wants and does not possess beauty?"

"Certainly not."

"Then would you still say that love is beautiful?"

Agathon replied: "I fear that I did not understand what I was saying."

"You made a very good speech, Agathon," replied Socrates; "but there is yet one small question which I would fain ask: Is not the good also the beautiful?"

"Yes."

"Then in wanting the beautiful, love wants also the good?"

"I cannot refute you, Socrates," said Agathon. "Let us assume that what you say is true."

"Say rather, beloved Agathon, that you cannot refute the truth."

[There now follows in the *Symposium* an eloquently told story by Socrates in which he describes Love as a great power that "lifts man from the passions of earth to a vision of the absolute beauty of God."]

From Book X of Plato's "Republic"

"Are you not aware," I [Socrates] said, "that the soul of man is immortal and imperishable?"

Glaucon looked at me in astonishment, and said: "No, by heaven! And are you really prepared to maintain this?"

"Yes," I said, "I ought to be, and you too—there is no difficulty in proving it."

"I see a great difficulty; but I should like to hear you state this argument of which you make so light."

"Listen, then."

"I am attending."

"There is a thing which you call good and another which you call evil?"

"Yes," he replied.

"Would you agree with me in thinking that the corrupting and destroying element is the evil, and the saving and improving element the good?"

"Yes."

"And you admit that everything has a good and also an evil; as ophthalmia is the evil of the eyes and disease of the whole body; as mildew is of corn, and rot of timber, or rust of copper and iron: in everything, or in almost everything, there is an inherent evil and disease?"

"Yes," he said.

"And anything which is infected by any of these evils is made evil, and at last wholly dissolves and dies?"

"True."

"The vice and evil which is inherent in each is the destruction of each; and if this does not destroy them there is nothing else that will; for good certainly will not destroy them, nor again, that which is neither good nor evil."

"Certainly not."

"If, then, we find any nature which having this inherent corruption cannot be dissolved or destroyed, we may be certain that of such a nature there is no destruction?"

"That may be assumed."

"Well," I said, "and is there no evil which corrupts the soul?"

"Yes," he said, "there are all the evils which we were just now passing in review: unrighteousness, intemperance, cowardice, ignorance."

"But does any of these dissolve or destroy her? And here do not let us fall into the error of supposing that the unjust and foolish man, when he is detected, perishes through his own injustice, which is an evil of the soul. Take the analogy of the body: The evil of the body is a disease which wastes and reduces and annihilates the body; and all the things of which we were just now speaking come to annihilation through their own corruption attaching to them and inhering in them and so destroying them. Is not this true?"

"Yes."

"Consider the soul in like manner. Does the injustice or other evil which exists in the soul waste and consume her? Do they by attaching to the soul and inhering in her at last bring her to death, and so separate her from the body?"

"Certainly not."

"And yet," I said, "it is unreasonable to suppose that anything can perish from without through affection of external evil which could not be destroyed from within by a corruption of its own?"

"It is," he replied.

"Consider," I said, "Glaucon, that even the badness of food, whether staleness, decomposition, or any other bad quality, when confined to the actual food, is not supposed to destroy the body; although, if the badness of food communicates corruption to the body, then we should say that the body has been destroyed by a corruption of itself, which is disease, brought on by the food; but that the body, being one thing, can be destroyed by the badness of food, which is another, and which does not engender any natural infection—this we shall absolutely deny?"

"Very true."

"And, on the same principle, unless some bodily evil can produce an evil of the soul, we must not suppose that the soul, which is one thing, can be dissolved by any merely external evil which belongs to another?"

"Yes," he said, "there is reason in that."

"Either, then, let us refute this conclusion, or, while it remains unrefuted, let us never say that fever, or any other disease, or the knife put to the throat, or even the cutting up of the whole body into the minutest pieces, can destroy the soul, until she herself is proved to become more unholy or unrighteous in consequence of these things being done to the body; but that the soul, or anything else if not destroyed by an internal evil, can be destroyed by an external one, is not to be affirmed by any man."

"And surely," he replied, "no one will ever prove that the souls of men become more unjust in consequence of death."

"But if someone who would rather not admit the immortality of the soul boldly denies this, and says that the dying do really become more evil and unrighteous, then, if the speaker is right, I suppose that injustice, like disease, must be assumed to be fatal to the unjust, and that those who take this disorder die by the natural inherent power of destruction which evil has, and which kills them sooner or later, but in quite another way from that in which, at present, the wicked receive death at the hands of others as the penalty of their deeds?"

"Nay," he said, "in that case injustice, if fatal to the unjust, will not be so very terrible to him, for he will be delivered from evil. But I rather suspect the opposite to be the truth, and that injustice which, if it have the power, will murder others, keeps the murderer alive—aye, and well awake too; so far removed is her dwelling-place from being a house of death."

"True," I said; "if the inherent natural vice or evil of the soul is unable to kill or destroy her, hardly will that which is appointed to be the destruction of some other body, destroy a soul or anything else except that of which it was appointed to be the destruction."

"Yes, that can hardly be."

"But the soul which cannot be destroyed by an evil, whether inherent or external, must exist forever, and if existing forever, must be immortal?"

"Certainly," agreed Glaucon.

[There now follows in Book X of the *Republic* further exploring of the conditions of human immortality and a soaring vision of the rewards of justice and wisdom in this life and the next.]

Comment on Edman's "First Lesson"

Half a century ago, according to his famous friend T. V. Smith, Professor A. E. Johnson liked to say that "education is the creation of finer human hungers." Most good teachers know that teaching students to think and evaluate is far more important than just giving them information. Often a great teacher stretches the minds of his students by asking disquieting questions or by challenging assumptions that have never been challenged before. Sometimes this is frustrating, even painful, to the student—but the reward is growth.

Irwin Edman (1896-1954) was a prominent American educator who for many years taught philosophy at Columbia University. The story that follows is his own account of how he stimulated his students to think, even the reluctant ones.

At the beginning of the hour some of the students are hostile, some are indifferent, and some are amused. At the end, most of them have been caught up in the challenge of thinking, even though it is a kind of game that the teacher is playing. Note that Professor Edman is a sort of modern Socrates. There is, however, a difference. Both ask provocative, leading questions; but Socrates in one way or another supplies most of the answers himself, whereas Professor Edman leaves many of the questions dangling unanswered, at least in this first lesson.

Questions for discussion: Is it sufficient for a teacher to maneuver his students into thinking, or is it also the teacher's responsibility to guide them to the right answers? Is it best if he sometimes does the one and sometimes the other? Are there "right answers" to all questions? Assuming that it is part of the work of the teacher, at least the great teacher, not only to ask questions that stretch the students' minds, but also to skillfully guide the students towards wise answers, is there evidence in Professor Edman's account that he accepts this as part of his responsibility, if not in the first lesson, then in the lessons that are to follow?

First Lesson

by Irwin Edman

Every autumn in normal times I walk, with rather deliberate briskness, into a classroom in which are gathered about forty young men who have voluntarily enrolled themselves in a course entitled "Introduction to Philosophy." They have come to this class not as they come to similar enterprises in physics, chemistry, or history. They come to those subjects expecting to find out more about what they already know something about. They come to this class hoping to find out by the end of the year what it is that they are studying. And, as I am a disciple of Socrates, I do not propose to tell them. I propose, by asking the proper questions, to have them tell me, and to assist them in the discovery that they have in essence always known what philosophy is.

I look around and light on the most likely looking candidate. I find a young man whom I know by sight, Alfred Jeremy, hitherto undebauched by philosophy.

"Mr. Jeremy," I say without preamble, "I suppose you believe you exist?"

Young Jeremy looks at me quizzically. I feel he is wondering if this is what professors of philosophy are paid to do.

"Of course I exist," he says, and I detect the slightest tone of impatience in his courteous and somewhat surprised tone.

"What makes you so sure?" I ask.

The large football player in the second row shifts his bulk impatiently in the seat too small for him, as if suddenly wondering what is going on here.

"Well," says Jeremy, "it's me. I mean I. I brought myself in here." The class smiles a little at that.

"How do you know it's you?" I say.

"I can pinch myself," he says. The football player does that very thing. Then he pinches his neighbor. I tap warningly on the table with a piece of chalk.

"I can feel my hands if I press them hard, and I have a pain in the crick of my neck."

"You mean you have sensations," I say. "But how do you know they're yours?"

"Well, whose else would they be?" asks Jeremy in great surprise.

"But who are you?" I insist. "Simply this cluster of sensations at the present moment?"

"Oh, no," says Jeremy. "I'm the guy, excuse me, the fellow, who went through the Horace Mann School, and who entered Columbia College last year as a freshman. I left the dormitory this morning and had breakfast at the Sandwich Shop, no, it was in the Lion's Den, and I had a class in advanced French, and I talked to a couple of guys, I mean fellows, and now I'm here."

"But all that was up to the present moment; it was all in the past, wasn't it?"

"Yes, sir," says Jeremy.

"It was pure memory," I say. "Might it not be false memory, pure fiction? You know how difficult it is to get a reliable witness of what has happened in the past. You can't be sure, can you, that it *was* you, can you now?"

"Who else could it be?" asks Jeremy.

"It might be a dream that you in the present are having of what you call the immediate past, mightn't it?"

During this colloquy some members of the class are sitting in absorbed attention. There is a bright-looking, very young man who can scarcely wait until I ask him a question. His hand is already up. The football player is not exactly absorbed, but he looks a little as if he would like really very much now to know what is going on here. The nice-looking boy in the third row seems vaguely troubled. Several look as if they think I am trying to play some trick on them.

The very young-looking boy can wait no longer.

"Well?" I say. (I recognize him, too. He had come to interview me yesterday for the college paper.) "Mr. Gottesman, what do *you* think?"

"Well, I not only remember, but I expect," he says, "I know for pretty certain that I'm going to be around tomorrow, having breakfast and lunch and coming to classes."

"But that," I say, "is mere expectation, is it not? It's an act of faith. You can't really believe you exist on the ground that somebody to whom unhappened things have not yet happened is going to be there to have them happen to him. And is that the ground for your believing that you now exist—because somebody not in existence is going to exist? That future 'you' does not yet exist, does he?"

"No," says young Gottesman ruefully, "I suppose he doesn't."

There is a hand raised in the back now. I look at the pleasant blue-eyed Irish face behind it.

"Your name, please."

"Farrell, John."

"Well, Mr. Farrell, what do you think? Why do *you* think you exist?"

"Because I can't think of myself not existing while I'm sitting here talking—or thinking," he adds after a moment's thought. "Who else is doing it?"

"Have you ever read Descartes?" I ask.

"Never heard of him," he says, almost in a tone of disclaiming unsavory acquaintance.

"Well, he is a famous French philosopher of three centuries ago. He would be inclined to agree with you."

"He would?" asks Farrell.

"Well, let's see where we are," I say. "The past is an illusion, the future a gamble. We have only ourselves of the moment—feeling, thinking, sensing—to be sure of. But surely, Mr. Farrell, you wouldn't call that enough to call 'Mr. Farrell,' would you? The John Farrell your parents know has a past and a future, hasn't he?"

"I sure hope so," says Mr. Farrell. "So do my parents, especially about the future."

"Well," I say, "let's take a vote for a moment. How many are willing to assume they exist?"

The class is unanimous in favor of their own existence.

"But it's only an assumption, mind," I say. "We haven't proved it yet. Now how about other people?"

John Farrell looks appraisingly at his neighbor to the left and then to the right. Many members of the class do the same. The football player looks appraisingly at me.

"How do we know other people exist?"

"How do we know other people exist?" Farrell repeats.

Jeremy raises his hand. I nod.

"Well, I hear them, I see them. Seeing is believing, as they say."

"Yes, but gentlemen, we are obviously often deceived. There are mirages in the desert; we think we see things that turn out to be not there, or to be something else. The man you see is not the one you thought you saw, but his brother. The stick looks broken in water, but it is the shadow, not the stick, that you see. Perhaps it is a devil who has masked as your friend and classmate. Perhaps it is a dream, or a nightmare."

The bright youngster in the front row looks at me as if he wondered if I were more than half joking.

"And how about *things*, this blackboard, this desk?" I ask, turning to Farrell, whose blue eyes seem to be speculating curiously on this panorama of illusion I have opened before him.

"Me?" he says, his attention recalled. "Well, the same thing as other people. I see it, I can touch it. The blackboard has a sort of odor, too."

I take the class on a little imaginary tour through the history of thought. I remind them how uneasy Plato was about the senses; how Berkeley whisked the world away into a semblance constituted by our ideas; how Schopenhauer emphasizes the dreamlike quality of existence, despite the regularity and order of the dream.

"But things," persists the bright young boy, "are there in space, and that blackboard will be there tomorrow when we come back. Or," he added, "if we don't."

The Role of Education

I had been rather waiting for this opening.

"What," I say, turning to Smith, having found his name next to his seat number, "what, Mr. Smith, *is space?*"

Mr. Smith considers a moment. He waves his hand comprehensively in the air. "Space is what everything else is in," he says.

The football player leans forward. "Yeah, like a box," he bursts out.

"But what," I say, "is space in?" Some of the boys look faintly disgusted, some perplexed.

"Yes, sir," says the football player slowly and ruefully, "what *is* it in?"

For the next fifteen minutes or so, without knowing the words, the young men, aided and abetted by myself, explore, in elementary form, some of the mysteries and paradoxes that Immanuel Kant turned up. We come out at about the same place he did. Perhaps space is just a way our mind has of arranging our sensations. Experience, we determine tentatively, is impossible without space, and yet it is impossible to find space in experience.

"Is it the same about time?" says a rather blasé youth in the third row who has not up to that point taken any part in the discussion.

"Well, surely the present is here," says Mr. Gottesman.

"And the past *has* been here," says the football player.

"And the future is surely going to be here," says Mr. Jeremy.

"You are going too fast for me, gentlemen," I interrupt. "Why are you so sure, Mr. Jeremy, that the past *was* here? Is it not, like yourself of yesterday, a memory? You cannot see the past clearly, can you? Or hear it? It's gone forever.

"And as for the future, you can bet, if you care to, that it is going to take place, but surely at the present moment it does not exist. If it did, it would be the present, wouldn't it? There's just this moment, isn't there? All the rest is memory or imagination."

"It doesn't leave us very much," says Mr. Smith.

There are several students who have not entered into the discussion at all. But I suspect I know what is going on in their heads. Some of them look bored, and I am not sure they will not change their registration after all. Some of them are pleasantly bewildered, some embarrassed by their bewilderment. The football player finally says, "But that's all very well, maybe, for philosophers. But for plain ordinary people, time and space and other people and themselves do exist, don't they now, professor? Right here now, aren't we in this actual room, talking to each other, today, Monday?"

For the next ten minutes we have quite a heated controversy. There are those who side with the football player, who take the side of common-sense men in all ages, who will have no traffic with such nonsense. In a class every sort of temperament in the history of mankind is likely to reveal itself. Young Gottesman is a kind of poet, and I can see already that he is impressed by the poetry and suasion of the idea that all we see and hear is a dream.

I intend myself before the term is over to try to show these young men that it would be silly to pretend that they need seriously doubt their own existence, that of the world, of time and space and other people and things. My purpose this morning has been to get them to look at these things with a difference. If only one can get them to be critical of their most usual preconceptions, one is on the road. A little later we'll see what we can do about good and evil, right and wrong, justice and injustice. These students are very young, but they are already full of age-old prejudices. At least an Introduction to Philosophy may start them on the quest for more rational standards of life, of knowledge, of action, of society.

The bell is ringing, announcing the end of the hour. Young Farrell leans forward. "But *do* we exist?" he says.

"Here endeth the first lesson," I say.

Selections from the Writings of the Author

Urged by others to do so, I have hesitantly decided to include here three selections from my own writings on education and the role of the teacher.

First is a little essay called "Seven Qualities of an Educated Person," which originally was written as part of a talk given in 1968 to the officers of the Rocky Mountain Modern Language Association:

Seven Qualities of an Educated Person

In all schools we are principally engaged, or should be, in *educating* people—not just filling their heads with information and preparing them for jobs, but truly educating them. And what is a truly educated person? It seems to me that whatever else he is or is not, he is characterized by seven qualities:

First, he places ideas over power. In a sense, of course, ideas are power, and the highest kind of power. But you all know what I mean. The educated person builds his life around ideas rather than around brawn or wealth or position.

Second, he places aesthetic and spiritual values above material possessions and sensual desires. I think I need comment no further on this.

Third, he has the ability to see the other person's point of view and both (or several) sides of a question. Almost always there are at least two sides to any issue, and one measure of the truly educated person is that he can see these sides in their complex reality. Narrowness, prejudice, and bigotry melt away under the warm light of many-sided understanding.

Fourth, he has the ability to disagree pleasantly. Because everybody is different from everybody else, disagreements are inevitable, and the world would be dull without them. Disagreement, however, need not mean anger, hostility, or quarreling. Educated people can disagree vigorously but still be friends and pleasant conversationalists. If the world were truly educated, quarrels between individuals and wars between nations would cease to exist. Perhaps this is too much to hope for, but at least we can be pleasant in disagreement with our friends, colleagues, neighbors, and families.

Fifth, he has the ability to like and get value from things with which he disagrees. I am thinking particularly of books. Too often when people say "I don't like this book; it isn't any good," they really mean "I disagree with what this book says." The kindergarten rule of literature is that there can be both enjoyment and value in reading books with which one disagrees. Some people dislike and find useless everything with which they disagree. But what a narrow world this makes! Generally a person can learn more from exploring several points of view than he can from merely re-experiencing his own. This is not to say, of course, that he should not hold firm to his convictions when he is sure they are right. He should, but he should also explore other points of view sufficiently to have an *informed* conviction, and to develop his own standards of good taste.

Sixth, the educated person gets angry over the right things. Note, I am not saying that an educated person does not or should not get angry. Everybody gets angry. Even God. But how educated and mature a person is can be measured by what makes him angry. Uneducated, immature, shallow, and character-thin people become angry over certain kinds of things. Different kinds of things—less selfish, less personal—arouse the anger of educated, mature, character-deep people.

Seventh, and finally, the educated person is concerned and cares, really cares, about what happens to people other than just himself, his family, and his immediate associates. It is so easy to be selfish and trivial, but it is so right to be unselfish and relevant! Our danger as educators is that we get so involved in the machinery of education—administrative chores, committee work, meetings, hallway shoptalk, social chit-chat, abstract philosophizing, and even classroom pedantry—that we have little time for more vital issues. Our world is torn with such urgent moral, racial, socio-economic, and ideological problems that unless as educators we give at least part of our energy to these matters we are missing our finest opportunity and most compelling responsibility. We may not be able to solve the problems, but every one of us can do at least something to bridge communication and deepen understanding.

Next is another little essay called "The Faces of Anger," which develops the thought touched on in item six of the preceding essay—that is, that everybody gets angry, but the educated person gets angry over the right things:

The Faces of Anger

The quality of a person is measured by what makes him angry.
If lust makes him angry, he is an animal. Pity him, and teach him self-control.
If greed makes him angry, he is a child. Be patient with him, and teach him unselfishness.

The Role of Education 61

If jealousy makes him angry, he is an adolescent. Comfort him, and encourage him to achieve.
If hunger for revenge makes him angry, the hate of the savage still flows in his veins. Forgive him, and teach him love.
If his own ignorance and prejudice make him angry, he is a victim of environment. Be tolerant with him, and feed him knowledge.
If the daily friction of personalities makes him angry, he is normal. Give him understanding, and guide him to understand others.
However, if unnecessary suffering makes him angry, he is a humanitarian. Help him.
If injustice among nations makes him angry, he is a statesman. Follow him.
If injustice among people makes him angry, he is a champion of principle. Stand firm by his side.
If the sins of the world make him angry, he is a prophet. Heed his counsel.
If the suppression of truth makes him angry, he is a scholar. Respect him.
If the suppression of thinking makes him angry, he is a teacher. Honor him, and be forever grateful.

Last are some excerpts from a longer essay called "The Challenge of Teaching." This was first published about five years ago and has been re-published in several places since then but now for the first time is made available for Church readers generally. No further introductory comment seems needful except to observe two things: First, although the essay was originally written for an audience of professional teachers at Brigham Young University, especially literature teachers, much of what is said about good and bad teaching applies equally to our teaching in the auxiliary organizations of the Church. Second, unless we reach *all* class members in our Church teaching, we fail just as much as the grade school or high school teacher who reaches only part of her students. In Sunday School, Primary, and M.I.A. the best answer to discipline problems is not to be so severe and harsh that some students are driven from the class or react negatively to what is going on. The best answer is to teach so vividly and excellently that even the most unruly or inattentive child is caught up in the excitement of learning.

Excerpts from "The Challenge of Teaching"

The responsibilities resting on the shoulders of a teacher, as any teacher knows, are both frightening and wonderful. No role, unless it is parenthood, provides a more awesome challenge than does teaching. And this is true no matter where the teaching is done—in grade school, in high school, in college, or in church. . . .

Because I am an English teacher, what I say will apply especially to the teaching of English; but I hope I have spread the focus enough to cover the broad field of teaching as a whole. Also, part of what I say will explore the challenges that all teachers share, and part will explore the special challenges peculiar to L.D.S. teachers.

As a beginning let me describe seven types of teachers that I feel we should determine with all our will power never to become:

(1) First is the sentimentalist—the teacher who reacts emotionally to everything and everyone he teaches. I don't believe a teacher can get away with gushy sentimentality even in grade school or in church. The children will see through it and mock it. Certainly in junior high and high school the weepy or saccharine teacher will be looked on by students as both shallow and weak. The ineffectiveness, indeed the harm, of such a teacher in college is so obvious as to need no comment. We cannot teach those who do not respect us, and no one respects the sentimentalist, not even his fellow sentimentalists. (I am not, of course, talking against genuine sentiment, which has its place in education as in life, and lies at the center of literature and religion. The difference between sentiment and sentimentality is the difference between emotion that is honest and emotion that is cheap, surfacy, and false.)

(2) Second is the cynic—the sophisticated intellectual egotist who believes in nothing, not even the subject that he teaches. He analyzes to scorn and examines to ridicule. Criticism for him means hyper-criticism. He is skilled at finding fault with all that he reads and with all of the students he teaches. In his role as teacher he is at the opposite extreme from the sentimentalist, scorning all forms of sentiment, both the true and the imitative; and in his dread of being regarded as "soft" or "wholesome" he sustains a pose of flippancy and snobbish boredom. Students may learn from such a teacher, but often he will do them harm greater than the help he gives them.

(3) The third undesirable type, the sadist, is a first cousin of the cynic. His attitude towards everything, including especially his students, is negative always, and he prides himself in failing as many students as possible, justifying himself by his "high academic standards." He delights in student blunders because they give him an opportunity to ridicule. His students are in the grip of his power, and he punishes them without mercy, finding fault equally with all that they do and all that they don't

do. . . . He enjoys the suffering of others, and seems even to get a masochistic pleasure out of his own sour attitude. Pessimism is his dominant mood, sarcasm is his main weapon, low grades are his principal threats, and his students are his victims.

(4) Fourth is the egoistic show-off, the teacher who uses his classroom mostly as a theater in which to parade his personality before a captive audience. He is so interested in himself that he has little concern for others, including especially his students. Whether they learn or don't learn, whether they fail or pass, is secondary to the marvelous experience they have of seeing and hearing him, and he hopes that they appreciate him as he deserves to be appreciated. In my criticism of such a teacher, I don't want to imply that teaching should be dull and flat. Quite the contrary, it should be as vivid as possible, and every good teacher is properly part showman, perhaps even with a tinge of the prima donna in his nature. But teaching that focuses on the teacher's desire to display himself rather than on the needs of the students will always, I think, be bad teaching.

(5) Fifth is the faddist, the hobby-horse rider, the teacher with narrow interests who cannot see beyond his own myopia. . . . Narrowness and prejudice can ruin an otherwise able teacher, who in his limited vision often becomes a cultist crusading to shape his students in his own narrow image and labeling as evil anyone who doesn't share his constricted views. . . . In religion, as in literature, as in art, as in education, as in life, the broad view should be cultivated, not at the sacrifice of truth or of critical standards, but with the reward of truth and of deepened critical standards. And all of this, I believe, is in harmony with the Prophet Joseph Smith's counsel that we should seek all things virtuous, lovely, and praiseworthy, getting the riches of the mind and spirit out of the world's best books.

(6) Sixth is the information-giver, the teacher who deludes himself into believing that he is fulfilling his teaching role when, like a machine, he feeds students a mass of facts and has them parrot the information back in examinations. . . . I am not suggesting that knowledge is unimportant. It is very important, both as an end in itself and as a tool. But beyond knowledge lie principles and relationships and thought-processes and value-judgments that should be the ultimate concern of both a teacher and his students. Ignorance is dangerous, but knowledge without responsibility may be more dangerous. More than to give information, a teacher needs to help guide a student's mind to think, and even beyond that, to help him shape his character. Giving information is easy. Forming a thinking mind is hard. And shaping a strong character is hardest of all, partly because it must be shaped mostly from within. Giving information is only the beginning of a teacher's responsibility; the end is to stimulate, excite, motivate, lift, challenge, inspire.

(7) Seventh is the "wage-earner teacher," the person for whom teaching is primarily just a job, just a way to make a living. I am not implying that a teacher should work for a sub-standard salary; he should not. As a highly trained professional person, he is worthy of an adequate salary and should get it. But if he is a first-quality teacher he will work for higher wages than money. His reward will be the growth of his students and of his own vision, and the satisfaction of unselfishly giving himself in the service of the human struggle upward. As teachers we must resist the trend of our time to demand more and more money for less and less work, and we should also resist a growing tendency among ourselves to waste our energy in complaining about salaries, and about the burden of papers to correct and students to advise and committees to serve on. We need to subdue any feeling within us that teaching is just a job and cultivate an attitude of dedication in our work. At least we must do this if we want to rise above being mere wage-earners and become great teachers. . . .

Up to this point I have been talking mostly about extreme attitudes that as teachers we should avoid. Let me shift ground a little now and talk more directly about our goals in teaching. First, I believe, we should recognize that above all else we exist professionally to serve our students. This means that we should be concerned about them and available to them, outside the classroom as well as in it, for much of our best teaching is done outside the classroom. If we hide from our students, making ourselves as inaccessible as possible, we are neglecting one of our major responsibilities.

Some say we should be as objective as possible in teaching, treating each student impersonally. To the extent that this applies to standards of grading, I agree that it is the proper and necessary attitude; but to the extent that it applies to our relationship with the personalities of the students, I am convinced that complete objectivity is inadequate, harmful, and also, fortunately, impossible. We must see them as individuals! Every student is a unique personality and must be approached uniquely. The right way of handling one student may well be the wrong way for another, and we must treat each as sensitively and wisely as possible.

I remember a boy suffering from cerebral palsy whose brilliant mind was hampered with spasms that weakened the control of his body. He needed special arrangements to complete his examinations, and I would have been inexcusably unfair if I had treated him the same as the other students.

That boy's uniqueness was, of course, visible and invited immediate sympathy. Sometimes the injury is hidden inside. I remember a Freshman English student who was so torn emotionally that she could not complete some of her assignments, mostly because of extreme hostilities within her family. . . . This girl had seen too much of life and too little

The Role of Education

of love. She needed the special understanding that a teacher can give when the parents have failed.

Sometimes, too, we must be firm and seemingly harsh. It is easier to be tenderly considerate than to be rigid, but sometimes rigidity is needed. I remember a boy who asked me to falsify a grade because he said he was suffering from an incurable disease and did not want to die with a "D" on his record. He was a brash boy who had never learned to be honest with himself; always he had found a way to maneuver around the truth. I told him that it was better to die with a "D" on his record than with a lie on his conscience. This is the cruellest thing I have ever told a student, but for him it was right. At least I *think* it was right.

These are dramatic examples. But, in less extreme ways, all of our students are unique personalities and need to be treated as such if we are to influence them beyond just feeding them information. I shall never forget the student who came to my office several years ago and said, "You are the worst teacher I ever had, and I've had some bad ones." I was stung by his comment, not by the falseness of it but because, as I thought the course over, it was true. I *was* his worst teacher. At least I was for him a bad teacher. He had special academic problems and I had failed to help him overcome them. I may have been a good teacher for other students in the class, but I was a bad teacher for this particular student. Our responsibility is not only to teach *part* of the students but to teach *all* of them who come to us. And when a student fails, a teacher fails also.

I suppose there has never been a teacher skilled and powerful enough to reach all his students, but we need to try. There is the student who sleeps with bored or weary eyes, and the one who sleeps with eyes open but mind closed; the one who says "I dare you to teach me," and the one who, like a sponge, uncritically absorbs everything; the girl who has learned to use her body more than her mind, and the boy who spends his time looking at her; the would-be writer who thinks that his small talent excuses him from learning anything, and the memorizer who mistakenly assumes that an accumulation of facts equals genuine knowledge; the girl who always has a sympathy-winning explanation for her failure to learn, and the boy who has brilliant possibilities but is so torn in the depths of his own thoughts that all we can see is a tangled mass of potentiality; the student who tries very hard and is very sweet but is obviously a slow learner, and the one who terrifies because he is obviously brighter than the teacher; the gregarious student whose personality makes him always the center of a circle, and the one who is a misfit in all groups and all situations; the student who never speaks because he has nothing to say, and the one who never speaks although he has much to say, and the one who speaks often even though he has little to say.

All of these and the hundreds of others equally diverse, all must be reached. At least we should try.

Part of our responsibility is to help students enjoy the excitement of learning. Perhaps teaching should at times be painful, but it should never be dull. . . . The best guarantee against poor discipline is good teaching. And this is true at all levels of teaching and in all situations, including both school and church. If the teaching is good enough, the students will be attentive and responsive. When students are bored and unruly, the best solution is not harsher rules but better teaching.

I would like to say a little more about the hard work of being a good teacher, because I think it *is* hard work—hard and long. Anyone who thinks otherwise can probably find and keep a job teaching, but he won't be a good teacher. One of the unfortunate things about teaching as a profession is that all teachers, whether strong or weak, energetic or lazy, inspired or dull, are paid about the same. Oh, we hear talk of merit pay, etc., but the truth is that the best teachers aren't paid much more than the worst teachers. They may be worth several times as much, but they won't be paid according to their worth. The strong ones will be paid too little, and the weak ones will be paid too much. Therefore, the rewards for a good teacher must be other than money. Fortunately, the rewards are abundant, and they are available daily, including the wonderful pleasure of teaching itself.

If we are good teachers we will have to work hard just to complete our daily tasks. Even so, I don't think most of us ever reach our potentiality as thinking, creative human beings. Most people, including both those of us who are teachers and those who are students, operate at about half efficiency, I fear. We sleep too much, eat too much, idle too much, and waste too much time in trivia. We need to work harder, think deeper, exchange ideas more constructively, and create more abundantly. . . .

As a final point I want to comment on what I feel are our special responsibilities as L.D.S. teachers, particularly for those of us who teach L.D.S. students in an L.D.S. school, or who teach within the auxiliary organizations of the Church. Above all, I think we have a special responsibility to live the Gospel, remaining as true as we can to its fundamental principles. I have heard some say that we have no more responsibility than do all members of the Church. But I don't feel this way. I feel that because we are selected to teach the youth of the Church we have a special responsibility to be loyal and spiritual in our personal lives. Our students need to observe our activity in the Church, to sense our faith, to hear our convictions. I do not mean that we should spend all our class time preaching to our students. Our responsibility if we are professional teachers is to teach the subject matter for which we are professionally trained, and besides, preaching tends only to alienate the most sensitive of the students. But occasionally we need to let students know where we stand on the vital issues of the spirit. They need to know that we have studied philosophy, literature, and science and remained strong in our faith in the Gospel. They need to know that we have explored the difficult questions with our testimonies intact. I am not asking that we betray our integrity. I am asking only that we fulfill and share it. . . . As L.D.S. teachers, we need to speak courageously our confidence that literature, art, and religion are comrades in arms against the common foes of selfishness, materialism, and all things maudlin, superficial, and gross. This is the goal of education at its best, and this is the challenge of the first-quality teacher.

I have been talking about the ideal teacher. My students will testify that as a teacher I too fall short. My only plea is that I too am human, and that, however inadequate, I see the vision.

Comment on "The Fish, the Man, and the Spirit"

The passages printed below are the first two sections of "The Fish, the Man, and the Spirit" by Leigh Hunt (1784-1859), English romantic poet and essayist. The stanzas are printed here for two reasons: first, to illustrate in an exaggerated but very clear way the point made in "Seven Qualities of an Educated Person" that part of being educated is the ability to see things from the other person's point of view; second, to inject a note of delightful satiric humor (but humor with a lesson) into this generally very serious section on education.

From "The Fish, the Man, and the Spirit"

Leigh Hunt

(A man speaks to a fish)
>You strange, astonished-looking, angle-faced,
>Dreary-mouthed, gaping wretches of the sea,
>Gulping salt-water everlastingly,
>Cold-blooded, though with red your blood be graced,
>And mute, though dwellers in the roaring waste;
>And you, all shapes beside, that fishy be,—
>Some round, some flat, some long, all devilry,
>Legless, unloving, infamously chaste:—
>
>O scaly, slippery, wet, swift, staring wights,
>What is't ye do? what life lead? eh, dull goggles?
>How do ye vary your vile days and nights?
>How pass your Sundays? Are ye still but joggles
>In ceaseless wash? Still nought but gapes and bites,
>And drinks, and stares, diversified with boggles?

(The fish answers)
>Amazing monster! that, for aught I know,
>With the first sight of thee didst make our race
>Forever stare! Oh flat and shocking face,
>Grimly divided from the breast below!
>Thou that on dry land horribly dost go
>With a split body and most ridiculous pace,
>Prong after prong, disgracer of all grace,
>Long-useless-finned, haired, upright, unwet, slow!

O breather of unbreathable, sword-sharp air,
How canst exist? How bear thyself, thou dry
And dreary sloth? What particle canst share
Of the only blessed life, the watery?
I sometimes see of ye an actual *pair*
Go by! linked fin by fin! most odiously.

Comment on "He Ate and Drank the Precious Words"

We will give Emily Dickinson the final word in this section on education as she talks about the power of books to liberate and give wings to the human spirit. After all that other people can say in essay and in speech, the poet—the great poet—can often say it better, and in fewer words, as Emily Dickinson does here:

He Ate and Drank the Precious Words

Emily Dickinson

He ate and drank the precious words,
His spirit grew robust;
He knew no more that he was poor,
Nor that his frame was dust.
He danced along the dingy days,
And this bequest of wings
Was but a book. What liberty
A loosened spirit brings!

SECTION THREE

The Problem of Communication

by Robert K. Thomas

"ADVICE TO A YOUNG ARTIST"
By Honoré Daumier
National Gallery of Art, Washington, D.C. · Gift of Duncan Phillips

Commentary by
Floyd E. Brienholt, Chairman, Department of Art,
Brigham Young University

Honoré Daumier at the age of seven decided to be an artist. To gain background for his chosen field, he frequented the poorer quarters of Paris and haunted the corridors of the Louvre. He studied Rembrandt and Michelangelo, nature, and the manners and customs of his period. Although he is better known as a lithographer and political cartoonist, it has been said that he was one of the greatest painters of the 19th Century.

Daumier expressed very deep feelings in a spirit of satire and ridicule. His caricatures are without hatred or spite, although they are biting. There is a direct simplicity in the expressions of what he saw and felt. All of his work has social significance. His art was and still is a very direct means of communication of ideas, a universal language. Artists today use art for propaganda purposes just as Daumier did in his time.

The painting, "Advice to a Young Artist," is perhaps more mild than many of his works. This is not a portrait of any two particular people but more a generalization of a typical situation in the world of work. We all learn from others who go before us, especially if they are willing to share their knowledge with us. In this very commonplace idea, expressed in a simple, earthy manner, one senses a certain kinship between the artist and the common working man, a certain reality that makes the commonplace beautiful when stripped to the bare essentials. None of his works is pretty. All tinsel and glitter have been left out and only simple truth remains. Perhaps this is why many have placed Daumier in the school of realism. All of his works, full of compassion for the downtrodden, are attempts at communicating the unvarnished truth as he saw it. As in all great art, Daumier in his work gives us not merely a photographic likeness of his subject but an interpretation of it in which he communicates what he knows, thinks, and feels.

THE PROBLEM OF COMMUNICATION

"There is no more sure tie between friends than when they are united in their objects and wishes."—Cicero

Introductory Comments

Current discussion of the "communication gap," which is blamed for everything from family bickering to international tension, seems to accept without question that the basic problem in poor communication is failure to be understood. Manuals that promise to increase our ability to speak or write effectively enjoy continuing popularity, and techniques that are intended to help us improve our methods of communication are widely discussed.

Almost lost in this stress upon communication as a tool is a connotation that this word originally carried—that is, sharing or making common an idea or an experience. To understand is not necessarily to agree; to be aware is not always to be united. If sophisticated ways of communication serve only to present our disagreements skillfully, we are stressing means at the expense of ends. Modern man has devised extraordinary techniques for disseminating information, and he has been equally ingenious in determining man's reactions; but the daily problems of harmony in a marriage, unselfishness in a family, and cooperation among friends seem to be hampered less by awkward methods than by unshared commitments and goals. Two small girls playing house need not speak their still unfocused hopes to know that they share them. "I love you" spoken sincerely doesn't need an ingenious setting.

The material we will consider in this section, therefore, will focus less on procedure than on result, and since examples of failure in communication are distressingly evident all about us, we will also emphasize positive examples of successful communication.

In our opening poem, "The Secret Heart," the father manages to convey love for his son in an unforgettable way, even though he is hardly conscious of doing it. With "Another April" we move to a tender but frustrating situation in which the relationship between an aged father and his daughter is heightened by the candid remarks of a child. This story is particularly effective in suggesting the limits upon certain types of communication that circumstances may dictate. Oliver Wendell Holmes' lines from *The Autocrat of the Breakfast Table* spend little time in discussing how one determines who is to have a key to his innermost feelings, but they portray graphically the result of being totally vulnerable to another human being.

In the rather informal "Can You Get Along With Your In-Laws?" there are some negative warnings, but these serve to highlight the positive suggestions at the practical base of this article. The selection of letters from Mark Twain to his wife and his wife's family lets us see a relationship in which extraordinary communication was achieved; and Willa Cather's story, "Neighbor Rosicky," presents not only a happy marriage but a loving family—including in-laws—and an exemplary account of friendship.

Scripture tells us that it takes the spirit to give life to the letter of the law. Note that the spirit doesn't substitute for the letter; it vitalizes it. Similarly, we should not expect to have the spirit by which we attempt to relate to one another assume the full burden of communication. Some of the devices and techniques currently available to facilitate sharing our world with others are blessings that were not available to our forebears. As we unite modes that partake of the present with the spirit that is eternal, we can establish that oneness that is the aim of all communication.

The Problem of Communication 77

The Secret Heart

by Robert P. Tristram Coffin

Across the years he could recall
His father one way best of all.
In the stillest hour of night
The boy awakened to a light.
Half in dreams, he saw his sire
With his great hands full of fire.
The man had struck a match to see
If his son slept peacefully.
He held his palms each side the spark
His love had kindled in the dark.
His two hands were curved apart
In the semblance of a heart.
He wore, it seemed to his small son,
A bare heart on his hidden one.
A heart that gave out such a glow
No son awake could bear to know.
It showed a look upon a face
Too tender for the day to trace.
One instant, it lit all about,
And then the secret heart went out.
But it shone long enough for one
To know that hands held up the sun.

Discussion of

"The Secret Heart"

While much of Robert P. Tristram Coffin's (1892-1955) poetry has the New England setting he loved and evoked so well, an occasional piece touches on a theme that transcends regional or even national boundaries. Such a poem is "The Secret Heart."

There is a ring of actuality in the situation that is depicted here: a small boy waking to see the lighted match in his father's cupped hands. Knowing that young Robert grew up on his father's farm and in a family characterized by a reserve appropriate to its northeastern location helps us appreciate the rather unusual form in which this poem is cast. These four stress couplets are at least one accent short of what is usually thought of as a normal speaking line. The clipped, laconic quality that results suggests Mr. Coffin's own New England childhood without being restricted to it.

Despite his Pulitzer Prize, his Rhodes Scholarship, and a lifetime of poetic and literary honors, Robert Coffin was an authentically simple man whose work always retained its common imagery, its straightforward language, and its optimistic tone. In less masculine hands the revelation of this childish memory might verge on the maudlin. How rare it is to find a picture of father-son devotion that is both appealing and convincing.

This poem is especially appropriate for this section since it is more a disclosure of communicated love than love itself. Even half awake, the boy has no difficulty in interpreting the glow on his father's face, and that moment becomes the basic memory he retains of his father. The final, almost cryptic, lines to this poem touch emphatically if almost casually upon the critical nature of expressed love. The son's whole universe takes on order and meaning in his *knowing* how deeply and tenderly his father's "secret heart" beats for him.

Another April

by Jesse Stuart

"Now, Pap, you won't get cold," Mom said as she put a heavy wool cap over his head.

"Huh, what did ye say?" Grandpa asked, holding his big hand cupped over his ear to catch the sound.

"Wait until I get your gloves," Mom said, hollering real loud in Grandpa's ear. Mom had forgotten about his gloves until he raised his big bare hand above his ear to catch the sound of Mom's voice.

"Don't get 'em," Grandpa said, "I won't ketch cold."

Mom didn't pay any attention to what Grandpa said. She went on to get the gloves anyway. Grandpa turned toward me. He saw that I was looking at him.

"Yer Ma's a-puttin' enough clothes on me to kill a man," Grandpa said, then he laughed a coarse laugh like March wind among the pine tops at his own words. I started laughing but not at Grandpa's words. He thought I was laughing at them and we both laughed together. It pleased Grandpa to think that I had laughed with him over something funny that he had said. But I was laughing at the way he was dressed. He looked like a picture of Santa Claus. But Grandpa's cheeks were not cherry-red like Santa Claus' cheeks. They were covered with white thin beard—and above his eyes were long white eyebrows almost as white as percoon petals and very much longer.

Grandpa was wearing a heavy wool suit that hung loosely about his big body but fitted him tightly round the waist where he was as big and as round as a flour barrel. His pant legs were as big round his pipe-stem legs as emptied meal sacks. And his big shoes, with his heavy wool socks dropping down over their tops, looked like sled runners. Grandpa wore a heavy wool shirt and over his wool shirt he wore a heavy wool sweater and then his coat over the top of all this. Over his coat he wore a heavy overcoat and about his neck he wore a wool scarf.

The way Mom had dressed Grandpa you'd think there was a heavy snow on the ground but there wasn't. April was here instead and the sun was shining on the green hills where the wild plums and the wild crab apples were in bloom enough to make you think there were big snow-drifts sprinkled over the green hills. When I looked at Grandpa and then looked out at the window at the sunshine and the green grass I laughed more. Grandpa laughed with me.

"I'm a-goin' to see my old friend," Grandpa said just as Mom came down the stairs with his gloves.

"Who is he, Grandpa?" I asked, but Grandpa just looked at my mouth working. He didn't know what I was saying. And he hated to ask me the second time.

Mom put the big wool gloves on Grandpa's hands. He stood there just like I had to do years ago, and let Mom put his gloves on. If Mom didn't get his fingers back in the glove-fingers exactly right Grandpa quarreled at Mom. And when Mom fixed his fingers exactly right in his gloves the way he wanted them Grandpa was pleased.

"I'll be a-goin' to see 'im," Grandpa said to Mom. "I know he'll still be there."

Mom opened our front door for Grandpa and he stepped out slowly, supporting himself with his big cane in one hand. With the other hand he held to the door facing. Mom let him out of the house just like she used to let me out in the spring. And when Grandpa left the house I wanted to go with him, but Mom wouldn't let me go. I wondered if he would get away from the house—get out of Mom's sight—and pull off his shoes and go barefooted and wade the creeks like I used to do when Mom let me out. Since Mom wouldn't let me go with Grandpa, I watched him as he walked slowly down the path in front of our house. Mom stood there watching Grandpa too. I think she was afraid that he would fall. But Mom was fooled; Grandpa toddled along the path better than my baby brother could.

"He used to be a powerful man," Mom said more to herself than she did to me. "He was a timber cutter. No man could cut more timber than my father; no man in the timber woods could sink an ax deeper into a log than my father. And no man could lift the end of a bigger saw log than Pap could."

"Who is Grandpa goin' to see, Mom?" I asked.

"He's not goin' to see anybody," Mom said.

"I heard 'im say that he was goin' to see an old friend," I told her.

"Oh, he was just a-talkin'," Mom said.

I watched Grandpa stop under the pine tree in our front yard. He set his cane against the pine tree trunk, pulled off his gloves and put them in his pocket. Then Grandpa stooped over slowly, as slowly as the wind bends down a sapling, and picked up a pine cone in his big soft fingers. Grandpa stood fondling the pine cone in his hand. Then, one by one, he pulled the little chips from the pine cone—tearing it to pieces like he was hunting for something in it—and after he had torn it to pieces he threw the pine-cone stem on the ground. Then he pulled pine needles from a low hanging pine bough and he felt of each pine needle between his fingers. He played with them a long time before he started down the path.

The Problem of Communication

"What's Grandpa doin'?" I asked Mom.

But Mom didn't answer me.

"How long has Grandpa been with us?" I asked Mom.

"Before you's born," she said. "Pap has been with us eleven years. He was eighty when he quit cuttin' timber and farmin'; now he's ninety-one."

I had heard her say that when she was a girl he'd walk out on the snow and ice barefooted and carry wood in the house and put it on the fire. He had shoes but he wouldn't bother to put them on. And I heard her say that he would cut timber on the coldest days without socks on his feet but with his feet stuck down in cold brogan shoes and he worked stripped above the waist so his arms would have freedom when he swung his double-bitted ax. I had heard her tell how he'd sweat and how the sweat in his beard would be icicles by the time he got home from work on the cold winter days. Now Mom wouldn't let him get out of the house for she wanted him to live a long time.

As I watched Grandpa go down the path toward the hog pen he stopped to examine every little thing along his path. Once he waved his cane at a butterfly as it zigzagged over his head, its polkadot wings fanning the blue April air. Grandpa would stand when a puff of wind came along, and hold his face against the wind and let the wind play with his white whiskers. I thought maybe his face was hot under his beard and he was letting the wind cool his face. When he reached the hog pen he called the hogs down to the fence. They came running and grunting to Grandpa just like they were talking to him. I knew that Grandpa couldn't hear them trying to talk to him but he could see their mouths working and he knew they were trying to say something. He leaned his cane against the hog pen, reached over the fence, and patted the hogs' heads. Grandpa didn't miss patting one of our seven hogs.

As he toddled up the little path alongside the hog pen he stopped under a blooming dogwood. He pulled a white blossom from a bough that swayed over the path above his head, and he leaned his big bundled body against the dogwood while he tore each petal from the blossom and examined it carefully. There wasn't anything his dim blue eyes missed. He stopped under a redbud tree before he reached the garden to break a tiny spray of redbud blossoms. He took each blossom from the spray and examined it carefully.

"Gee, it's funny to watch Grandpa," I said to Mom, then I laughed.

"Poor Pap," Mom said, "he's seen a lot of Aprils come and go. He's seen more Aprils than he will ever see again."

I don't think Grandpa missed a thing on the little circle he took before he reached the house. He played with a bumblebee that was bending a windflower blossom that grew near our corncrib beside a big bluff. But Grandpa didn't try to catch the bumblebee in his big bare hand. I wondered if he would and if the bumblebee would sting him, and if he would holler. Grandpa even pulled a butterfly cocoon from a blackberry briar that grew beside his path. I saw him try to tear it into shreds but he couldn't. There wasn't any butterfly in it, for I'd seen it before. I wondered if the butterfly with the polka-dot wings, that Grandpa waved his cane at when he first left the house, had come from this cocoon. I laughed when Grandpa couldn't tear the cocoon apart.

"I'll bet I can tear that cocoon apart for Grandpa if you'd let me go help him," I said to Mom.

"You leave your Grandpa alone," Mom said. "Let 'im enjoy April."

Then I knew that this was the first time Mom had let Grandpa out of the house all winter. I knew that Grandpa loved the sunshine and the fresh April air that blew from the redbud and dogwood blossoms. He loved the bumblebees, the hogs, the pine cones, and pine needles. Grandpa didn't miss a thing along his walk. And every day from now on until just before frost Grandpa would take this little walk. He'd stop along and look at everything as he had done summers before. But each year he didn't take as long a walk as he had taken the year before. Now this spring he didn't go down to the lower end of the hog pen as he had done last year. And when I could first remember Grandpa going on his walks he used to go out of sight. He'd go all over the farm. And he'd come to the house and take me on his knee and tell me about all that he had seen. Now Grandpa wasn't getting out of sight. I could see him from the window along all of his walk.

Grandpa didn't come back into the house at the front door. He tottered around back of the house toward the smokehouse and I ran through the living room to the dining room so I could look out at the window and watch him.

"Where's Grandpa goin'?" I asked Mom.

"Now never mind," Mom said. "Leave your Grandpa alone. Don't go out there and disturb him."

"I won't bother 'im, Mom," I said. "I just want to watch 'im."

"All right," Mom said.

But Mom wanted to be sure that I didn't bother him so she followed me into the dining room. Maybe she wanted to see what Grandpa was going to do. She stood by the window and we watched Grandpa as he walked down beside our smokehouse and the tall sassafras. Above was a blue April sky—so high you couldn't see the sky-roof. It was just blue space and little white clouds floated upon this blue.

When Grandpa reached the smokehouse he leaned his cane against

The Problem of Communication 83

the sassafras tree. He let himself down slowly to his knees as he looked carefully at the ground. Grandpa was looking at something and I wondered what it was. I just didn't think or I would have known.

"There you are, my good old friend," Grandpa said.

"Who is his friend, Mom?" I asked.

Mom didn't say anything. Then I saw.

"He's playin' with that old terrapin, Mom," I said.

"I know he is," Mom said.

"The terrapin doesn't mind if Grandpa strokes his head with his hand," I said.

"I know it," Mom said.

"But the old terrapin won't let me do it," I said. "Why does he let Grandpa?"

"The terrapin knows your Grandpa."

"He ought to know me," I said, "but when I try to stroke his head with my hand, he closes up in his shell."

Mom didn't say anything. She stood by the window watching Grandpa and listening to Grandpa talk to the terrapin.

"My old friend, how do you like the sunshine?" Grandpa asked the terrapin.

The terrapin turned his fleshless face to one side like a hen does when she looks at you in the sunlight. He was trying to talk to Grandpa; maybe the terrapin could understand what Grandpa was saying.

"Old fellow, it's been a hard winter," Grandpa said. "How have you fared under the smokehouse floor?"

"Does the terrapin know what Grandpa is sayin?" I asked Mom.

"I don't know," she said.

"I'm awfully glad to see you, old fellow," Grandpa said.

He didn't offer to bite Grandpa's big soft hand as he stroked his head.

"Looks like the terrapin would bite Grandpa," I said.

"That terrapin has spent the winters under that smokehouse for fifteen years," Mom said. "Pap has been acquainted with him for eleven years. He's been talkin' to that terrapin every spring."

"How does Grandpa know the terrapin is old?" I asked Mom.

"It's got 1847 cut on its shell," Mom said. "We know he's ninety-five years old. He's older than that. We don't know how old he was when that date was cut on his back."

"Who cut 1847 on his back, Mom?"

"I don't know, child," she said, "but I'd say whoever cut that date on his back has long been under the ground."

Then I wondered how a terrapin could get that old and what kind of a looking person he was who cut the date on the terrapin's back. I wondered where it happened—if it happened near where our house stood. I wondered who lived here on this land then, what kind of a house they lived in, and if they had a sassafras with tiny thin April leaves on its top growing in their yard, and if the person that cut the date on the terrapin's back was buried at Plum Grove, if he had farmed these hills where we lived to-day and cut timber like Grandpa had—and if he had seen the Aprils pass like Grandpa had seen them and if he enjoyed them like Grandpa was enjoying this April. I wondered if he had looked at the dogwood blossoms, the redbud blossoms, and talked to this same terrapin.

"Are you well, old fellow?" Grandpa asked the terrapin.

The terrapin just looked at Grandpa.

"I'm well as common for a man of my age," Grandpa said.

"Did the terrapin ask Grandpa if he was well?" I asked Mom.

"I don't know," Mom said. "I can't talk to a terrapin."

"But Grandpa can."

"Yes."

"Wait until tomatoes get ripe and we'll go to the garden together," Grandpa said.

"Does a terrapin eat tomatoes?" I asked Mom.

"Yes, that terrapin has been eatin' tomatoes from our garden for fifteen years," Mom said. "When Mick was tossin' the terrapins out of the tomato patch, he picked up this one and found the date cut on his back. He put him back in the patch and told him to help himself. He lives from our garden every year. We don't bother him and don't allow anybody else to bother him. He spends his winters under our smokehouse floor buried in the dry ground."

"Gee, Grandpa looks like the terrapin," I said.

Mom didn't say anything; tears came to her eyes. She wiped them from her eyes with the corner of her apron.

"I'll be back to see you," Grandpa said. "I'm a-gettin' a little chilly; I'll be gettin' back to the house."

The terrapin twisted his wrinkled neck without moving his big body, poking his head deeper into the April wind as Grandpa pulled his bundled body up by holding to the sassafras tree trunk.

"Good-by, old friend!"

The terrapin poked his head deeper into the wind, holding one eye on Grandpa, for I could see his eye shining in the sinking sunlight.

Grandpa got his cane that was leaned against the sassafras tree trunk and hobbled slowly toward the house. The terrapin looked at him with first one eye and then the other.

Discussion of

"Another April"

Jesse Stuart (1908-   ) was born at Riverton, Kentucky, the scene of many of his stories. As we see in "Another April" the characters he handles most skillfully are those simple hill folk who speak to him from his home country and who speak to us in language that seems to have grown from the earth as naturally as vegetation.

In using a child as his narrator, Stuart makes appropriate the simple, forthright dialogue by which the various levels of communication in this story are revealed. The candor of a youngster who is not yet in his teens is often disconcerting. He knows his grandfather as only another child could. He understands the frustration of being bundled up before he can go out, and with the casual objectivity of the young he compares his grandfather's walk to the toddling of a yet-younger brother.

The mother of the boy is both mother and daughter to her father. She remembers the man who could cut more timber than anyone else, and she knows his need to "enjoy April." She is not hurt by the child's laughter, but his blunt identification of the old man and the aged terrapin brings tears to her eyes. As a farm wife she is not romantic about age or death. In her son's words she simply wants her father "to live a long time," and she cares for him with the realistic devotion that her tender but essentially reticent nature dictates.

Perhaps the most successful part of this story is Stuart's handling of the terrapin. Giving human characteristics to animals is rarely effective in a short story, and the terrapin is kept carefully in character. He responds to the slow caress of the old man naturally, and the daughter's matter-of-fact explanation of their long relationship is convincing. The grandson's easy identification of old tortoise and old man prevents us from taking the terrapin too seriously as a symbol. The extent to which these two really communicate is questionable. But the grandfather does react so totally to the burgeoning spring into which he is stepping—perhaps for the last time—that we share his wonder and concern.

From The Autocrat of the Breakfast Table

by Oliver Wendell Holmes

VI

—Every person's feelings have a front-door and a side-door by which they may be entered. The front-door is on the street. Some keep it always open; some keep it latched; some, locked; some, bolted,—with a chain that will let you peep in, but not get in; and some nail it up, so that nothing can pass its threshold. This front-door leads into a passage which opens into an anteroom and this into the interior apartments. The side-door opens at once into the sacred chambers.

There is almost always at least one key to this side-door. This is carried for years hidden in a mother's bosom. Fathers, brothers, sisters, and friends, often, but by no means so universally, have duplicates of it. The wedding-ring conveys a right to one; alas, if none is given with it!

If nature or accident has put one of these keys into the hands of a person who has the torturing instinct, I can only solemnly pronounce the words that Justice utters over its doomed victim—The Lord have mercy on your soul! You will probably go mad within a reasonable time, —or, if you are a man, run off and die with your head on a curb-stone, in Melbourne or San Francisco,—or, if you are a woman, quarrel and break your heart, or turn into a pale, jointed petrifaction that moves about as if it were alive, or play some real life tragedy or other.

Be very careful to whom you trust one of these keys of the side-door. The fact of possessing one renders those even who are dear to you very terrible at times. You can keep the world out from your front-door, or receive visitors only when you are ready for them; but those of your own flesh and blood, or of certain grades of intimacy, can come in at the side-door, if they will, at any hour and in any mood. Some of them have a scale of your whole nervous sytem, and can play all the gamut of your sensibilities in semitones,—touching the naked nerve-pulps as a pianist strikes the keys of his instrument. I am satisfied that there are as great masters of this nerve-playing as Vieuxtemps or Thalberg in their lines of performance. Married life is the school in which the most accomplished artists in this department are found. A delicate woman is the best instrument; she has such a magnificent compass of sensibilities! From the deep inward moan which follows pressure on the great nerves of right, to the sharp cry as the filaments of taste are struck with a crashing sweep, is a range which no other instrument possesses. A few exercises on it daily at home fit a man wonderfully for his habitual labors, and refresh him immensely as he returns from them. No stranger can get a great many notes of torture out of a human soul; it takes one that knows it well,—parent, child, brother, sister, intimate. Be very careful to whom you give a side-door key; too many have them already.

Discussion of
The Autocrat of the Breakfast Table

In volume four of *Out of the Best Books*, Oliver Wendell Holmes (1809-1894) is represented by one of his most famous poems. In this volume we are reprinting a few lines from the series of informal essays that were collected under the title *The Autocrat of the Breakfast Table*. Using as a setting a boardinghouse, at whose table he presides, Holmes indulges his penchant for a buoyant, witty prose that ranges from outrageous punning to serious commentary. In the paragraphs selected for this section Holmes probes the vulnerability that any close relationship between two or more persons establishes.

If only briefly, it is worth noting that failure to communicate effectively may be less of a problem than full but destructive communication. In elaborating his metaphor of the front and side doors to everyone's feelings, Holmes suggests that the success in opening ourselves to intimates which we often crave may exact a fearful toll. Only those who know us well can hurt us deeply, and we always give them the key that unlocks our innermost feelings.

Holmes' language may be a little dramatic as he recounts the way in which a truly sensitive person may be wounded by someone who is close to him, but awareness of the negative possibilities that successful communication makes possible can keep us from being duped by the specious promises sometimes made in the name of group therapy.

Limits of taste and self-respect should inhibit the intimacies we share. Confession is not a shortcut to that communication earned by trust, rooted in similar commitment, and justified by joint responsibility.

Can You Get Along With Your In-Laws?

Edward D. Fales, Jr.

It was a long time coming, but it's happened at last. Science is beginning to look at mothers-in-law to see (1) if they're really as dangerous as some people think, and (2), if so, why?

Here at Cornell University a brave and pioneering investigation has put the parents-in-law under a microscope. Yes, they've given fathers-in-law a quick look, too! Because the things some wives are saying about him have given more than a hint that father often is the real villain on the domestic scene! Researchers think maybe somebody ought to investigate him more thoroughly.

If you're plagued by too many in-law troubles, however, stop right now and look in a mirror. There may be something YOU can learn from the survey that will increase your happiness.

For the people who DO get along, the Cornell survey showed, are people who—right from the start—accept their in-laws, with a big grin, right into the family. They say, in effect: "We're all on the same side; it's all one family!"

The survey showed that a surprising number of couples DO get along with their in-laws. This does not obscure the sad fact that mother-in-law trouble goes hand in hand with divorce.

Young Wives Helped

It was this fact that prompted the study. Cornell's College of Home Economics started a big job—in a small way.

As a starter, an astute young wife, Mrs. Peggy Schiffman Marcus, a Cornell researcher in family relationships, called on a Mothers' Club for help, then shot out questionnaires to 150 young wives, all married 11 years or less.

Each was asked frankly (and secretly) what she thought of her in-laws. No one signed her name, and each had 16 whole pages in which to tell a lot.

Here are some of the findings which are important to you:

More than half of the husbands and wives loved and respected both Mother & Father Smith and Mother & Father Jones! This was a surprising discovery. The ratio was far higher than expected.

Of the others, *almost all* had managed to work out a "good adjustment" with their in-laws. Only a minor 6% were on really poor terms! Some of these, however, were really bad.

Almost invariably, when the score indicated "fair" or "poor" in-law adjustment, daughters-in-law seemed to blame their in-laws.

But here, the Cornell study showed, something is wrong. You can't acquire in-laws without becoming one. And so findings of the investigation were divided into two groups: one for daughters-in-law and one for parents-in-law.

Advice for Daughters-in-Law

Let's start with you—daughter-in-law. (And you, too, son-in-law!) Then we'll come to you—parents-in-law. Here's what Cornell suggests:

1. Call your parents-in-law "Mom," or "Mother" and "Dad." Or, by some other name of *affection*. In most cases they'll like it and feel warmer toward you! (If you want trouble, just don't name them at all when you speak to them!)

2. Live alone, apart from any relatives, if you possibly can. You will want to be boss of your household, even if you must live in a shack. Only people of exceptionally warm and "giving" natures can live with in-laws!

3. Make friends with your in-laws before you marry. A girl has two strikes against her if, without warning, she walks in with her new spouse and lets him drop the bombshell: "Mother, Dad —this is my wife, Mary!" According to the study, the third strike may not be far in the offing.

4. Learn all you can about marriage before you marry! The study showed that wives who took marriage courses in school had a slight edge.

5. Choose a husband with at *least* as much education as you have. Things are evening up, but today *he's* still supposed to be the brains of the family.

6. Look out for interfaith marriages. It's sad but true, the study showed, that in-law trouble still breeds here.

7. Marry a man whose parents are happy. If they're happy together, they won't cling to him.

Advice for Parents-in-Law

Now for the parents: If you parents want your son's marriage to stick—and statistics show you do a lot toward making or breaking it— here are some Cornell suggestions.

1. DON'T MEDDLE. Unasked advice stands out head and shoulders above all other trouble-makers. "My parents-in-law give us too free and too frequent advice," was a repeated complaint.

The Problem of Communication

Yet many fortunate wives reported over and over to this effect: "*My in-laws never have interferred, but they have given us the secure feeling that they WOULD help us if we needed it."*

2. DON'T CLING: After your son is married, you are no longer Number One interest in his life! If you are alone, find some outside interest.

3. But DON'T keep hands off to the extent of ignoring your grandchildren. Proud young parents demand recognition for their children. "They ignore the baby," wailed one young mother. This, it seems, is a serious offense!

4. DON'T FAIL to call your daughter-in-law by some name of affection, and encourage her to do likewise! This is top insurance.

5. DON'T address your letters just to your son, or your daughter, but to BOTH of them.

So much for DON'T. Now for some DO's.

Do speak and think of your in-law son or daughter not as an "in-law" at all but as "one of the family."

DO try to give them a feeling of acceptance right from the beginning.

DO keep on trying! Among those who had most in-law trouble were people—young and old—who gave up too easily!

DO sit with the baby (although your young folks must remember that this is often hard on you—especially as you grow older).

DO give them advice out of your experience *if they ask for it*, but let them decide freely whether or not to follow your suggestions.

DO give them financial help if they need it and you can spare it, but NEVER make them feel obligated.

Finances Cause Headaches

Money, often a trouble-maker, has spoiled many a happy in-law picture. One young couple reported: "They help us but we wish it were unnecessary. The obligation felt is overwhelming."

Yet read these comments by happier daughters:

"They are very generous and we are grateful—though they never make us feel obligated."

"No obligation felt. The things we do for them in return, we would do anyway."

"They are so decent about it all, but we do expect to return these loans."

America's millions of in-laws may well hope that Cornell will probe even deeper. A handful of earlier researchers had stressed the difficulties; Cornell's survey showed that even in the worst cases there IS hope.

If you have in-law problems, don't despair. Cornell found that people who broke many of the rules still had no trouble. Why? They were people who refused to think of their relatives as "in-laws" but only as "members of *our* family!"

This seems to be the one greatest lesson in the survey. It's the point of view that made it possible for one wife to write on her questionnaire:

"*No adjustment to my in-laws had been necessary. We are one family. We feel warmth of relationship—and know that it is mutual!*"

Discussion of "Can You Get Along With Your In-Laws?"

Edward D. Fales, Jr. (1906 -   ) has been associated with *Parade, U.S. Camera,* and *Science Illustrated* magazines. Before moving to the editorial positions he held with these publications, he did news and picture assignments for Associated News.

In the popular style affected by the magazine he now represents, Fales summarizes the findings of a Cornell University study of parents-in-law. The results of this study should not be surprising to those who have not let themselves be conditioned by jokes and comedy routines that poke heavy-handed fun at in-laws. For, in spite of some detailed lists of "do's" and "don'ts," the real key to happy relationships with those who become part of a family through marriage is loving acceptance by all concerned.

Such acceptance keeps communication problems from developing. Respect and affection cannot be successfully feigned, and they are never really misunderstood. Few things are easier to declare than devotion, and mutual devotion inspires the confidence that characterizes developing communication.

Mark Twain's Family Letters

Few famous marriages have been happier than that achieved by Samuel Clemens (alias Mark Twain) and Olivia Langdon. The romantic story in which young Samuel sees a miniature of "Livy," as her family called her, may be mildly exaggerated, but there is no denying the vehemence of and constancy of his love from the very beginning. Indeed, in his autobiography forty years later, Mark remembers that on his first official call he arrived at ten in the morning and stayed thirteen hours!

Livy's wealthy, adoring family were not unsympathetic to the siege for her heart that the already well-known humorist was determined upon; but Jervis Langdon, Livy's father, suggested that Mark proceed more slowly with his courtship. The following excerpt from a letter to Mr. Langdon has the authentic Twain ring but is also touching in its desire to please and be understood:

December 29, 1868

Dear Mr. Langdon:

I wrote to the Metropolitan Hotel for your letter and it overtook me two or three days ago at Charlotte, Mich. . . .

I am not hurrying my love—it is my love that is hurrying *me* — and surely no one is better able to comprehend that than you. I fancy that Mrs. Langdon was the counterpart of her daughter at twenty-three— and so I refer you to the past for explanation and for pardon of my conduct. At your time of life, and being, like you, the object of an assured regard, I shall be able to urge moderation upon younger people, and shall do so relentlessly—but now I feel a larger charity for such. Your heart is big enough to feel all the force of that remark, — and so believing, you will not be surprised to find me thus boldly knocking at it. It does not seem to me that I am otherwise than moderate—it cannot seem so from my point of view—and so while I continue as moderate as I am now and have been, I think it is fair to hope that you will not turn away from me your countenance or deny me your friendly toleration, even though it be under a mild protest. . . .

To Livy herself Mark was far less restrained. Having asked her to marry him in September, and having been rejected, he contented himself with several carefully decorous letters in which he refers to her as his "honored sister" during the following few weeks. But by the last of November he is pouring out his heart in the most impetuous terms.

November 28, 1868

My dear, dear Livy:

I do love, love, *love* you, Livy! My whole being is permeated, is renewed, is leavened with this love, and with every breath I draw its noble influence makes of me a better man. And I shall yet be worthy of your priceless love, Livy. It is the glad task of my life—it is the purest ambition and the most exalted that ever I have known, and I shall never, never swerve from the path it has marked out for me. . . .

By January, when some disturbing reports about his earlier activities in California had reached the Langdons, Mark is especially grateful to hear from Livy that her trust in him remains unshaken. After assuring her that there is nothing in his past life that is seriously reprehensible, he continues as follows:

As far as what I have been is concerned, I am only sorry that I did not tell all of that, in full and relentless detail, to your father and your mother, and to you, Livy—for it would be all the better that you knew it also.

I would not seem to have been that which I was not. If I am speaking carelessly or untruly now, I am doing a fearful thing, for before I began this letter I offered up that prayer which has passed my lips many and many a time during these latter months: that I might be guarded from ever unconsciously or unwittingly saying anything to you which you might construe and be thereby deceived—and that I might not be guilty of any taint or shadow of hypocrisy, however refined, in my dealings with you—that I might be wholly true and frank and open with you, even though it cost me your priceless love, and the life that is now so inestimably valuable to me become in that moment a blank and hated captivity. Wherefore I now speak to you standing in the presence of God. And I say that what I have been I am not now; that I am striving and shall strive to reach the highest altitude of worth, the highest Christian excellence; that I know of nothing in my past career that I would conceal from your parents, howsoever, I might blush to speak the words; & that it is my strong conviction that, married to you, I would never desire to roam again while I lived. The circumstances under which I say these things, make the statements as grave & weighty as if I endorsed them with an oath.

The Problem of Communication

These opening letters in their courtship begin a fascinating disclosure of how two sensitive people developed the love that had to stand an unusual strain in the years to come. It is revealing, however, to see Mark feel secure enough to tease Livy a bit and then retreat in terror lest he has gone too far. Mark had early found that Livy was careless in her spelling. Up to this point he hadn't teased her about it, but he can't resist in talking to her about his sister:

> My sister is a good woman, familiar with grief, though bearing it bravely & giving no sign upon the surface; & she is kind-hearted, void of folly or vanity, perfectly unacquainted with deceit or dissimulation, diffident about her own faults, & slow to discover those of others.
>
> She isn't such a gem as you; (by a long shot) & neither is any other woman, but then she is a very, very excellent woman anyway. You'll like her, Livy—she don't seem to spell worth a cent. You see she spells cow with a k. And she has spelled "tripped" with only one p, & she puts only one t in "delighted," & only two s's in "expression," I can stand those little blunders well enough, but I do hate to see anybody spell John with a G. I look upon that as perfectly awful. I notice that you always spell John with a G.—Now forgive me, Livy, darling—you know I wouldn't poke fun at you to save a man's life if I thought it would wound you. I don't care a straw how you spell, Livy dear—I hardly ever notice when you make a mistake—& bless you I am just as proud of you as if you could beat the Unabridged dictionary spelling. It would be a pity indeed if I presumed to criticize your spelling—I who am sown as thick with faults as you are with merits, & shining virtues, & beautiful traits of character; & yet you have found it in your heart to take me just as I am & lift me up & bless me with your priceless love— I never can be *your* critic, my loved and honored Livy.

After several years of marriage, the birth of two children and the death of one, Mark's letters from abroad are still adoring:

**Off Queenstown, Ireland,
August 29/72**

Livy darling, I have little or nothing to write, except that I love you & think of you night & day, & wonder where you are, & what you are doing, & how the Muggins comes on, & whether she ever speaks of me—& whether Mother is cheerful & happy. I hope & trust & pray that you are all well & enjoying yourselves—but I can't say that I have been enjoying myself, greatly, lost in a vast ship where our 40 or 50 passengers flit about in the great dim distances like vagrant spirits. But latterly our small clique have had a somewhat better time of it, though if one is absent there can be no whist.

I have given the purser a ten-dollar telegram of 3 words to send to you from Queenstown, & also my journal in 2 envelopes—& now I'll rush & give him this—consider, my dear, that I am standing high on the stern of the ship, looking westward, with my hands to my mouth, trumpet fashion, yelling across the tossing waste of waves, "I LOVE YOU, LIVY DARLING!!!!"

Livy's letters to Mark during this decade of their marriage are gently cautionary. She is afraid his impetuous nature will lead him into thoughtless and ungenerous remarks:

Elmira, July 29th, '77

My Darling—Two letters came from you today, and I assure you it was a mighty delight to get them— I am so thankful that all the arrangements about the play suit you so well, how I do wish that I was going to be with you on the opening night. I want to hear your speech and I want to be with you—I love you—. We had such a wonderful evening last evening, beautiful cloud effects at sunset and then such a beautiful sky with the moon and clouds in the evening, I did wish so very much for you—.

Youth I want to caution you about one thing, don't say harsh things about Mr. Harte, don't talk against Mr. Harte to people, it is much better that you be reticent about him, don't let anybody trap you into talking freely of him—We are so desperately happy, our paths lie in such pleasant places, and he is so miserable, we can easily afford to be magnanimous toward him—but I am afraid that my desire to have you quiet is not from generosity to him, but from my selfish desires toward you. I don't want you in the position of having talked against him—be careful my darling.

It is not until financial and personal catastrophe bludgeons the Twains, however, that we begin to understand how deep their love is and how perfect their communication. By 1893 two business ventures which Mark was backing heavily had thrown him into debt and would soon drive him to the brink of bankruptcy. In some despondency he writes his wife, even remembering an earlier day when he had appeared to jeopardize Livy's security in other ways:

Thursday, Sept. 21/93

Sweetheart, I am waiting patiently to see what is going to happen. If there had been any news of a cabling sort you would have had a cable before this, of course, I should not have forgotten; I would not lose any time in sharing good news with you if I had any.

Late last night I was smitten suddenly with shame & remorse in remembering how I forced you to drive through the thunder & lightning & rain that night that you were so frightened & wanted to stop at the Water Cure. I have remembered that brutality many a time since, & cursed myself for it. It is at times like these that I also visit with deep & honest curses the memory of those various people who plucked me from the water when I was a lad & drowning.

A few days later he continues in much the same vein:

It breaks my heart to write these things to you & I kept still as long as there was nothing definite to say; for as long as the offer was going to be made but the size of it not named, there was hope that it might be large enough to enable us to get out of our horrible hole alive. It may be that the offer will be enlarged a little but I don't expect it.

I do love you so, & it does hurt me so to send you such news when you are away off there, lonely among strangers. I love you deep deep down.

During this gloomy time, Livy's letters are consistently hopeful and loyal. Addressing him by her pet name for him, "Youth," she tries her best to cheer him:

December 17th, 1893

Youth My Darling: Your dispatch reached me last night and greatly rejoiced my heart because it does look as if perhaps you were going to be able to come here some day. Thank you so much for sending it. It also seems as if perhaps you were beginning to see your way through financially. How is Webster & Co. situated now? Are they working out of debt?

You should have been here today to see Clara imitate you telling them stories and eating at the same time, it was just as funny as it could be. She bit a piece of bread exactly as you bit it. She said, "I don't know what it is but Papa always seems to be having a quarrel with his piece of bread to make it let go."

We have just had visit from our new doctor. He has examined Susy most thoroughly, he says there is some extension of the cells of the lungs, he thinks it comes from enemia and will not long resist treatment. I like him exceedingly. He says that one great trouble with her is that she is not sufficiently developed, particularly her chest he is going to have her take gymnastics for developing that, and also masage. I hope now she will soon be on the road to health. It has been very pitiful to see her look so miserable. And sometimes it has been hard to keep cheerful with her so down hearted.

Can it be that pretty soon I shall have a cable stating when you are coming won't that be glorious.

Good night, many kisses and hugs and may the sense of my great love for you, give you comfort.

Despite some shrewd help from a few friends, the Twains' financial condition became more and more desperate. Notable at this difficult time is Livy's concern that Mark do the scrupulously honest thing. She is obviously fearful that the burdens her husband is now carrying—and the advice he may be getting from some of his new friends—might be too much for him. Mark is obviously reacting to her anxiety in the following letter:

The Players, July 23/94

My darling, I note carefully everything you say in yours of the 12th; I note it reverently & loving, honoring you & loving you for what you say & for the high position which you take. You can take no other position; I would not wish you to take any other, I could not bear to have you take any other.

My own position must necessarily differ from yours in one or two details. My first duty is to you & the children—my second is to those others. I must protect you first—protect you against yourself. That accomplished I mean to take the fullest possible care of those others. And at the right moment I shall tell them so.

They are all acting handsomely—even the bank. Everything is agreed upon except your royalty for Pudd'n head. I mean to see to it that if they strenuously object to 20 percent, they shall have the book for less. That detail arranged I am free from legal persecution for one year. Mr. Rogers is still detained in Washington. He expects to get back tonight. Then I hope the papers can be signed tomorrow. I think nothing is wanting but his signature. After the papers are signed, I will ask him to let me tell the creditors—but he won't. He will probably say: "It could make them lax; let them alone—they'll work the harder; a year hence will be time enough."

Mind you, dearheart, nobody can charge me with dishonorable con-

The Problem of Communication

duct; I have not been guilty of any; I shall not be guilty of any until I desert my family to take care of those others. Whenever I do that, it will be time for people to call me names; up to that time they can't call me names. Those creditors forced me to make an assignment—goodness knows I didn't want to do it. They must stand part of the hardship of their own act. They did me a very great kindness, & I am grateful to them for it & shall try to see that they lose no penny by it.

It is only when the children are stricken that Mark and Livy almost go under. Susy Clemens died while Mark was on a world lecture tour in an attempt to pay off his creditors. Livy and their daughter, Clara, did not hear of her death for several days. The following letter was sent to prepare them:

**Guildford, Friday, Aug. 21
(1896)**

Oh poor Livy darling at 8 tomorrow morning your heart will break, the Lord God knows I am pitying you. Smythe & I have done what we could—cabled Mr. Rogers to have Dr. Rice at the ship & keep all other friends prudently out of sight—for if you saw them on the dock you would know; and you would swoon before Rice could get to you to help you.

Hour by hour my sense of calamity that has overtaken us closes down heavier & heavier upon me; & now for 48 hours there is a form of words that runs in my head with ceaseless iteration—without stop or pause— "I shall never see her again, I shall never see her again." You will see the sacred face once more—I am so thankful for that.

But though my heart break I will still say she was fortunate; & I would not call her back if I could.

I eat—because you wish it; I go on living—because you wish it; I play billiards, and billiards, & billiards, till I am ready to drop—to keep from going mad with grief & with resentful thinkings.

You will find my health perfect—for your sake—when you come.

I know where you will be, tomorrow and Sunday, & in spirit I shall be at your side & taking step by step with you.

Give my love to Clara & Jean. We have that much of our fortune left.

I love you with all my whole heart.

Shortly after the blow of Susy's death it was found that one of their remaining children, Jean, was epileptic. She lingered on until 1909, but was never well again. Livy died in 1904. To the last, Twain was strengthened and encouraged by her support and her example. The epitaph he suggested that Adam might have put on Eve's grave is a beautifully appropriate expression of his own love:

"Wheresoever she was, *there* was Eden."

Neighbor Rosicky

by Willa Cather

I

When Doctor Burleigh told neighbor Rosicky he had a bad heart, Rosicky protested.

"So? No, I guess my heart was always pretty good. I got a little asthma, maybe. Just a awful short breath when I was pitchin' hay last summer, dat's all."

"Well now, Rosicky, if you know more about it than I do, what did you come to me for? It's your heart that makes you short of breath, I tell you. You're sixty-five years old, and you've always worked hard, and your heart's tired. You've got to be careful from now on, and you can't do heavy work any more. You've got five boys at home to do it for you."

The old farmer looked up at the Doctor with a gleam of amusement in his queer, triangular-shaped eyes. His eyes were large and lively, but the lids were caught up in the middle in a curious way, so that they formed a triangle. He did not look like a sick man. His brown face was creased but not wrinkled, he had a ruddy color in his smooth-shaven cheeks and in his lips, under his long brown moustache. His hair was thin and ragged around his ears, but very little grey. His forehead, naturally high and crossed by deep parallel lines, now ran all the way up to his pointed crown. Rosicky's face had the habit of looking interested,—suggested a contented disposition and a reflective quality that was gay rather than grave. This gave him a certain detachment, the easy manner of an onlooker and observer.

"Well, I guess you ain't got no pills for a bad heart, Doctor Ed. I guess the only thing is fur me to git me a new one."

Doctor Burleigh swung around in his desk-chair and frowned at the old farmer. "I think if I were you I'd take a little care of the old one, Rosicky."

Rosicky shrugged. "Maybe I don't know how, I expect you mean fur me not to drink my coffee no more."

"I wouldn't, in your place. But you'll do as you choose about that. I've never yet been able to separate a Bohemian from his coffee or his pipe. I've quit trying. But the sure thing is you've got to cut out farm work. You can feed the stock and do chores about the barn, but you can't do anything in the fields that makes you short of breath."

"How about shelling corn?"

"Of course not!"

Rosicky considered with puckered brows.

"I can't make my heart go no longer'n it wants to, can I, Doctor Ed?"

"I think it's good for five or six years yet, maybe more, if you'll take the strain off it. Sit around the house and help Mary. If I had a good wife like yours, I'd want to stay around the house."

His patient chuckled. "It ain't no place fur a man. I don't like no old man hanging around the kitchen too much. An' my wife, she's a awful hard worker her own self."

"That's it; you can help her a little. My Lord, Rosicky, you are one of the few men I know who has a family he can get some comfort out of; happy dispositions, never quarrel among themselves, and they treat you right. I want to see you live a few years and enjoy them."

"Oh they're good kids, all right." Rosicky assented.

The Doctor wrote him a prescription and asked him how his oldest son, Rudolph, who had married in the spring, was getting on. Rudolph had struck out for himself, on rented land. "And how's Polly? I was afraid Mary mightn't like an American daughter-in-law, but it seems to be working out all right."

"Yes, she's a fine girl. Dat widder woman bring her daughters up very nice. Polly gots lots of spunk, an' she got some style, too. Da's nice, for young folks to have some style." Rosicky inclined his head gallantly. His voice and his twinkly smile were an affectionate compliment to his daughter-in-law.

"It looks like a storm, and you'd better be getting home before it comes. In town in the car?" Doctor Burleigh rose.

"No, I'm in de wagon. When you got five boys, you ain't got much chance to ride around in de Ford. I ain't much for cars, noway."

"Well, it's a good road out to your place; but I don't want you bumping around in a wagon much. And never again on a hay-rake, remember!"

Rosicky placed the Doctor's fee delicately behind the desk-telephone, looking the other way, as if this were an absent-minded gesture. He put on his plush cap and his corduroy jacket with a sheepskin collar, and went out.

The Doctor picked up his stethoscope and frowned at it as if he were seriously annoyed with the instrument. He wished it had been telling tales about some other man's heart, some old man who didn't look the Doctor in the eye so knowingly, or hold out such a warm brown hand when he said good-bye. Doctor Burleigh had been a poor boy in the country before he went away to medical school; he had known Rosicky almost ever since he could remember, and he had a deep affection for Mrs. Rosicky.

Only last winter he had had such a good breakfast at Rosicky's, and that when he needed it. He had been out all night on a long, hard confinement case at Tom Marshall's,—a big rich farm where there was plenty of stock and plenty of feed and a great deal of expensive farm machinery of the newest model, and no comfort whatever. The woman had too many children and too much work, and she was no manager. When the baby was born at last, and handed over to the assisting neighbor woman, and the mother was properly attended to, Burleigh refused any breakfast in that slovenly house, and drove his buggy—the snow was too deep for a car—eight miles to Anton Rosicky's place. He didn't know another farm-house where a man could get such a warm welcome, and such good strong coffee with rich cream. No wonder the old chap didn't want to give up his coffee!

He had driven in just when the boys had come back from the barn and were washing up for breakfast. The long table, covered with a bright oilcloth, was set out with dishes waiting for them, and the warm kitchen was full of the smell of coffee and hot biscuits and sausage.

Five big handsome boys, running from twenty to twelve, all with what Burleigh called natural good manners,—they hadn't a bit of the painful self-consciousness he himself had to struggle with when he was a lad. One ran to put his horse away, another helped him off with his fur coat and hung it up, and Josephine, the youngest child and the only daughter, quickly set another place under her mother's direction.

With Mary, to feed creatures was the natural expression of affection,—her chickens, the calves, her big hungry boys. It was a rare pleasure to feed a young man whom she seldom saw and of whom she was as proud as if he belonged to her. Some country housekeepers would have stopped to spread a white cloth over the oilcloth, to change the thick cups and plates for their best china, and the wooden-handled knives for plated ones, but not Mary.

"You must take us as you find us, Doctor Ed. I'd be glad to put out my good things for you if you was expected, but I'm glad to get you any way at all."

He knew she was glad,—she threw back her head and spoke out as if she were announcing him to the whole prairie. Rosicky hadn't said anything at all; he merely smiled his twinkling smile, put some more coal on the fire, and went into his own room to pour the Doctor a little drink in a medicine glass. When they were all seated, he watched his wife's face from his end of the table and spoke to her in Czech. Then, with the instinct of politeness which seldom failed him, he turned to the Doctor and said slyly, "I was just tellin' her not to ask you no questions about Mrs. Marshall till you eat some breakfast. My wife, she's terrible fur to ask questions."

The boys laughed, and so did Mary. She watched the Doctor devour her biscuit and sausage, too much excited to eat anything herself. She drank her coffee and sat taking in everything about her visitor. She had known him when he was a poor country boy, and was boastfully proud of his success, always saying: "What do people go to Omaha for, to see a doctor, when we got the best one in the State right here?" If Mary liked people at all, she felt physical pleasure in the sight of them, personal exultation in any good fortune that came to them. Burleigh didn't know many women like that, but he knew she was like that.

When his hunger was satisfied, he did, of course, have to tell them about Mrs. Marshall, and he noticed what a friendly interest the boys took in the matter.

Rudolph, the oldest one (he was still living at home then,) said: "The last time I was over there, she was lifting them big heavy milk-cans, and I knew she ought not to be doing it."

"Yes, Rudolph told me about that when he come home, and I said it wasn't right," Mary put in warmly. "It was all right for me to do them things up to the last, for I was terrible strong, but that woman's weakly. And do you think she'll be able to nurse it, Ed?" She sometimes forgot to give him the title she was so proud of. "And to think of your being up all night and then not able to get a decent breakfast! I don't know what's the matter with such people."

"Why, mother," said one of the boys, "if Doctor Ed had got breakfast there, we wouldn't have him here. So you ought to be glad."

"He knows I'm glad to have him, John, any time. But I'm sorry for that poor woman, how bad she'll feel the Doctor had to go away in the cold without his breakfast."

"I wish I'd been in practice when these were getting born." The doctor looked down the row of close-clipped heads. "I missed some good breakfasts by not being."

The boys began to laugh at their mother because she flushed so red, but she stood her ground and threw up her head. "I don't care, you wouldn't have got away from this house without breakfast. No doctor ever did. I'd have had something ready fixed that Anton could warm up for you."

The boys laughed harder than ever, and exclaimed at her. "I'll bet you would!" "She would, that!"

"Father, did you get breakfast for the doctor when we were born?"

"Yes, and he used to bring me my breakfast, too, might nice. I was always hungry!" Mary admitted with a guilty laugh.

While the boys were getting the Doctor's horse, he went to the window to examine the house plants. "What do you do to your geraniums to keep them blooming all winter, Mary? I never pass this house that from the road I don't see your windows full of flowers."

She snapped off a dark red one, and a ruffled new green leaf, and put them in his buttonhole. "There, that looks better. You look too solemn for a young man, Ed. Why don't you git married? I'm worried about you. Settin' at breakfast, I looked at you real hard, and I seen you've got some grey hairs already."

"Oh, yes! They're coming. Maybe they'd come faster if I married."

"Don't talk so. You'll ruin your health eating at the hotel. I could send your wife a nice loaf of nut bread, if you only had one. I don't like to see a young man getting grey. I'll tell you something, Ed; you make some strong black tea and keep it handy in a bowl, and every morning just brush it into your hair, an' it'll keep the grey from showin' much. That's the way I do!"

Sometimes the Doctor heard the gossipers in the drugstore wondering why Rosicky didn't get on faster. He was industrious, and so were his boys, but they were rather free and easy, weren't pushers, and they didn't always show good judgment. They were comfortable, they were out of debt, but they didn't get much ahead. Maybe, Doctor Burleigh reflected, people as generous and warmhearted and affectionate as the Rosickys never got ahead much; maybe you could not enjoy your life and put it into the bank, too.

II

When Rosicky left Doctor Burleigh's office, he went into the farm-implement store to light his pipe and put on his glasses and read over the list Mary had given him. Then he went into the general merchandise place next door and stood about until the pretty girl with the plucked eyebrows, who always waited on him, was free. Those eyebrows, two thin India-ink strokes, amused him, because he remembered how they used to be.

Rosicky always prolonged his shopping by a little joking; the girl knew the old fellow admired her, and she liked to chaff with him.

"Seems to me about every other week you buy ticking, Mr. Rosicky, and always the best quality." she remarked as she measured off the heavy bolt with red stripes.

"You see, my wife is always makin' goose-fedder pillows, and de'thin stuff don't hold in dem little down-fedders."

"You must have lots of pillows at your house."

"Sure, she makes quilts of dem, too. We sleeps easy. Now she's makin' a fedder quilt for my son's wife. You know Polly, that married my Rudolph. How much my bill, Miss Pearl?"

"Eight eighty-five."

"Chust make it nine, and put in some candy fur de woman."

"As usual. I never did see a man buy so much candy for his wife. First thing you know, she'll be getting too fat."

"I'd like dat. I ain't much fur all dem slim women like what de style is now."

"That's one for me, I suppose, Mr. Bohunk!" Pearl sniffed and elevated her India-ink strokes.

When Rosicky went out to his wagon, it was beginning to snow, —the first snow of the season, and he was glad to see it. He rattled out of town and along the highway through a wonderfully rich stretch of country, the finest farms in the county.

He admired this High Prairie, as it was called, and always liked to drive through it. His own place lay in a rougher territory, where there was some clay in the soil and it was not too productive. When he bought his land, he hadn't the money to buy on High Prairie; so he told his boys, when they grumbled, that if their land hadn't some clay in it, they wouldn't own it at all. All the same, he enjoyed looking at these fine farms, as he enjoyed looking at a prize bull.

After he had gone eight miles, he came to the graveyard, which lay just at the edge of his own hay-land. There he stopped his horses and sat still on his wagon seat, looking about the snowfall. Over yonder on the hill he could see his own house, crouching low, with the clump of orchard behind the windmill before, and all down the gentle hill-slope the rows of pale gold cornstalks stood out against the white field. The snow was falling over the cornfield and the pasture and the hay-land, steadily, with very little wind,—a nice dry snow. The graveyard had only a light wire fence about it, and was all overgrown with long red grass. The fine snow, settling into this red grass and upon the few little evergreens and the headstones, looked very pretty.

It was a nice graveyard, Rosicky reflected, sort of snug and homelike, not cramped or mournful,—a big sweep all around it. A man could lie down in the long grass and see the complete arch of the sky over him, hear the wagons go by; in summer the mowing-machine rattle right up to the wire fence. And it was so near home. Over there across the cornstalks his own roof and windmill looked so good to him that he promised himself to mind the Doctor and take care of himself. He was awful fond of his place, he admitted. He wasn't anxious to leave it.

And it was a comfort to think that he would never have to go farther than the edge of his own hayfield. The snow, falling over his barnyard and the graveyard, seemed to draw things together like. And they were all old neighbors in the graveyard, most of them friends; there was nothing to feel awkward or embarrassed about. Embarrassment was the most disagreeable feeling Rosicky knew. He didn't often have it,—only with certain people whom he didn't understand at all.

Well, it was a nice snowstorm; a fine sight to see the snow falling so quietly and graciously over so much open country. On his cap and shoulders, on the horses' backs and manes, light, delicate, mysterious it fell; and with it a dry cool fragrance was released into the air. It meant rest for vegetation and men and beasts, for the ground itself; a season of long nights for sleep, leisurely breakfasts, peace by the fire. This and much more went through Rosicky's mind, but he merely told himself that winter was coming, clucked to his horses, and drove on.

When he reached home, John, the youngest boy, ran out to put away his team for him, and he met Mary coming up from the outside cellar with her apron full of carrots. They went into the house together. On the table, covered with oilcloth figured with clusters of blue grapes, a place was set, and he smelled hot coffee-cake of some kind. Anton never lunched in town; he thought that extravagant, and anyhow he didn't like the food. So Mary always had something ready for him when he got home.

After he was settled in his chair, stirring his coffee in a big cup, Mary took out of the oven a pan of *kolache* stuffed with apricots, examined them anxiously to see whether they had got too dry, put them beside his plate, and then sat down opposite him.

Rosicky asked her in Czech if she wasn't going to have any coffee.

She replied in English, as being somehow the right language for transacting business: "Now what did Doctor Ed say, Anton? You tell me what."

"He said I was to tell you some compliments, but I forgot 'em." Rosicky's eyes twinkled.

"About you, I mean, What did he say about your asthma?"

"He says I ain't got no asthma." Rosicky took one of the little rolls in his broad brown fingers. The thickened nail of his right thumb told the story of his past.

"Well, what is the matter? And don't try to put me off."

"He don't say nothing much, only I'm a little older, and my heart ain't so good like it used to be."

Mary started and brushed her hair back from her temples with both hands as if she were a little out of her mind. From the way she glared, she might have been in a rage with him.

"He says there's something the matter with your heart? Doctor Ed says so?"

"Now don't yell at me like I was a hog in de garden, Mary. You know I always did like to hear a woman talk soft. He didn't say anything de matter wid my heart, only it ain't so young like it used to be, an' he tell me not to pitch hay or run de cornsheller."

Mary wanted to jump up, but she sat still. She admired the way he never under any circumstances raised his voice or spoke roughly. He was city-bred, and she was country-bred; she often said she wanted her boys to have their papa's nice ways.

"You never have no pain there, do you? It's your breathing and your stomach that's been wrong. I wouldn't believe nobody but Doctor Ed about it. I guess I'll go see him myself. Didn't he give you no advice?"

"Chust to take it easy like, an' stay round de house dis winter. I guess you got some carpenter work for me to do. I kin make some new shelves for you, and I want dis long time to build a closet in de boys' room and make dem two little fellers keep dere clo'es hung up."

Rosicky drank his coffee from time to time, while he considered. His moustache was of the soft long variety and came down over his mouth like the teeth of a buggy-rake over a bundle of hay. Each time he put down his cup, he ran his blue handkerchief over his lips. When he took a drink of water, he managed very neatly with the back of his hand.

Mary sat watching him intently, trying to find any change in his face. It is hard to see anyone who has become like your own body to you. Yes, his hair had got thin, and his high forehead and deep lines running from left to right. But his neck, always clean-shaven except in the busiest seasons, was not loose or baggy.

It was burned a dark reddish brown, and there were deep creases in it, but it looked firm and full of blood. His cheeks had a good color. On either side of his mouth, there was a half-moon down the length of his cheek, not wrinkles, but two lines that had come there from his habitual expression. He was shorter and broader than when she married him; his back had grown broad and curved, a good deal like the shell of an old turtle, and his arms and legs were short.

He was fifteen years older than Mary, but she had hardly ever thought about it before. He was her man, and the kind of man she liked. She was rough, and he was gentle,—city-bred, as she always said. They had been shipmates on a rough voyage and had stood by each other in trying times. Life had gone well with them because, at bottom, they had the same ideas about life. They agreed, without discussion, as to what was most important and what was secondary. They didn't often exchange opinions, even in Czech,—it was as if they had thought the same thought together. A good deal had to be sacrificed and thrown overboard in a hard life like theirs, and they had never disagreed as to the things that could go. It had been a hard life, and a soft life, too. There wasn't anything brutal in the short, broad-backed man with the three-cornered eyes and the forehead that went on to the top of his skull. He was a city man, a gentle man, and though he had married a rough farm girl, he had never touched her without gentleness.

They had been at one accord not to hurry through life, not to be always skimping and saving. They saw their neighbors buy more land and feed more stock than they did, without discontent.

Once when the creamery agent came to the Rosickys to persuade them to sell their cream, he told them how much money the Fasslers, their nearest neighbors, had made on their cream last year.

"Yes," said Mary, "and look at them Fassler children! Pale, pinched little things, they look like skimmed milk. I had rather put some color into my children's faces than put money into the bank."

The agent shrugged and turned to Anton.

"I guess we'll do like she says," said Rosicky.

III

Mary very soon got into town to see Doctor Ed, and then she had a talk with her boys and set a guard over Rosicky. Even John, the youngest, had his father on his mind. If Rosicky went to throw hay down from the loft, one of the boys ran up the ladder and took the fork from him. He sometimes complained that though he was getting to be an old man, he wasn't an old woman yet.

That winter he stayed in the house in the afternoon and carpentered, or sat in the chair between the window full of plants and the wooden bench where the two pails of drinking-water stood. This spot was called "Father's corner," though it was not a corner at all. He had a shelf there, where he kept his Bohemian papers and his pipes and tobacco, and his shears and needles and thread and tailor's thimble. Having been a tailor in his youth, he couldn't bear to see a woman patching at his clothes, or at the boys'. He liked tailoring, and always patched all the overalls and jackets and work shirts. Occasionally he made over a pair of pants one of the older boys had outgrown, for the little fellow.

While he sewed, he let his mind run back over his life. He had a good deal to remember, really, life in three countries. The only part of his youth he didn't like to remember was the two years he had spent in London, in Cheapside, working for a German tailor who was wretchedly poor. Those days, when he was nearly always hungry, when his clothes were dropping off him for dirt, and the sound of a strange language kept him on continual bewilderment, had left a sore spot in his mind that wouldn't bear touching.

He was twenty when he landed at Castle Garden in New York, and he had a protector who got him work in a tailor shop in Vesey Street, down near the Washington Market. He looked upon that part of his life as very happy. He became a good workman, he was industrious, and his wages were increased from time to time. He minded his own business and envied nobody's good fortune. He went to night school and learned to read English. He often did overtime work and was well paid for it, but somehow he never saved anything. He couldn't refuse a loan to a friend, and he was self-indulgent. He liked a good dinner, and a little went for beer, a little for tobacco; a good deal went to the girls. He often stood through an opera on Saturday nights; he could get standingroom for a dollar. Those were the great days of opera in New York, and it gave a fellow something to think about for the rest of the week. Rosicky had a quick ear, and a childish love of all the stage splendor; the scenery, the costumes, the ballet.

He usually went with a chum, and after the performance they had beer, and maybe some oysters somewhere. It was a fine life; for the first five years or so it satisfied him completely. He was never hungry or cold or dirty, and everything amused him; a fire, a dog fight, a parade, a storm, or ferry ride. He thought New York the finest, richest, friendliest city in the world.

Moreover, he had what he called a happy home life. Very near the tailorshop was a small furniture-factory where an old Austrian, Loeffler, employed a few skilled men and made unusal furniture, most of it to order, for the rich German housewives, uptown. The top floor of Loeffler's five story factory was a loft, where he kept his choice lumber and stored the odd pieces of furniture left on his hands. One of the young workmen he employed was a Czech, and he and Rosicky became fast friends. They persuaded Loeffler to let them have a sleeping-room in one corner of the loft. They bought good beds and bedding and had their pick of the furniture kept up there. The loft was low-pitched, but light and airy, full of windows, and good-smelling by reason of the fine lumber put up there to season. Old Loeffler used to go down to the docks and buy wood from South America and the East from the sea captains. The young men were as foolish about their house as a bridal pair. Zichec, the young cabinet-maker, devised every sort of convenience, and Rosicky kept their clothes in order. At night and on Sunday, when the quiver of machinery underneath was still, it was the quietest place in the world, and on summer nights all the sea winds blew in. Zichec often practiced on his flute in the evening. They were both fond of music and went to the opera together. Rosicky thought he wanted to live like that forever.

But as the years passed, all alike, he began to get a little restless. When spring came around, he would begin to feel fretted, and he got to drinking. He was likely to drink too much of a Saturday night. On Sunday, he was languid and heavy, getting over his spree. On Monday he plunged into work again. So he never had time to figure out what ailed him, although he knew something did. When the grass turned green in Park Place, and the lilac hedge at the back of Trinity churchyard put out its blossoms, he was tormented by a longing to run away. That was why he drank too much, to get a temporary illusion of freedom and wide horizons.

Rosicky, the old Rosicky, could remember as if it were yesterday the day when the young Rosicky found out what was the matter with him. It was on a Fourth of July afternoon, and he was sitting in Park Place in the sun. The lower part of New York was empty. Wall Street, Liberty Street, Broadway, all empty. So much stone and asphalt with nothing going on, so many empty windows. The emptiness was intense, like the stillness in a great factory when the machinery stops and the belts and bands cease running. It was too great a change, it took all the strength out of one. Those blank buildings, without the stream of life pouring through them, were like empty jails. It struck young Rosicky that this was the trouble with big cities; they built you in from the earth itself, cemented you away from any contact with the ground. You lived in an unnatural world, like the fish in an aquarium, who were probably much more comfortable than they ever were in the sea.

On that very day he began to think seriously about the articles he had read in the Bohemian papers, describing prosperous Czech farming communities in the West. He believed he would like to go out there as a farmhand; it was hardly possible that he could ever have land of his own. His people had always been workmen; his father and grandfather had worked in shops. His mothers' parents had lived in the country, but they rented their farm and had a hard time to get along. Nobody in his family had ever owned any land,—that belong to a different station of life altogether. Anton's mother died when he was little, and he was sent into the country to her parents. He stayed with them until he was twelve, and formed those ties with the earth and the farm animals and growing things which are never made at all unless they are made early. After his grandfather died, he went back to live with his father and stepmother, but she was very hard on him, and his father helped him to get passage to London.

After that Fourth of July day in Park Place, the desire to return to the country never left him. To work on another man's farm would be all he asked; to see the sun rise and set and to plant things and watch them grow. He was a very simple man. He was like a tree that has not many roots, but one tap root that goes down deep. He subscribed for a Bohemian paper printed in Chicago, then for one printed in Omaha. His mind got farther and farther west. He began to save a little money to buy his liberty. When he was thirty-five, there was a great meeting in New York of Bohemian athletic societies, and Rosicky left the tailor shop and went home with the Omaha delegates to try his fortune in another part of the world.

IV

Perhaps the fact that his own youth was well over before he began to have a family was one reason why Rosicky was so fond of his boys. He had almost a grandfather's indulgence for them. He had never had to worry about any of them—except, just now, a little about Rudolph.

On Saturday night the boys always piled into the Ford, took little Josephine, and went to town to the moving-picture show. One Saturday morning they were talking at the breakfast table about starting early that evening, so that they would have an hour or so to see the Christmas things in the stores before the show began. Rosicky looked down the table.

"I hope you boys ain't disappointed, but I want you to let me have de car tonight. Maybe some of you can go in with de neighbors."

Their faces fell. They worked hard all week, and they were still like children. A new jack-knife or a box of candy pleased the older ones as much as the little fellow.

"If you and Mother are going to town," Frank said, "maybe you could take a couple of us along with you, anyway."

"No, I want to take de car down to Rudolph's, and let him an' Polly go in to de show. She don't git into town enough, and' I'm afraid she's gittin' lonesome, an' he can't afford no car yet."

That settled it. The boys were a good deal dashed. Their father took another piece of apple-cake and went on: "Maybe next Saturday night de two little fellers can go along wid dem."

"Oh, is Rudolph going to have the car every Saturday night?"

Rosicky did not reply at once; then he began to speak seriously: "Listen, boys; Polly ain't lookin' so good. I don't like to see nobody lookin' sad. It comes hard fur a town girl to be a farmer's wife. I don't want no trouble to start in Rudolph's family. When it starts, it ain't so easy to stop. An American girl don't git used to our ways all at once. I like to tell Polly she and Rudolph can have the car every Saturday night till after New Years, if it's all right with you boys."

"Sure it's all right, Papa," Mary cut in. "And it's good you thought about that. Town girls is used to more than country girls. I lay awake nights, scared she'll make Rudolph discontented with the farm."

The boys put as good a face on it as they could. They surely looked foward to their Saturday nights in town. That evening Rosicky drove the car the half-mile down the road to Rudolph's new, bare little house.

Polly was in a short-sleeved gingham dress, clearing away the supper dishes. She was a trim, slim little thing, with blue eyes and shingled yellow hair, and her eyebrows were reduced to a mere brush-stroke, like Miss Pearl's.

"Good evening, Mr. Rosicky. Rudolph's at the barn, I guess." She never called him father, or Mary mother. She was sensitive about having married a foreigner. She never in the world would have done it if Rudolph hadn't been such a handsome, persuasive fellow and such a gallant lover. He had graduated in her class in the high school in town, and their friendship began in the ninth grade.

Rosicky went in, though he wasn't exactly asked. "My boys ain't goin' to town to-night, an' I brought de car over fur you two to go in to de picture show."

Polly, carrying dishes to the sink, looked over her shoulder at him. "Thank you, but I'm late with my work tonight, and pretty tired. Maybe Rudolph would like to go in with you."

"Oh, I don't go to de shows! I'm too old-fashioned. You won't feel so tired after you ride in de air a ways. It's a nice clear night, an' it ain't cold. You go an' fix yourself up, Polly, an' I'll wash de dishes an' leave everything nice fur you."

Polly blushed and tossed her bob. "I couldn't let you do that, Mr. Rosicky, I wouldn't think of it."

Rosicky said nothing. He found a bib apron on a nail behind the kitchen door. He slipped it over his head and then took Polly by her two elbows and pushed her gently toward the door of her own room. "I washed up de kitchen many times for my wife, when de babies was sick or somethin'. You go an' make yourself look nice. I like you to look prettier'n any of dem town girls when you go in. De young folks must have some fun, an' I'm goin' to look out fur you, Polly."

That kind, reassuring grip on her elbows, the old man's funny bright eyes, made Polly want to drop her head on his shoulder for a second. She restrained herself, but she lingered in his grasp at the door of her room, murmuring tearfully: "You always lived in the city when you were young, didn't you? Don't you ever get lonesome out here?"

As she turned round to him, her hand fell naturally into his, and he stood holding it, and smiling onto her face with his peculiar, knowing, indulgent smile without a shadow of reproach in it. "Dem big cities is all right fur de rich, but dey is terrible fur de poor."

"I don't know. Sometimes I think I'd like to take a chance. You lived in New York, didn't you?"

"An' London. Da's bigger still. I learned my trade dere. Here's Rudolph comin', you better hurry."

"Will you tell me about London sometime?"

"Maybe. Only I ain't no talker, Polly; run an' dress yourself up."

The bedroom door closed behind her, and Rudolph came in from the outside, looking anxious. He had seen the car and was sorry any of his family should come just then. Supper hadn't been a very pleasant occasion. Halting in the doorway, he saw his father in a kitchen apron, carrying dishes to the sink. He flushed crimson and something flashed in his eye. Rosicky held up a warning finger.

"I brought de car over fur you an' Polly to go to de picture show, an' I made her let me finish here so you won't be late. You go put on a clean shirt, quick!"

"But don't the boys want the car, father?"

"Not tonight dey don't," Rosicky fumbled under his apron and found his pants pocket. He took out a silver dollar and said in a hurried whisper: "You go an' buy dat girl some ice cream an' candy tonight, like you was courtin'. She's awful good friends wid me."

Rudolph was very short of cash, but he took the money as if it hurt him. There had been a crop failure all over the country. He had more than once been sorry he'd married this year.

In a few minutes, the young people came out, looking clean and a little stiff. Rosicky hurried them off, and then he took his own time with the dishes. He scoured the pots and pans and put away the milk and swept the kitchen. He put some coal in the stove and shut off the draughts, so the place would be warm for them when they got home late at night. Then he sat down and had a pipe and listened to the clock tick.

Generally speaking, marrying an American girl was certainly a risk. A Czech should marry a Czech. It was lucky that Polly was the daughter of a poor widow woman; Rudolph was proud, and if she had a prosperous family to throw up at him, they could never make it go. Polly was one of four sisters, and they all worked; one was bookkeeper in the bank, one taught music, and Polly and her younger sister had been clerks, like Miss Pearl. All four of them were musical, had pretty voices, and sang in the Methodist choir, which the eldest sister directed.

Polly missed the sociability of a store position. She missed the choir, and the company of her sisters. She didn't dislike housework, but she disliked so much of it. Rosicky was a little anxious about this pair. He was afraid Polly would grow so discontented that Rudy would quit the farm and take a factory job in Omaha. He had worked for a winter up there, two years ago, to get money to marry on. He had done very well, and they would always take him back at the stockyards. But to Rosicky that meant the end of everything for his son. To be a landless man was to be a wage-earner, a slave, all your life; to have nothing, to be nothing.

Rosicky thought he would come over and do a little carpentering for Polly after the New Year. He guessed she needed jollying. Rudolph was a serious short of chap, serious in love and serious about his work.

Rosicky shook out his pipe and walked home across the fields. Ahead of him the lamplight shone from his kitchen windows. Suppose he were still in a tailor shop on Vesey Street, with a bunch of pale, narrow-chested sons working on machines, all coming home tired and sullen to eat supper in a kitchen that was a parlor also; with another crowded, angry family quarrelling just across the dumb waiter shaft, and squeaking pulleys at the windows where dirty washings hung on dirty lines above a court full of old brooms and mops and ash-cans. . .

He stopped by the windmill to look up at the frosty winter stars and draw a long breath before he went inside. That kitchen with the shining windows was dear to him; but the sleeping fields and bright stars and the noble darkness were dearer still.

V

On the day before Christmas the weather set in very cold; no snow, but a bitter, biting wind that whistled and sang over the flat land and lashed one's face like fine wires. There was baking going on in the Rosicky kitchen all day, and Rosicky sat inside, making over a coat that Albert had outgrown into an overcoat for John. Mary had a big red geranium in bloom for Christmas and a row of Jerusalem cherry trees, full of berries. It was the first year she had ever grown these; Doctor Ed brought her the seeds from Omaha when he went to some medical convention. They reminded Rosicky of plants he had seen in England; and all afternoon, as he stitched, he sat thinking about those two years in London, which his mind usually shrank from even after all this while.

He was a lad of eighteen when he dropped down into London, with no money and no connections except the address of a cousin who was supposed to be working at a confectioner's.

When he went to the pastry shop, however, he found that the cousin had gone to America. Anton tramped the streets for several days, sleeping in doorways and on the Embankment, until he was in utter despair. He knew no English, and the sound of the strange language all about him confused him. By chance he met a poor German tailor who had learned his trade in Vienna, and could speak a little Czech. This tailor, Lifschnitz, kept a repair shop in a Cheapside basement, underneath a cobbler. He didn't much need an apprentice, but he was sorry for the boy and took him in for no wages but his keep and what he could pick up. The pickings were supposed to be coppers given you when you took work home to a customer. But most of the customers called for their clothes themselves, and the coppers that came Anton's way were very few. He had, however, a place to sleep. The tailor's family lived upstairs in three rooms; a kitchen, a bedroom, where Lifschnitz and his wife and five children slept, and a living room, Two corners of this living-room were curtained off for lodgers; in one Rosicky slept on an old horsehair sofa, with a feather quilt to wrap himself in. The other corner was rented to a wretched, dirty boy, who was studying the violin. He actually practiced there. Rosicky was dirty, too. There was no way to be anything else. Mrs. Lifschnitz got the water she cooked and washed with from a pump in a brick court, four flights down. There were bugs in the place and multitudes of fleas, though the poor woman did the best she could. Rosicky knew she often went empty to give another potato or a spoonful of dripping to the two hungry, sad-eyed boys who lodged with her. He used to think he would never get out of there, never get a clean shirt to his back again. What would he do, he wondered, when his clothes actually dropped to pieces and the worn cloth wouldn't hold patches any longer?

It was still early when the old farmer put aside his sewing and his recollections. The sky had been a dark grey all day, with not a gleam of sun, and the light failed at four o'clock. He went to shave and change his shirt while the turkey was roasting. Rudolph and Polly were coming over for supper.

After supper they sat round in the kitchen, and the younger boys were saying how sorry they were it hadn't snowed. Everybody was sorry. They wanted a deep snow that would lie long and keep the wheat warm, and leave the ground soaked when it melted.

"Yes, sir!" Rudolph broke out fiercely; "If we have another dry year like last year, there's going to be hard times in this country."

Rosicky filled his pipe. "You boys don't know what hard times is. You don't owe nobody, you got plenty to eat an' keep warm, an' plenty water to keep clean. When you got them, you can't have it very hard."

Rudolph frowned, opened and shut his big right hand, and dropped it clenched upon his knee. "I've got to have a good deal more than that, Father, or I'll quit this farming gamble. I can always make good wages railroading or at the packing house, and be sure of my money."

"Maybe so," his father answered dryly.

Mary, who had just come in from the pantry, and was wiping her hands on the roller towel, thought Rudy and his father were getting too serious. She brought her darning-basket and sat down in the middle of the group.

"I ain't much afraid of hard times, Rudy," she said heartily, "we've had a plenty, but we've always come through. Your father wouldn't never take nothing very hard, not even hard times. I got a mind to tell you a story on him. Maybe you boys can't hardly remember the year we had that terrible hot wind, that burned up everything, on the Fourth of July? All the corn an' the gardens. An' that was in the days when we didn't have alfalfa yet,—I guess it wasn't invented.

The Problem of Communication

"Well, that very day your father was out cultivatin' corn, and I was here in the kitchen makin' plum preserves. We had bushels of plums that year. I noticed it was terrible hot, but it's always hot in the kitchen when you're preservin' an' I was too busy with my plums to mind. Anton come in from the field about three o'clock, an' I asked him what was the matter.

" 'Nothin',' he says, 'but it's pretty hot, an' I think I won't work no more today.' He stood round for a few minutes, an' then he says: 'Ain't you near through? I want you should git up a nice supper for us tonight. It's Fourth of July.'

"I told him to git along, that I was right in the middle of preservin', but the plums would taste good on hot biscuit. 'I'm goin' to have fried chicken, too,' he says, and he went off and killed a couple. You three oldest boys was little fellers, playin' round outside, real hot an' sweaty, an' your father took you to the horse tank down by the windmill an' took off your clothes an' put you in. Them two box-elder trees was little then, but they made shade over the tank. Then he took off all his own clothes, an' got in with you. While he was playin' in the water with you, the Methodist preacher drove into our place to say how all the neighbors was goin' to meet at the schoolhouse that night, and there was your father and you three with no clothes on. I was in the kitchen door, an' I had to laugh, for the preacher acted like he ain't never seen a naked man before. He surely was embarrassed, an' your father couldn't get to his clothes; they was all hangin' up on the windmill to let the sweat dry out of 'em. So he laid in the tank where he was, an' put one of you boys on top of him to cover him a little, an' talked to the preacher.

"When you got through playin' in the water, he put clean clothes on you and a clean shirt on himself, and by that time I'd begun to get supper. He says: 'It's too hot in here to eat comfortable. Let's have a picnic in the orchard. We'll eat our supper behind the mulberry hedge, under them linden trees.'

"So he carried our supper down, an' a bottle of my wild-grape wine, an' everything tasted good, I can tell you. The wind got cooler as the sun was goin' down, and it turned out pleasant, only I noticed how the leaves was curled up on the linden trees.' That made me think, an' I asked your father if that hot wind all day hadn't been terrible hard on the gardens an' the corn.

"'Corn,' he says, 'there ain't no corn.'

"'What you talkin' about?' I said. 'Ain't we got forty acres?'"

"'We ain't got an ear,' he says, 'nor anybody else ain't got none. All the corn in this country was cooked by three o'clock today, like you'd roasted it in an oven.'

"'You mean you won't get no crop at all?' I asked him. I couldn't believe it, after he'd worked so hard.

"'No crop this year,' he says. 'That's why we're havin' a picnic. We might as well enjoy what we got.'

"An' that's how your father behaved, when all the neighbors was so discouraged they couldn't look you in the face. An' we enjoyed ourselves that year, poor as we was, an' our neighbors wasn't a bit better off for bein' miserable. Some of 'em grieved till they got poor digestions and couldn't relish what they did have."

The younger boys said they thought their father had the best of it. But Rudolph was thinking that, all the same, the neighbors had managed to get ahead more, in the fifteen years since that time. There must be something wrong about his father's way of doing things. He wished he knew what was going on in the back of Polly's mind. He knew she liked his father, but he knew, too, that she was afraid of something. When his mother sent over coffee-cake or prune tarts or a loaf of fresh bread, Polly seemed to regard them with a certain suspicion. When she observed to him that his brothers had nice manners, her tone implied that it was remarkable they should have. With his mother she was stiff and on her guard. Mary's hearty frankness and gusts of good humor irritated her. Polly was afraid of being unusual or conspicuous in any way, of being "ordinary," as she said!

When Mary had finished her story, Rosicky laid aside his pipe.

"You boys like me to tell you about some of dem hard times I been through in London?" Warmly encouraged, he sat rubbing his forehead along the deep creases. It was bothersome to tell a long story in English (he nearly always talked to the boys in Czech), but he wanted Polly to hear this one.

"Well, you know about dat tailor shop I worked in in London? I had one Christmas dere I ain't never forgot. Times was awful bad before Christmas; de boss ain't got much work, an' have it awful hard to pay his rent. It ain't so much fun, bein' poor in a big city like London, I'll say! All de windows is full of good t'ings to eat, an' all de pushcarts in de streets is full, an' you smell 'em all de time, an' you ain't got no money,—not a damn bit. I didn't mind de cold so much, though I didn't have no overcoat, chust a short jacket I'd outgrowed so it wouldn't meet on me, an' my hands was chapped raw. But I always had a good appetite, like you all know, an' de sight of dem pork pies in de windows was awful fur me.

"Day before Christmas was terrible foggy dat year, an' dat fog gits into your bones and makes you all damp like. Mrs. Lifschnitz did not give us nothing' but a little bread an' drippin' for supper, because she was savin' to try for to give us a good dinner on Christmas Day.

The Problem of Communication

After supper de boss say I can go an' enjoy myself, so I went into de streets to listen to de Christmas singers. Dey sang old songs an' make very nice music, an' I run round after dem a good ways, till I got awful hungry. I t'ink maybe if I go home, I can sleep till morning an' forgit my belly.

"I went into my corner real quiet, and roll up in my fedder quilt. But I ain't got my head down, till I smell somet'ing good. Seem like it git stronger, an' I can't git to sleep noway. I can't understand dat smell. Dere was a gas light in a hall across de court, dey always shine in at my window a little. I got up an' look around. I got a little wooden box in my corner fur a stool, cause I ain't got no chair. I picks up dat box, and under it dere is a roast goose on a platter! I can't believe my eyes. I carry it to de window where de light comes in, an' touch it and smell it to find out, an' den I taste it to be sure. I say, I will eat chust one little bit of dat goose, so I can go to sleep and tomorrow I won't eat none at all, but I tell you boys, when I stop, one half of dat goose was gone!"

The narrator bowed his head, and the boys shouted. But little Josephine slipped behind his chair and kissed him on the neck beneath his ear.

"Poor little Papa, I don't want him to be hungry."

"Da's long ago, child, I ain't never been hungry since I had your mudder to cook fur me."

"Go on and tell us the rest, please," said Polly.

"Well, when I come to realize what I done, of course, I felt terrible. I felt better in de stomach, but very bad in de heart. I set on my bed wid dat platter on my knees, ain't it all come to me; how hard dat poor woman save to buy dat goose, and how she got some neighbor to cook it dat got more fire, an' how she put it in my corner to keep it away from dem hungry children. Dey was an old carpet hung up to shut my corner off, an' de children wasn't allowed to go in dere. An' I know she put it in my corner because she trust me more'n she did de violin boy. I can't stand it to face her after I spoil de Christmas. So I put on my shoes and go out into de city. I tell myself I better throw myself in de river; but I guess I ain't dat kind of a boy.

"It was after twelve o'clock, an' terrible cold, an' I start out to walk about London all night. I walk de river awhile, but dey was lots of drunks all along; men, and women, too. I chust move along to keep away from the police. I get onto de Strand, an' den over to New Oxford Street, where dere was a big German restaurant, on de ground floor, wid big windows all fixed up fine, an' I could see de people havin' parties inside. While I was lookin' in, two men and two ladies come out, laughin' and talkin' and feelin' happy about all dey been eatin' an' drinkin' an' dey was speaking Czech,—not like de Austrians, but like de home folks talk it.

"I guess I went crazy, an' I done what I ain't never done before nor since. I went right up to dem gay people an' begun to beg dem, 'Fellow countrymen, for God's sake, give me money enough to buy a goose!'

"Dey laugh, of course, but de ladies speak awful kind to me, an' day take me back into de restaurant and give me hot coffee and cakes, an' make me tell all about how, I happened to come to London, an' what I was doin' dere. Dey take my name and where I work down on paper, an' both of dem ladies give me ten shillings.

"De big market at Covent Garden ain't very far away, an' by dat time it was open. I go dere an' buy a big goose an' some pork pies, an' potatoes and onions, an' cakes an' oranges fur de children,—all I could carry! When I git home, everybody is still asleep. I pile all I bought on de kitchen table, an' go in an' lay down on my bed, an' I ain't waken up till I hear dat woman scream when she come out into her kitchen. My goodness, but she was surprise! She laugh an' cry at de same time, an' hug me an' waken all de children. She ain't stop fur no breakfast; she git de Christmas dinner ready dat morning, and we all sit down an' eat all we can hold. I ain't never seen dat violin boy have all he can hold before.

"Two three days after dat, de two men come to hunt me up, an' dey ask my boss, and he give me a good report an' tell dem I was a steady boy all right. One of dem Bohemians was very smart an' run a Bohemian newspaper in New York, an' de odder was a rich man, in de importing business, an' day been travelling togedder. Dey told me how t'ings was easier in New York, an' offered to pay my passage when dey was goin' home soon on a boat. My boss say to me: 'You go. You ain't got no chance here, an' I like to see you git ahead, fur you always been a good boy to my woman, and fur dat fine Christmas dinner you give us all.' An' da's how I got to New York."

That night when Rudolph and Polly, arm in arm, were running home across the fields with the bitter wind at their backs, his heart leaped for joy when she said she thought they might have his family over for supper on New Year's Eve. "Let's get up a nice supper, and not let your mother help at all; make her be company for once."

"That would be lovely of you, Polly," he said humbly. He was a very simple, modest boy, and he, too, felt vaguely that Polly and her sisters were more experienced and worldly than his people.

VI

The winter turned out badly for farmers. It was bitterly cold, and after the first light snows before Christmas there was no snow at all,

—and no rain. March was as bitter as February. On those days when the wind fairly punished the country, Rosicky sat by his window. In the fall he and the boys had put in a big wheat planting, and now the seed had frozen in the ground. All that land would have to be ploughed up and planted over again, planted in corn. It had happened before, but he was younger then, and he never worried about what had to be. He was sure of himself and of Mary, he knew they could bear what they had to bear, that they would always pull through somehow. But he was not sure about the young ones, and he felt troubled because Rudolph and Polly were having such a hard start.

Sitting beside his flowering window while the panes rattled and the wind blew in under the door, Rosicky gave himself to reflection as he had not done since those Sundays in the loft of the furniture-factory in New York, long ago. Then he was trying to find what he wanted in life for himself; now he was trying to find what he wanted for his boys, and why it was he so hungered to feel sure they would be here, working this very land, after he was gone.

They would have to work hard on the farm, and probably they would never do much more than make a living. But if he could think of them as staying here on the land, he wouldn't have to fear any great unkindness for them. Hardships, certainly; it was a hardship to have the wheat freeze in the ground when seed was so high; and to have to sell your stock because you had no feed. But there would be other years when everything came along right, and you caught up. And what you had was your own. You didn't have to choose between bosses and strikers, and go wrong either way. You didn't have to do with dishonest and cruel people. They were the only things in his experience he had found terrifying and horrible; the look in the eyes of a dishonest and crafty man, of a scheming and rapacious woman.

In the country, if you had a mean neighbor, you could keep off his land and make him keep off yours. But in the city, all the foulness and misery and brutality of your neighbors was part of your life. The worst things he had come upon in his journey through the world were human —depraved and poisonous specimens of man. To this day he could recall certain terrible faces in the London streets. There were mean people everywhere, to be sure, even in their own country town here. But they weren't tempered, hardened, sharpened, like the treacherous people in cities who live by grinding or cheating or poisoning their fellowmen. He had helped to bury two of his fellow-workmen in the tailoring trade, and he was distrustful of the organized industries that seek one out of the world in big cities. Here, if you were sick, you had Doctor Ed to look after you; and if you died, fat Mr. Haycock, the kindest man in the world, buried you.

It seemed to Rosicky that for good, honest boys like his, the worst they could do on the farm was better than the best they could do in the city. If he'd had a mean boy, now, one who was crooked and sharp and tried to put anything over on his brothers, then town would be the place for him. But he had no such boy. As for Rudolph, the discontented one, he would give the shirt off his back to anyone who touched his heart. What Rosicky really hoped for his boys was that they could get through the world without ever knowing much about the cruelty of human beings. "Their mother an' me ain't prepared them for that," he sometimes said to himself.

These thoughts brought him back to a grateful consideration of his own case. What an escape he had had, to be sure! He, too, in his time, had had to take money for repair work from the hand of a hungry child who let it go so wistfully; because it was money due his boss. And now, in all these years, he had never had to take a cent from anyone in bitter need, — never had to look at the face of a woman become like a wolf's from struggle and famine. When he thought of these things, Rosicky would put on his cap and jacket and slip down to the barn and give his work-horses a little extra oats, letting them eat it out of his hand in their slobbery fashion. It was his way of expressing what he felt, and made him chuckle with pleasure.

The spring came warm, with blue skies,—but dry, dry as a bone. The boys began ploughing up the wheat-fields to plant them over in corn. Rosicky would stand at the fence corner and watch them, and the earth was so dry it blew up in clouds of brown dust that hid horses and the sulky plough and the driver. It was a bad outlook.

The big alfalfa-field that lay between the home place and Rudolph's came up green, but Rosicky was worried because during that open windy winter a great many Russian thistle plants had blown in there and lodged. He kept asking the boys to rake them out; he was afraid that their seed would root and "take the alfalfa." Rudolph said that was nonsense. The boys were working so hard planting corn, their father felt he couldn't insist about the thistles, but he set great store by that big alfalfa field. It was a feed you could depend on,—and there was some deeper reason, vague, but strong. The peculiar green of that clover woke early memories in old Rosicky, went back to something in his childhood in the old world. When he was a little boy, he had played in fields of that strong blue-green color.

One morning, when Rudolph had gone to town in the car, leaving a work-team idle in his barn, Rosicky went over to his son's place, put the horses to the buggy rake, and set about quietly raking up those thistles. He behaved with guilty caution, and rather enjoyed stealing a march on Doctor Ed, who was just then taking his first vacation in seven years of practice and was attending a clinic in Chicago. Rosicky got the thistles raked up, but did not stop to burn them. That would take some time, and his breath was pretty short, so he thought he had better get the horses back to the barn.

He got them into the barn and to their stalls, but the pain had come on so sharp in his chest that he didn't try to take the harness off. He started for the house, bending lower with every step. The cramp in his chest was shutting him up like a jack-knife. When he reached the windmill, he swayed and caught at the ladder. He saw Polly coming down the hill, running with the swiftness of a slim grey-hound. In a flash she had her shoulder under his armpit.

"Lean on me, Father, hard! Don't be afraid. We can get to the house all right."

Somehow they did, though Rosicky became blind with pain; he could keep on his legs, but he couldn't steer his course. The next thing he was conscious of was lying on Polly's bed, and Polly bending over him wringing out bath towels in hot water and putting them on his chest. She stopped only to throw coal into the stove, and she kept the tea-kettle and the black pot going. She put these hot applications on him for nearly an hour, she told him afterwards, and all that time he was drawn up stiff and blue, with the sweat pouring off him.

As the pain gradually loosed its grip, the stiffness went out of his jaws, the black circles round his eyes disappeared, and a little of his natural color came back. When his daughter-in-law buttoned his shirt over his chest at last, he sighed.

"Da's fine, de way I feel now, Polly. It was a awful bad spell, an' I was so sorry it all come on you like it did."

Polly was flushed and excited. "Is the pain really gone? Can I leave you long enough to telephone over to your place?"

Rosicky's eyelids fluttered. "Don't telephone, Polly. It ain't no use to scare my wife. It's nice and quiet here, an' if I ain't too much trouble to you, just let me lay still till I feel like myself. I ain't got no pain now. It's nice here."

Polly bent over him and wiped the moisture from his face. "Oh, I'm so glad it's over!" She broke out impulsively. "It just broke my heart to see you suffer so, Father."

Rosicky motioned her to sit down on the chair where the tea-kettle had been, and looked up at her with that lively affectionate gleam in his eyes. "You was awful good to me, I won't ever forgit dat. I hate it to be sick on you like dis. Down at de barn I say to myself, dat young girl ain't had much experience in sickness, I don't want to scare her, an' maybe she's got a baby comin' or somet'ing."

Polly took his hand. He was looking at her so intently and affectionately and confidingly; his eyes seemed to caress her face, to regard it with pleasure. She frowned with her funny streaks of eyebrows, and then smiled back at him.

"I guess maybe there is something of that kind going to happen. But I haven't told anyone yet, not my mother or Rudolph. You'll be the first to know."

"I like mighty well to see dat little child, Polly," was all he said. Then he closed his eyes and lay half-smiling. But Polly sat still, thinking hard. She had a sudden feeling that nobody in the world, not her mother, not Rudolph, or anyone, really loved her as much as old Rosicky did. It perplexed her. She sat frowning and trying to puzzle it out. It was as if Rosicky had a special gift for loving people, something that was like an ear for music or an eye for color. It was quiet, unobtrusive; it was merely there. You saw it in his eyes,—perhaps that was why they were merry. You felt it in his hands, too. After he dropped off to sleep, she sat holding his warm, broad, flexible brown hand. She had never seen another in the least like it. She wondered if it wasn't a kind of gypsy hand, it was so alive and quick and light in its communications, —very strange in a farmer. Nearly all the farmers she knew had huge lumps of fists, like mauls, or they were knotty and bony and uncomfortable-looking, with stiff fingers. But Rosicky's hand was like quicksilver, flexible, muscular, about the color of a pale cigar, with deep, deep creases across the palm. It wasn't nervous, it wasn't a stupid lump; it was a warm brown human hand, with some cleverness in it, a great deal of generosity, and something else which Polly could only call "gypsylike," —something nimble and lively and sure, in the way that animals are.

Polly remembered that hour long afterward; it had been like an awakening to her. It seemed to her that she never learned so much about life from anything as from old Rosicky's hand. It brought her to herself; it communicated some direct and untranslatable message.

When she heard Rudolph coming in the car, she ran out to meet him.

"Oh, Rudy, your Father's been awful sick! He raked up those thistles he's been worrying about, and afterwards he could hardly get to the house. He suffered so I was afraid he was going to die."

Rudolph jumped to the ground. "Where is he now?"

"On the bed, He's asleep. I was terribly scared, because you know, I'm so fond of your father." She slipped her arm through his and they went into the house. That afternoon, they took Rosicky home and put him to bed, though he protested that he was quite well again.

The next morning he got up and dressed and sat down to breakfast with his family. He told Mary that his coffee tasted better than usual to him, and he warned the boys not to bear any tales to Doctor Ed when he got home. After breakfast he sat down by his window to do some patching and asked Mary to thread several needles for him before she went to feed her chickens,—her eyes were better than his, and her hands steadier. He lit his pipe and took up John's overalls, Mary had been watching him anxiously all morning, and as she went out of the door with her bucket of scraps, she saw he was smiling. He was thinking, indeed, about Polly, and how he might never have known what a tender heart she had if he hadn't got sick over there. Girls nowadays didn't wear their heart on their sleeve. But now he knew Polly would make a fine woman after the foolishness wore off. Either a woman had that sweetness at her heart or she hadn't. You couldn't always tell by the look of them; but if they had that, everything came out right in the end.

After he had taken a few stitches, the cramp began in his chest, like yesterday. He put his pipe cautiously down on the window-sill and bent over to ease the pull. No use, —he had better try to get to his bed if he could. He rose and groped his way across the familiar floor, which was rising and falling like the deck of a ship. At the door he fell. When Mary came in, she found him lying there, and the moment she touched him she knew that he was gone.

Doctor Ed was away when Rosicky died, and for the first few weeks after he got home he was hard driven. Every day he said to himself that he must get out to see the family that had lost their father. One soft, warm moonlight night in early summer he started for the farm. His mind was on other things, and not until his road ran by the graveyard did he realize that Rosicky wasn't over there on the hill where the red lamp-light shone, but here, in the moonlight. He stopped his car, shut off the engine, and sat there for a while.

A sudden hush had fallen on his soul. Everything here seemed strangely moving and significant, though signifying what, he did not know. Close by the wire fence stood Rosicky's mowing-machine, where one of the boys had been cutting hay that afternoon; his own work-horses had been going up and down there. The new-cut hay perfumed all the night air. The moonlight silvering the long, billowy grass that grew over the graves and hit the fence; the few little evergreens stood out black in it, like shadows in a pool. The sky was very blue and soft, the stars rather faint because the moon was full.

For the first time it struck Doctor Ed that this was really a beautiful graveyard. He thought of city cemeteries; acres of shrubbery and heavy world. Cities of the dead, indeed; cities of the forgotten, of the "put away." But this was open and free, this little square of long grass which the wind for ever stirred. Nothing but the sky overhead, and the many-colored fields running on until they met that sky. The horses worked here in summer; the neighbors passed on their way to town; and over yonder, in the cornfield, Rosicky's own cattle would be eating fodder as winter came on. Nothing could be more undeathlike than this place; nothing could be more right for a man who had helped to do the work of great cities and had always longed for the open country and had got to it at last. Rosicky's life seemed to him complete and beautiful.

Discussion of "Neighbor Rosicky"

Willa Cather (1876 - 1947) has already been studied in volume two of *Out of the Best Books.* The story used then, "The Sculptor's Funeral," could hardly be in greater contrast with "Neighbor Rosicky." Where most of the characters we met earlier are petty, mean, and callous, it is difficult to find a single person in "Neighbor Rosicky" who is not admirable.

Although longer than most selections that we have used heretofore, this story is such a great one that it must be included in any extended discussion of communication, for most of the relationships that challenge our effectiveness as human beings are seen at their acme here.

Dr. Burleigh, a friend of the Rosicky family, appropriately opens and closes this condensed saga of a remarkable group of people. We know little of the Doctor to begin with, but he becomes a convenient device to introduce all the participants in this household drama naturally. Such is Miss Cather's skill, however, that Dr. Burleigh is more than a frame for a story. His developing awareness of how truly unusual the Rosickys are corresponds with our growing appreciation of what this simple Czech family stands for. In the beginning, Dr. Burleigh reflects on the possibility that "Maybe you couldn't enjoy your life and put it in the bank too." After Anton Rosicky's death, it finally occurs to the Doctor that here was one life that was "complete and beautiful."

From his dawning awareness that other values might take precedence over "getting on" to his final realization that a life such as neighbor Rosicky's even took the terror out of death, "Dr. Ed" grows in understanding of himself as much as he comes to appreciate others.

No finer communication between friends is possible, for we need to know others that we might know ourselves. In the mutual revelation that true friendship brings, we grow to meet the ideal that is compounded of our own and our friends' estimates of our potential.

In Rosicky's relationship with his daughter-in-law, Polly, we see illustrated the conclusion reached by the Cornell study of in-law relationships mentioned earlier in this section. To begin with, Polly is uneasy about her connection with the Rosicky family. The financial difficulties she and Rudolph are experiencing add to her insecurity. It is only when she realizes, suddenly, how totally her father-in-law loves her that she loses that focus on herself which has been in the way of any real fulfillment as a wife, a mother-to-be, and an accepted part of the Rosicky family.

The feelings between the Rosicky children are mentioned almost casually, but they are persuasively appropriate. It isn't easy for them to accept the fact that Rudolph and Polly are to get the car every Saturday night for a number of weeks. But they *can* accept it, for they know that their parents are equally concerned about every child. In the stories their mother tells of early, difficult days on the farm or in their father's account of his youth in London and New York, there is unmistakable evidence that *family* means more than anything else. No child has to be coerced into accepting what is necessary at the moment, for where there is no ambiguity in family acceptance, there are no unanswered questions about one's worth in the family.

The really supreme example of human communication in this story, however, lies in the relationship of Anton and Mary Rosicky. They are not close in age and their backgrounds are different, but they have achieved a sensitivity to each other that is born of shared ideals. In the opening verse of the twenty-fifth chapter of Ecclesiasticus we are told that the Lord finds three things particularly pleasing; "The unity of brethren, the love of neighbors, and a man and a wife who agree together." The same final point is made beautifully in this story:

> They had been shipmates on a rough voyage and had stood by eath other in trying times. Life had gone well with them because, at bottom, they had the same ideas about life. They agreed, without discussion as to what was most important and what was secondary . . . a good deal had to be sacrificed and thrown overboard in a hard life like theirs, and they had never disagreed as to the things that could go.

In an ultimate sense, communication among the sons and daughters of God is preparation for that oneness with our Father in heaven which will be achieved only as we become like him. Our most sensitive efforts and our most skillful techniques must be unified by that love and compassion that characterizes him and distinguishes his patriarchal order.

SECTION FOUR

The Place of Entertainment

by Bruce B. Clark

THE PLACE OF ENTERTAINMENT

Any pleasure which keeps the heart from God will be fatal to the soul.
—Richard Fuller

Introductory Comments

There is a long tradition among some churches, going back through centuries of medieval Christianity, which assumes that God is not pleased when people enjoy themselves with the pleasures of this world. Under such a philosophy, money is regarded as evil, love between men and women is thought of as tainted with sin, art and recreation are looked on with suspicion. Through centuries of history some churches have banned dancing and drama as forbidden evils, some have legislated that their religious leaders must not marry, and some have prescribed heavy, drab clothing as the only dress suitable to express religious devotion. Philosophically a whole intellectual movement known as asceticism flourished for centuries advocating strict self-denial as a means of spiritual self-discipline. Severe "mortifications of the flesh" were practiced, apparently under the supposition that God is somehow pleased with human self-punishment.

This is not, however, the position of The Church of Jesus Christ of Latter-day Saints. The Church teaches that God wants people to be happy and enjoy themselves, in *this* life as well as in the life to come. "Men are that they might have joy" is one of the great principles expressed in the Book of Mormon. Money sometimes does promote evil but need not do so if used for good purposes. Love between men and women sanctified by marriage provides the richest source of genuine happiness, both in this life and eternally. Art and recreation when in good taste abundantly enrich life and are in harmony with the fullness of the gospel plan.

The key words in the preceding sentence are "when in good taste." From the beginning the Church has not only permitted but actually sponsored extensive programs in music, drama, dance, literature, and athletics. Always, however, emphasis has been upon encouraging refinement, wholesomeness, and "good taste"—good taste in dress styles, good taste in music, good taste in dancing, etc. A word of caution, though: "good taste" should not be interpreted as an excuse for one person to impose his personal taste upon another. Within the broad scope of art and entertainment, one person may like one thing, and another person may like something else—and each should be hesitant to call something bad simply because he personally does not like it. There are limits to what is in good taste, but the limits are often broader than one person's likes and dislikes.

Reading, as millions of readers know, provides an inexhaustible and wonderfully varied storehouse of entertainment. In addition to all of the aesthetic values of literature and all its rich insights into people, ideas, and problems, we should never forget that one of its great and valid functions is to entertain. We live in a world of pressures and problems. How wonderful that we can draw upon literature for the relaxation and delight it provides in addition to its many other values!

From Aristophanes in ancient Greek times to writers such as E.B. White,[1] James Thurber, and Al Capp in our own century, every era has had its great humorists. Thousands of delightful stories, novels, poems, dramas, and essays are available to illustrate the rich entertainment literature can provide. Most of the time through the four preceding volumes, and in this volume too, we have printed "serious" literature, concerned with problems, values, ideals, etc. Now in this one

---

[1] Read, for example, the charming essay "Farewell, My Lovely!" by E. B. White (with Richard Lee Strout as co-author) celebrating the wonderful era of the Model T Ford with all of the wonders and eccentricities of the old "flivver" itself. For anyone over 40 who remembers the Model T, this essay is one of the most delightful things ever written.

section we want to emphasize the power of literature to entertain. Unfortunately, we cannot print all of the thousands of wonderful things available. Instead, we can only do a little sampling, and as our samples we now present two short stories and some brief excerpts from the writings of Mark Twain and Charles Lamb—mostly for fun!

The Devil and Daniel Webster

by Stephen Vincent Benét

It's a story they tell in the border country, where Massachusetts joins Vermont and New Hampshire.

Yes, Dan'l Webster's dead—or, at least, they buried him. But every time there's a thunderstorm around Marshfield, they say you can hear his rolling voice in the hollows of the sky. And they say that if you go to his grave and speak loud and clear, "Dan'l Webster—Dan'l Webster!" the ground'll begin to shiver and the trees begin to shake. And after a while you'll hear a deep voice saying, "Neighbor, how stands the Union?" Then you better answer the Union stands as she stood, rock bottomed and copper sheathed, one and indivisible, or he's liable to rear right out of the ground. At least, that's what I was told when I was a youngster.

You see, for a while, he was the biggest man in the country. He never got to be President, but he was the biggest man. There were thousands that trusted in him right next to God almighty, and they told stories about him and all the things that belonged to him that were like the stories of patriarchs and such. They said, when he stood up to speak, stars and stripes came right out in the sky, and once he spoke against a river and made it sink into the ground. They said, when he walked the woods with his fishing rod, Killall, the trout would jump out of the streams right into his pockets, for they knew it was no use putting up a fight against him; and, when he argued a case, he could turn on the harps of the blessed and the shaking of the earth underground. That was the kind of man he was, and his big farm up at Marshfield was suitable to him. The chickens he raised were all white meat down through the drumsticks, the cows were tended like children, and the big ram he called Goliath had horns with a curl like a morning-glory vine and could butt through an iron door. But Dan'l wasn't one of your gentlemen farmers; he knew all the ways of the land, and he'd be up by candlelight to see that the chores got done. A man with a mouth like a mastiff, a brow like a mountain and eyes like burning anthracite—that was Dan'l Webster in his prime. And the biggest case he argued never got written down in the books, for he argued it against the devil, nip and tuck and no holds barred. And this is the way I used to hear it told.

There was a man named Jabez Stone, lived at Cross Corners, New Hampshire. He wasn't a bad man to start with, but he was an unlucky man. If he planted corn, he got borers; if he planted potatoes, he got blight. He had good-enough land, but it didn't prosper him; he had a decent wife and children, but the more children he had, the less there

The Place of Entertainment

was to feed them. If stones cropped up in his neighbor's field, boulders boiled up in his; if he had a horse with the spavins, he'd trade it for one with the staggers and give something extra. There's some folks bound to be like that, apparently. But one day Jabez Stone got sick of the whole business.

He'd been plowing that morning and he'd just broke the plowshare on a rock that he could have sworn hadn't been there yesterday. And, as he stood looking at the plowshare, the off horse began to cough—that ropy kind of cough that means sickness and horse doctors. There were two children down with the measles, his wife was ailing, and he had a whitlow on his thumb. It was about the last straw for Jabez Stone. "I vow," he said, and he looked around him kind of desperate, "I vow it's enough to make a man want to sell his soul to the devil! And I would, too, for two cents!"

Then he felt a kind of queerness come over him at having said what he'd said; though naturally, being a New Hampshireman, he wouldn't take it back. But, all the same, when it got to be evening and, as far as he could see, no notice had been taken, he felt relieved in his mind, for he was a religious man. But notice is always taken, sooner or later, just like the Good Book says. And, sure enough, next day, about suppertime, a soft-spoken, dark-dressed stranger drove up in a handsome buggy and asked for Jabez Stone.

Well, Jabez told his family it was a lawyer, come to see him about a legacy. But he knew who it was. He didn't like the looks of the stranger, nor the way he smiled with his teeth. They were white teeth, and plentiful—some say they were filed to a point, but I wouldn't vouch for that. And he didn't like it when the dog took one look at the stranger and ran away howling, with his tail between his legs. But having passed the word, more or less, he stuck to it, and they went out behind the barn and made their bargain. Jabez Stone had to prick his finger to sign, and the stranger lent him a silver pin. The wound healed clean, but it left a little white scar.

After that, all of a sudden, things began to pick up and prosper for Jabez Stone. His cows got fat and his horses sleek, his crops were the envy of the neighborhood, and lightning might strike all over the valley, but it wouldn't strike his barn. Pretty soon he was one of the prosperous people of the county; they asked him to stand for selectman, and he stood for it; there began to be talk of running him for state senate. All in all, you might say the Stone family was as happy and contented as cats in a dairy. And so they were, except for Jabez Stone.

He'd been contented enough for the first few years. It's a great thing when bad luck turns; it drives most other things out of your head. True, every now and then, especially in rainy weather, the little white scar on his finger would give him a twinge. And once a year, punctual as clockwork, the stranger with the handsome buggy would come driving by. But the sixth year the stranger lighted, and, after that, his peace was over for Jabez Stone.

The stranger came up through the lower field, switching his boots with a cane—they were handsome black boots, but Jabez Stone never liked the look of them, particularly the toes. And, after he'd passed the time of day, he said, "Well, Mr. Stone, you're a hummer! It's a very pretty property you've got here, Mr. Stone."

"Well, some might favor it and others might not," said Jabez Stone, for he was a New Hampshireman.

"Oh, no need to decry your industry!" said the stranger, very easy, showing his teeth in a smile. "After all, we know what's been done, and it's been according to contract and specifications. So when—ahem—the mortgage falls due next year, you shouldn't have any regrets."

"Speaking of that mortgage, mister," said Jabez Stone, and he looked around for help to the earth and the sky, "I'm beginning to have one or two doubts about it."

"Doubts?" said the stranger not quite so pleasantly.

"Why, yes," said Jabez Stone. "This being the U.S.A. and me always having been a religious man." He cleared his throat and got bolder. "Yes sir," he said, "I'm beginning to have considerable doubts as to that mortgage holding in court."

"There's courts and courts," said the stranger, clicking his teeth. "Still, we might as well have a look at the original document." And he hauled out a big black pocketbook, full of papers. "Sherwin, Slater, Stevens, Stone," he muttered. " 'I, Jabez Stone, for a term of seven years—' Oh, it's quite in order, I think."

But Jabez Stone wasn't listening, for he saw something else flutter out of the black pocketbook. It was something that looked like a moth, but it wasn't a moth. And as Jabez Stone stared at it, it seemed to speak to him in a small sort of piping voice, terrible small and thin, but terrible human. "Neighbor Stone!" it squeaked. "Neighbor Stone! Help me! Help me!"

But before Jabez Stone could stir hand or foot, the stranger whipped out a big bandanna handkerchief, caught the creature in it, just like a butterfly, and started tying up the ends of the bandanna.

"Sorry for the interruption," he said. "As I was saying—"

But Jabez Stone was shaking all over like a scared horse.

"That's Miser Stevens' voice!" he said in a croak. "And you've got him in your handkerchief!"

The stranger looked a little embarrassed.

"Yes, I really should have transferred him to the collecting box," he said with a simper, "but there were some rather unusual specimens there and I don't want them crowded. Well, well, these little contretemps will occur."

The Place of Entertainment 137

"I don't know what you mean by contertan," said Jabez Stone, "but that was Miser Stevens' voice! And he ain't dead! You can't tell me he is! He was just as spry and mean as a woodchuck Tuesday!"

"In the midst of life . . ." said the stranger, kind of pious. "Listen!" Then a bell began to toll in the valley and Jabez Stone listened, with the sweat running down his face. For he knew it was tolled for Miser Stevens and that he was dead.

"These long-standing accounts," said the stranger with a sigh; "one really hates to close them. But business is business."

He still had the bandanna in his hand, and Jabez Stone felt sick as he saw the cloth struggle and flutter.

"Are they all as small as that?" he asked hoarsely.

"Small?" said the stranger. "Oh, I see what you mean. Why, they vary." He measured Jabez Stone with his eyes, and his teeth showed. "Don't worry, Mr. Stone," he said. "You'll go with a very good grade. I wouldn't trust you outside the collecting box. Now, a man like Dan'l Webster, of course—well, we'd have to build a special box for him, and even at that, I imagine the wing spread would astonish you. He'd certainly be a prize. I wish we could see our way clear to him. But, in your case, as I was saying—"

"Put that handkerchief away!" said Jabez Stone, and he began to beg and to pray. But the best he could get at the end was a three years' extension, with conditions.

But till you make a bargain like that, you've got no idea of how fast four years can run. By the last months of those years Jabez Stone's known all over the state and there's talk of running him for governor—and it's dust and ashes in his mouth. For every day, when he gets up, he thinks, "There's one more night gone," and every night, when he lies down, he thinks of the black pocketbook and the soul of Miser Stevens, and it makes him sick at heart. Till finally, he can't bear it any longer, and, in the last days of the last year, he hitches up his horse and drives off to seek Dan'l Webster. For Dan'l was born in New Hampshire, only a few miles from Cross Corners, and it's well known that he has a particular soft spot for old neighbors.

It was early in the morning when he got to Marshfield, but Dan'l was up already, talking Latin to the farm hands and wrestling with the ram, Goliath, and trying out a new trotter and working up speeches to make against John C. Calhoun. But when he heard a New Hampshireman had come to see him, he dropped everything else he was doing, for that was Dan'l's way. He gave Jabez Stone a breakfast that five men couldn't eat, went into the living history of every man and woman in Cross Corners, and finally asked him how he could serve him.

Jabez Stone allowed that it was a kind of mortgage case.

"Well, I haven't pleaded a mortgage case in a long time, and I don't generally plead now, except before the Supreme Court," said Dan'l, "but if I can, I'll help you."

"Then I've got hope for the first time in ten years," said Jabez Stone and told him the details.

Dan'l walked up and down as he listened, hands behind his back, now and then asking a question, now and then plunging his eyes at the floor, as if they'd bore through it like gimlets. When Jabez Stone had finished, Dan'l puffed out his cheeks and blew. Then he turned to Jabez Stone and a smile broke over his face like the sunrise over Monadnock.

"You've certainly given yourself the devil's own row to hoe, Neighbor Stone," he said, "but I'll take your case."

"You'll take it?" said Jabez Stone, hardly daring to believe.

"Yes," said Dan'l Webster. "I've got about seventy-five other things to do and the Missouri Compromise to straighten out, but I'll take your case. For if two New Hampshiremen aren't a match for the devil, we might as well give the country back to the Indians."

Then he shook Jabez Stone by the hand and said, "Did you come down here in a hurry?"

"Well, I admit I made time," said Jabez Stone.

"You'll go back faster," said Dan'l Webster, and he told 'em to hitch up Constitution and Constellation to the carriage. They were matched grays with one white forefoot, and they stepped like greased lightning.

Well, I won't describe how excited and pleased the whole Stone family was to have the great Dan'l Webster for a guest, when they finally got there. Jabez Stone had lost his hat on the way, blown off when they overtook a wind, but he didn't take much account of that. But after supper he sent the family off to bed, for he had most particular business with Mr. Webster. Mrs. Stone wanted him to sit in the front parlor, but Dan'l Webster knew front parlors and said he preferred the kitchen. So it was there they sat, waiting for the stranger, with a jug on the table between them and a bright fire on the hearth—the stranger being scheduled to show up on the stroke of midnight, according to specification.

Well, most men wouldn't have asked for better company than Dan'l Webster and a jug. But with every tick of the clock Jabez Stone got sadder and sadder. His eyes roved round, and though he sampled the jug you could see he couldn't taste it. Finally, on the stroke of 11:30 he reached over and grabbed Dan'l Webster by the arm.

"Mr. Webster, Mr. Webster!" he said, and his voice was shaking with fear and a desperate courage. "Please, Mr. Webster, harness your horses and get away from this place while you can!"

"You've brought me a long way, neighbor, to tell me you don't like my company," said Dan'l Webster, quite peaceable, pulling at the jug.

The Place of Entertainment

"Miserable wretch that I am!" groaned Jabez Stone. "I've brought you a devilish way, and now I see my folly. Let him take me if he wills. I don't hanker after it, I must say, but I can stand it. But you're the Union's stay and New Hampshire's pride! He mustn't get you, Mr. Webster! He mustn't get you!"

Dan'l Webster looked at the distracted man, all gray and shaking in the firelight, and laid a hand on his shoulder.

"I'm obliged to you, Neighbor Stone," he said gently. "It's kindly thought of. But there's a jug on the table and a case in hand. And I never left a jug or a case half finished in my life."

And just at that moment there was a sharp rap on the door.

"Ah," said Dan'l Webster very coolly, "I thought your clock was a trifle slow, Neighbor Stone." He stepped to the door and opened it. "Come in!" he said.

The stranger came in—very dark and tall he looked in the firelight. He was carrying a box under his arm—a black japanned box with little air holes in the lid. At the sight of the box Jabez Stone gave a low cry and shrank into a corner of the room.

"Mr. Webster, I presume," said the stranger, very polite, but with his eyes glowing like a fox's deep in the woods.

"Attorney of record for Jabez Stone," said Dan'l Webster, but his eyes were glowing too. "Might I ask your name?"

"I've gone by a good many," said the stranger carelessly. "Perhaps Scratch will do for the evening. I'm often called that in these regions."

Then he sat down at the table and poured himself a drink from the jug. The liquor was cold in the jug, but it came steaming into the glass.

"And now," said the stranger, smiling and showing his teeth, "I shall call upon you, as a law-abiding citizen, to assist me in taking possession of my property."

Well, with that the argument began—and it went hot and heavy. At first Jabez Stone had a flicker of hope, but when he saw Dan'l Webster being forced back at point after point, he just sat scrunched in his corner, with his eyes on that japanned box. For there wasn't any doubt as to the deed or the signature—that was the worst of it. Dan'l Webster twisted and turned and thumped his fist on the table, but he couldn't get away from that. He offered to compromise the case; the stranger wouldn't hear of it. He pointed out the property had increased in value, and state senators ought to be worth more; the stranger stuck to the letter of the law. He was a great lawyer, Dan'l Webster, but we know who's the King of Lawyers, as the Good Book tells us, and it seemed as if, for the first time, Dan'l Webster had met his match.

Finally, the stranger yawned a little. "Your spirited efforts on behalf of your client do you credit, Mr. Webster," he said, "but if you have no more arguments to adduce, I'm rather pressed for time . . ." and Jabez Stone shuddered.

Dan'l Webster's brow looked dark as a thundercloud.

"Pressed or not, you shall not have this man!" he thundered. "Mr. Stone is an American citizen, and no American citizen may be forced into the service of a foreign prince. We fought England for that in '12 and we'll fight all hell for it again!"

"Foreign?" said the stranger. "And who calls me a foreigner?"

"Well, I never yet heard of the dev—of your claiming American citizenship," said Dan'l Webster with surprise.

"And who with better right?" said the stranger with one of his terrible smiles. "When the first wrong was done to the first Indian, I was there. When the first slaver put out for the Congo, I stood on her deck. Am I not in your books and stories and beliefs, from the first settlements on? Am I not spoken of still in every church in New England? 'Tis true the North claims me for a Southerner and the South for a Northerner, but I am neither. I am merely an honest American like yourself—and of the best descent—for, to tell the truth, Mr. Webster, though I don't like to boast of it, my name is older in this country than yours."

"Aha!" said Dan'l Webster with the veins standing out in his forehead. "Then I stand on the Constitution! I demand a trial for my client!"

"The case is hardly one for an ordinary court," said the stranger, his eyes flickering. "And, indeed, the lateness of the hour—"

"Let it be any court you choose, so it is an American judge and an American jury!" said Dan'l Webster in his pride. "Let it be the quick or the dead; I'll abide the issue!"

"You have said it," said the stranger, and pointed his finger at the door. And with that, and all of a sudden, there was a rushing of wind outside and a noise of footsteps. They came, clear and distinct, through the night. And yet they were not like the footsteps of living men.

"What's that? Who comes by so late?" cried Jabez Stone in an ague of fear.

"The jury Mr. Webster demands," said the stranger, sipping at his boiling glass. "You must pardon the rough appearance of one or two; they will have come a long way."

And with that the fire burned blue and the door blew open and twelve men entered, one by one.

If Jabez Stone had been sick with terror before, he was blind with terror now. For there was Walter Butler, the loyalist, who spread fire and horror through the Mohawk Valley in the times of the Revolution; and there was Simon Girty, the renegade, who saw white men burned at the stake and whooped with the Indians to see them burn. His eyes were green, like a catamount's, and the stains on his hunting shirt did not come from the blood of the deer. King Philip was there, wild and proud as he had been in life, with the great gash in his head that gave him his death wound, and cruel Governor Dale, who broke men on the wheel. There was Morton of Merry Mount, who so vexed the Plymouth Colony, with his flushed, loose, handsome face and his hate of the godly. There was Teach, the bloody pirate, with his black beard curling on his breast. The Reverend John Smeet, with his strangler's hands and his Geneva gown, walked as daintily as he had to the gallows. The red print of the rope was still around his neck, but he carried a perfumed handkerchief in one hand. One and all, they came into the room with the fires of hell still upon them, and the stranger named their names and their deeds as they came, till the tale of twelve was told. Yet the stranger had told the truth—they had all played a part in America.

"Are you satisfied with the jury, Mr. Webster?" said the stranger mockingly, when they had taken their places.

The sweat stood upon Dan'l Webster's brow, but his voice was clear.

"Quite satisfied," he said. "Though I miss General Arnold from the company."

"Benedict Arnold is engaged upon other business," said the stranger with a glower. "Ah, you asked for a justice, I believe."

He pointed his finger once more, and a tall man, soberly clad in Puritan garb, with the burning gaze of the fanatic, stalked into the room and took his judge's place.

"Justice Hathorne is a jurist of experience," said the stranger. "He presided at certain witch trials once held in Salem. There were others who repented of the business later, but not he."

"Repent of such notable wonders and undertakings?" said the stern old justice. "Nay, hang them—hang them all!" And he muttered to himself in a way that struck ice into the soul of Jabez Stone.

Then the trial began, and, as you might expect, it didn't look anyways good for the defense. And Jabez Stone didn't make much of a witness in his own behalf. He took one look at Simon Girty and screeched, and they had to put him back in his corner in a kind of swoon.

It didn't halt the trial though; the trial went on, as trials do. Dan'l Webster had faced some hard juries and hanging judges in his time, but this was the hardest he'd ever faced, and he knew it. They sat there with a kind of glitter in their eyes, and the stranger's smooth voice went on and on. Every time he'd raise an objection, it'd be "Objection sustained," but whenever Dan'l objected, it'd be "Objection denied." Well, you couldn't expect fair play from a fellow like this Mr. Scratch.

It got to Dan'l in the end, and he began to heat, like iron in the forge. When he got up to speak he was going to flay that stranger with every trick known to the law, and the judge and jury too. He didn't care if it was contempt of court or what would happen to him for it. He didn't care any more what happened to Jabez Stone. He just got madder and madder, thinking of what he'd say. And yet, curiously enough, the more he thought about it, the less he was able to arrange his speech in his mind.

Till, finally, it was time for him to get up on his feet, and he did so, all ready to bust out with lightnings and denunciations. But before he started he looked over the judge and jury for a moment, such being his custom. And he noticed the glitter in their eyes was twice as strong as before, and they all leaned forward. Like hounds just before they get the fox, they looked, and the blue mist of evil in the room thickened as he watched them. Then he saw what he'd been about to do, and he wiped his forehead, as a man might who's just escaped falling into a pit in the dark.

For it was him they'd come for, not only Jabez Stone. He read it in the glitter of their eyes and in the way the stranger hid his mouth with one hand. And if he fought them with their own weapons, he'd fall into their power; he knew that, though he couldn't have told you how. It was his own anger and horror that burned in their eyes; and he'd have to wipe that out or the case was lost. He stood there for a moment, his black eyes burning like anthracite. And then he began to speak.

He started off in a low voice, though you could hear every word. They say he could call on the harps of the blessed when he chose. And this was just as simple and easy as a man could talk. But he didn't start out by condemning or reviling. He was talking about the things that make a country a country and a man a man.

And he began with the simple things that everybody's known and felt—the freshness of a fine morning when you're young, and the taste of food when you're hungry, and the new day that's every day when you're a child. He took them up and he turned them in his hands. They were good things for any man. But without freedom they sickened. And when he talked of those enslaved, and the sorrows of slavery, his voice got like a big bell. He talked of the early days of America and the men who had made those days. It wasn't a spread-eagle speech, but he made you see it. He admitted all the wrong that had ever been done. But he showed how, out of the wrong and the right, the suffering and the starvations, something new had come. And everybody had played a part in it, even the traitors.

Then he turned to Jabez Stone and showed him as he was—an ordinary man who'd had hard luck and wanted to change it. And, because he'd wanted to change it, now he was going to be punished for all eternity. And yet there was good in Jabez Stone, and he showed that good. He was hard and mean, in some ways, but he was a man. There was sadness in being a man, but it was a proud thing too. And he showed what the pride of it was till you couldn't help feeling it. Yes, even in hell, if a man was a man, you'd know it. And he wasn't pleading for any one person any more, though his voice rang like an organ. He was telling the story and the failures and the endless journey of mankind.

The Place of Entertainment

They got tricked and trapped and bamboozled, but it was a great journey. And no demon that was ever foaled could know the inwardness of it—it took a man to do that.

The fire began to die on the hearth and the wind before morning to blow. The light was getting gray in the room when Dan'l Webster finished. And his words came back at the end to New Hampshire ground, and the one spot of land that each man loves and clings to. He painted a picture of that, and to each one of that jury he spoke of things long forgotten. For his voice could search the heart, and that was his gift and his strength. And to one his voice was like the forest and its secrecy, and to another like the sea and the storms of the sea; and one heard the cry of his lost nation in it, and another saw a little harmless scene he hadn't remembered for years. But each saw something. And when Dan'l Webster finished he didn't know whether or not he'd saved Jabez Stone. But he knew he'd done a miracle. For the glitter was gone from the eyes of judge and jury, and, for the moment, they were men again, and knew they were men.

"The defense rests," said Dan'l Webster and stood there like a mountain. His ears were still ringing with his speech, and he didn't hear anything else till he heard Judge Hathorne say, "The jury will retire to consider its verdict."

Walter Butler rose in his place and his face had a dark, gay pride on it. "The jury has considered its verdict," he said and looked the stranger full in the eye. "We find for the defendant, Jabez Stone."

With that, the smile left the stranger's face, but Walter Butler did not flinch. "Perhaps 'tis not strictly in accordance with the evidence," he said, "but even the damned may salute the eloquence of Mr. Webster."

With that, the long crow of a rooster split the gray morning sky, and judge and jury were gone from the room like a puff of smoke and as if they had never been there. The stranger turned to Dan'l Webster, smiling wryly.

"Major Butler was always a bold man," he said. "I had not thought him quite so bold. Nevertheless, my congratulations, as between two gentlemen."

"I'll have that paper first, if you please," said Dan'l Webster, and he took it and tore it into four pieces. It was queerly warm to the touch. "And now," he said, "I'll have you!" and his hand came down like a bear trap on the stranger's arm. For he knew that once you bested anybody like Mr. Scratch in fair fight, his power on you was gone. And he could see that Mr. Scratch knew it too.

The stranger twisted and wriggled, but he couldn't get out of that grip. "Come, come, Mr. Webster," he said, smiling palely. "This sort of thing is ridic—ouch!—is ridiculous. If you're worried about the costs of the case, naturally, I'd be glad to pay—"

"And so you shall!" said Dan'l Webster, shaking him till his teeth rattled. "For you'll sit right down at that table and draw up a document, promising never to bother Jabez Stone nor his heirs or assigns nor any other New Hampshireman till doomsday! For any hades we want to raise in this state, we can raise ourselves, without assistance from strangers."

"Ouch!" said the stranger. "Ouch! Well, they never did run very big to the barrel, but—ouch!—I agree!"

So he sat down and drew up the document. But Dan'l Webster kept his hand on his coat collar all the time.

"And now may I go?" said the stranger, quite humble, when Dan'l'd seen the documents in proper and legal form.

"Go?" said Dan'l, giving him another shake. "I'm still trying to figure out what I'll do with you. For you've settled the costs of the case, but you haven't settled with me. I think I'll take you back to Marshfield," he said, kind of reflective. "I've got a ram there named Goliath that can butt through an iron door. I'd kind of like to turn you loose in his field and see what he'd do."

Well, with that the stranger began to beg and to plead. And he begged and he pled so humble that finally Dan'l, who was naturally kindhearted, agreed to let him go. The stranger seemed terrible grateful for that and said, just to show they were friends, he'd tell Dan'l's fortune before leaving. So Dan'l agreed to that, though he didn't take much stock in fortune-tellers ordinarily. But, naturally, the stranger was a little different.

Well, he pried and he peered at the lines in Dan'l's hands. And he told him one thing and another that was quite remarkable. But they were all in the past.

"Yes, all that's true, and it happened," said Dan'l Webster. "But what's to come in the future?"

The stranger grinned, kind of happily, and shook his head.

"The future's not as you think it," he said. "It's dark. You have a great ambition, Mr. Webster."

"I have," said Dan'l firmly, for everybody knew he wanted to be President.

"It seems almost within your grasp," said the stranger, "but you will not attain it. Lesser men will be made President and you will be passed over."

"And, if I am, I'll still be Daniel Webster," said Dan'l. "Say on."

"You have two strong sons," said the stranger, shaking his head. "You look to found a line. But each will die in war and neither reach greatness."

"Live or die, they are still my sons," said Dan'l Webster. "Say on."

"You have made great speeches," said the stranger. "You will make more."

"Ah," said Dan'l Webster.

"But the last great speech you make will turn many of your own against you," said the stranger. "They will call you Ichabod; they will call you by other names. Even in New England some will say you have turned your coat and sold your country, and their voices will be loud against you till you die."

"So it is an honest speech, it does not matter what men say," said Dan'l Webster. Then he looked at the stranger and their glances locked.

"One question," he said. "I have fought for the Union all my life. Will I see that fight won against those who would tear it apart?"

"Not while you live," said the stranger grimly, "but it will be won. And after you are dead, there are thousands who will fight for your cause, because of words that you spoke."

"Why, then, you long-barreled, slab-sided, lantern-jawed, fortune-telling note shaver," said Dan'l Webster with a great roar of laughter, "be off with you to your own place before I put my mark on you! For, by the thirteen original colonies, I'd go to the Pit itself to save the Union!"

And with that he drew back his foot for a kick that would have stunned a horse. It was only the tip of his shoe that caught the stranger, but he went flying out of the door with his collecting box under his arm.

"And now," said Dan'l Webster, seeing Jabez Stone beginning to rouse from his swoon, "let's see what's left in the jug, for it's dry work talking all night. I hope there's pie for breakfast, Neighbor Stone."

But they say that whenever the devil comes near Marshfield, even now, he gives it a wide berth. And he hasn't been seen in the state of New Hampshire from that day to this.

I'm not talking about Massachusetts or Vermont.

Discussion of "The Devil and Daniel Webster"

In addition to being a first-rate poet, novelist, and short-story writer, Stephen Vincent Benét (1898-1943) is one of the great patriot-idealists of America. Although he has written many works, throughout them all one theme dominates—the wonder and glory of the American dream, envisioning a world in which all people are free and all can achieve. Perhaps his most widely acclaimed work is *John Brown's Body,* an epic-narrative poem of the American Civil War which was awarded the Pulitzer Prize in 1929. Dozens of other stories and poems are also excellent, however, notable especially for their interweaving of history, folk-legend, fantasy, and idealism: poetry volumes such as *A Ballad of William Sycamore, The Barefoot Saint, A Book of Americans* (with Rosemary Benét), and *Western Star;* stories such as "By the Waters of Babylon," "Doc Mellhorn and the Pearly Gates," "Freedom's a Hard-bought Thing," and "Johnny Pye and the Fool-Killer." In earlier volumes we have already studied two stories by Benét—"Too Early Spring" in Volume II and "Jacob and the Indians" in Volume III. Now we read his best-known story of all, "The Devil and Daniel Webster."

This famous story is an example of literature at its entertaining best—delightful, compelling, clever, yet also very wholesome, and rich with meaning. Cleverness of some kind can be found in almost every sentence, making the story great fun when read silently, and even greater fun when read aloud, as tens of thousands of readers and listeners throughout the world already know.

Why was the story written? Surely for at least three reasons: First, to eulogize Daniel Webster, making him emerge out of the pages of history as a vivid folk-hero of America—courageous, dynamic, idealistic, eloquent, and bigger-than-life, in the Paul Bunyan tradition. Second, to glorify the American ideal of freedom and human dignity—the beautiful dream of America. Third, simply to delight the reader, to entertain as literature and literature alone can do. Some works of literature live primarily through their message. Some live primarily through their power to entertain. When we have important meaning combined with wonderful entertainment, as in this story, then we have a great story.

Several suggestions may be helpful to teachers and to all who read the story:

(1) Although a good deal is said about the devil (Mr. Scratch) and about human souls being turned into little moth-like creatures, readers should remember that these matters are handled as folklore and are not intended as a realistic portrayal of the appearance and workings of the devil. This caution is perhaps not needed but is given nevertheless so

that no discussion group will get involved in debating whether or not Satan is portrayed realistically.

(2) A great deal of American history is woven into the story: Daniel Webster and his career, including his personality, his family, some of his great speeches, etc.; the world of the New England states and the background of the Civil War; famous and infamous men who played a part in the American past, including Walter Butler, Simon Girty, King Philip, Governor Dale, Morton of Merry Mount, Teach the Pirate, the Reverend John Smeet, Benedict Arnold, Justice Hathorne. The more readers know some details of American history, the more they will find meaning and fun in this rich story. It is filled with fantasy, but it is also filled with the growth of America as a young nation.

(3) Since the story is loosely based on the old Faust legend of the man who sold his soul to the devil in return for some temporary benefits, some awareness of this old legend will also enrich the reading.

(4) Although the story is wonderfully entertaining, part of its purpose will be lost if it is read purely for entertainment. The beautiful section of seriousness near the end when Daniel Webster talks about ideals of freedom and about the dignity and glory of mankind is one of the finest passages Benét ever wrote.

(5) Some valuable psychological insight is given into the problem of subduing hostility. Had Daniel Webster fought hostility with hostility, as he almost did, he would have lost the debate. When he met hostility with persuasion and hate with an appeal to idealism, he won. Surely there is a lesson here for all readers.

(6) Although the story contains a great message that should not be missed, it would also be a mistake to concentrate on the message to the extent of missing the delight that fills the tale from beginning to end. In fact, it both begins and ends primarily as entertainment, with some special fun for New Hampshire readers. I'm not talking about readers from Massachusetts or Vermont.

Haircut

by Ring Lardner

I got another barber that comes over from Carterville and helps me out Saturdays, but the rest of the time I can get along all right alone. You can see for yourself that this ain't no New York City and besides that, the most of the boys works all day and don't have no leisure to drop in here and get themselves prettied up.

You're a newcomer, ain't you? I thought I hadn't seen you around before. I hope you like it good enough to stay. As I say, we ain't no New York City or Chicago, but we have pretty good times. Not as good, though, since Jim Kendall got killed. When he was alive, him and Hod Meyers used to keep this town in an uproar. I bet they was more laughin' done here than any town its size in America.

Jim was comical, and Hod was pretty near a match for him. Since Jim's gone, Hod tries to hold his end up just the same as ever, but it's tough goin' when you ain't got nobody to kind of work with.

They used to be plenty fun in here Saturdays. This place is jampacked Saturdays, from four o'clock on. Jim and Hod would show up right after their supper round six o'clock. Jim would set himself down in that big chair, nearest the blue spittoon. Whoever had been settin' in that chair, why they'd get up when Jim come in and give it to him.

You'd of thought it was a reserved seat like they have sometimes in a theayter. Hod would generally always stand or walk up and down, or some Saturdays, of course, he'd be settin' in this chair part of the time, gettin' a haircut.

Well, Jim would set there a w'ile without openin' his mouth only to spit, and then finally he'd say to me, "Whitey,"—my right name, that is, my right first name, is Dick, but everybody round here calls me Whitey—Jim would say, "Whitey, your nose looks like a rosebud tonight. You must of been drinkin' some of your aw de cologne."

So I'd say, "No, Jim, but you look like you'd been drinkin' somethin' of that kind or somethin' worse."

Jim would have to laugh at that, but then he'd speak up and say, "No, I ain't had nothin' to drink, but that ain't sayin' I wouldn't like somethin'. I wouldn't even mind if it was wood alcohol."

Then Hod Meyers would say, "Neither would your wife." That would set everybody to laughin' because Jim and his wife wasn't on very good terms. She'd of divorced him only they wasn't no chance to get alimony and she didn't have no way to take care of herself and the kids. She couldn't never understand Jim. He was kind of rough, but a good fella at heart.

The Place of Entertainment

Him and Hod had all kinds of sport with Milt Sheppard. I don't suppose you've seen Milt. Well, he's got an Adam's apple that looks more like a mushmelon. So I'd be shavin' Milt and when I'd start to shave down here on his neck, Hod would holler, "Hey, Whitey, wait a minute! Before you cut into it, let's make up a pool and see who can guess closest to the number of seeds."

And Jim would say, "If Milt hadn't of been so hoggish, he'd of ordered a half a cantaloupe instead of a whole one and it might not of stuck in his throat."

All the boys would roar at this and Milt himself would force a smile, though the joke was on him. Jim certainly was a card!

There's his shavin' mug, settin' on the shelf, right next to Charley Vail's "Charles M. Vail." That's the druggist. He comes in regular for his shave, three times a week. And Jim's is the cup next to Charley's. "James H. Kendall." Jim won't need no shavin' mug no more, but I'll leave it there just the same for old time's sake. Jim certainly was a character!

Years ago, Jim used to travel for a canned goods concern over in Carterville. They sold canned goods. Jim had the whole northern half of the State and was on the road five days out of every week. He'd drop in here Saturdays and tell his experiences for that week. It was rich.

I guess he paid more attention to playin' jokes than makin' sales. Finally the concern let him out and he come right home here and told everybody he'd been fired instead of sayin' he'd resigned like most fellas would of.

It was a Saturday and the shop was full and Jim got up out of that chair and says, "Gentlemen, I got an important announcement to make. I been fired from my job."

Well, they asked him if he was in earnest and he said he was and nobody could think of nothin' to say till Jim finally broke the ice himself. He says, "I been sellin' canned goods and now I'm canned goods myself."

You see, the concern he'd been workin' for was a factory that made canned goods. Over in Carterville. And now Jim said he was canned himself. He was certainly a card!

Jim had a great trick that he used to play w'ile he was travelin'. For instance, he'd be ridin' on a train and they'd come to some little town like, well, like, we'll say, like Benton. Jim would look out the train window and read the signs on the stores.

For instance, they'd be a sign, "Henry Smith, Dry Goods." Well, Jim would write down the name and the name of the town and when he got to wherever he was goin' he'd mail back a postal card to Henry Smith at Benton and not sign no name to it, but he'd write on the card, well, somethin' like "Ask your wife about that book agent that spent the afternoon last week," or "Ask your Missus who kept her from gettin' lonesome the last time you was in Carterville." And he'd sign the card, "A Friend."

Of course, he never knew what really come of none of these jokes, but he could picture what *probably* happened and that was enough.

Jim didn't work very steady after he lost his position with the Carterville people. What he did earn, doin' odd jobs round town, why he spent pretty near all of it on gin and his family might of starved if the stores hadn't of carried them along. Jim's wife tried her hand at dressmakin', but they ain't nobody goin' to get rich makin' dresses in this town.

As I say, she'd of divorced Jim, only she seen that she couldn't support herself and the kids and she was always hopin' that some day Jim would cut out his habits and give her more than two or three dollars a week.

They was a time when she would go to whoever he was workin' for and ask them to give her his wages, but after she had done this once or twice, he beat her to it by borrowin' most of his pay in advance. He told it all round town, how he had outfoxed his Missus. He certainly was a caution!

But he wasn't satisfied with just outwittin' her. He was sore the way she had acted, tryin' to grab off his pay. And he made up his mind he'd get even. Well, he waited till Evans's Circus was advertised to come to town. Then he told his wife and two kiddies that he was goin' to take them to the circus. The day of the circus, he told them he would get the tickets and meet them outside the entrance to the tent.

Well, he didn't have no intentions of bein' there or buyin' tickets or nothin'. He got full of gin and laid round Wright's poolroom all day. His wife and the kids waited and waited and of course he didn't show up. His wife didn't have a dime with her, or nowhere else, I guess. So she finally had to tell the kids it was all off and they cried like they wasn't never goin' to stop.

Well, it seems, w'ile they was cryin', Doc Stair came along and he asked what was the matter, but Mrs. Kendall was stubborn and wouldn't tell him, but the kids told him and he insisted on takin' them and their mother in the show. Jim found this out afterwards and it was one reason why he had it in for Doc Stair.

Doc Stair come here about a year and a half ago. He's a mighty handsome young fella and his clothes always look like he has them made to order. He goes to Detroit two or three times a year and w'ile he's there he must have a tailor take his measure and then make him a suit to order. They cost pretty near twice as much, but they fit a whole lot better than if you just bought them in a store.

For a w'ile everybody was wonderin' why a young doctor like Doc Stair should come to a town like this where we already got old Doc

Gamble and Doc Foote that's both been here for years and all the practice in town was always divided between the two of them.

Then they was a story got round that Doc Stair's gal had throwed him over, a gal up in the Northern Peninsula somewheres, and the reason he came here was to hide himself away and forget it. He said himself that he thought they wasn't nothin' like general practice in a place like ours to fit a man to be a good all round doctor. And that's why he'd came.

Anyways, it wasn't long before he was makin' enough to live on, though they tell me that he never dunned nobody for what they owed him, and the folks here certainly has got the owin' habit, even in my business. If I had all that was comin' to me for just shaves alone, I could go to Carterville and put up at the Mercer for a week and see a different picture every night. For instance, they's old George Purdy—but I guess I shouldn't ought to be gossipin'.

Well, last year, our coroner died, died of the flu. Ken Beatty, that was his name. He was the coroner. So they had to choose another man to be coroner in his place and they picked Doc Stair. He laughed at first and said he didn't want it, but they made him take it. It ain't no job that anybody would fight for and what a man makes out of it in a year would just about buy seeds for their garden. Doc's the kind, though, that can't say no to nothin' if you keep at him long enough.

But I was goin' to tell you about a poor boy we got here in town— Paul Dickson. He fell out of a tree when he was about ten years old. Lit on his head and it done somethin' to him and he ain't never been right. No harm in him, but just silly. Jim Kendall used to call him cuckoo; that's a name Jim had for anybody that was off their head, only he called people's head their bean. That was another of his gags, callin' head bean and callin' crazy people cuckoo. Only poor Paul ain't crazy, but just silly.

You can imagine that Jim used to have all kinds of fun with Paul. He'd send him to the White Front Garage for a left-handed monkey wrench. Of course they ain't no such a thing as a left-handed monkey wrench.

And once we had a kind of a fair here and they was a baseball game between the fats and the leans and before the game started Jim called Paul over and sent him way down to Schrader's hardware store to get a key for the pitcher's box.

They wasn't nothin' in the way of gags that Jim couldn't think up, when he put his mind to it.

Poor Paul was always kind of suspicious of people, maybe on account of how Jim had kept foolin' him. Paul wouldn't have much to do with anybody only his own mother and Doc Stair and a girl here in town named Julie Gregg. That is, she ain't a girl no more, but pretty near thirty or over.

When Doc first come to town, Paul seemed to feel like here was a real friend and he hung round Doc's office most of the w'ile; the only time he wasn't there was when he'd go home to eat or sleep or when he seen Julie Gregg doin' her shoppin'.

When he looked out Doc's window and seen her, he'd run downstairs and join her and tag along with her to the different stores. The poor boy was crazy about Julie and she always treated him mighty nice and made him feel like he was welcome, though of course it wasn't nothin' but pity on her side.

Doc done all he could to improve Paul's mind and he told me once that he really thought the boy was gettin' better, that they was times when he was as bright and sensible as anybody else.

But I was goin' to tell you about Julie Gregg. Old Man Gregg was in the lumber business, but got to drinkin' and lost the most of his money and when he died, he didn't leave nothin' but the house and just enough insurance for the girl to skimp along on.

Her mother was a kind of a half invalid and didn't hardly ever leave the house. Julie wanted to sell the place and move somewheres else after the old man died, but the mother said she was born here and would die here. It was tough on Julie, as the young people round this town—well, she's too good for them.

She's been away to school and Chicago and New York and different places and they ain't no subject she can't talk on, where you take the rest of the young folks here and you mention anything to them outside of Gloria Swanson or Tommy Meighan and they think you're delirious. Did you see Gloria in Wages of Virtue? You missed somethin'!

Well, Doc Stair hadn't been here more than a week when he come in one day to get shaved and I recognized who he was as he had been pointed out to me, so I told him about my old lady. She's been ailin' for a couple years and either Doc Gamble or Doc Foote, neither one, seemed to be helpin' her. So he said he would come out and see her, but if she was able to get out herself, it would be better to bring her to his office where he could make a completer examination.

So I took her to his office and w'ile I was waitin' for her in the reception room, in come Julie Gregg. When somebody comes in Doc Stair's office, they's a bell that rings in his inside office so as he can tell they's somebody to see him.

So he left my old lady inside and come out to the front office and that's the first time him and Julie met and I guess it was what they call love at first sight. But it wasn't fifty-fifty. This young fella was the slickest lookin' fella she'd ever seen in this town and she went wild over him. To him she was just a young lady that wanted to see the doctor.

She'd came on about the same business I had. Her mother had been doctorin' for years with Doc Gamble and Doc Foote and without

The Place of Entertainment

no results. So she'd heard they was a new doc in town and decided to give him a try. He promised to call and see her mother that same day.

I said a minute ago that it was love at first sight on her part. I'm not only judgin' by how she acted afterwards but how she looked at him that first day in his office. I ain't no mind reader, but it was wrote all over her face that she was gone.

Now Jim Kendall, besides bein' a jokesmith and a pretty good drinker, well, Jim was quite a lady-killer. I guess he run pretty wild durin' the time he was on the road for them Carterville people, and besides that, he'd had a couple little affairs of the heart right here in town. As I say, his wife could of divorced him only she couldn't.

But Jim was like the majority of men, and women, too, I guess. He wanted what he couldn't get. He wanted Julie Gregg and worked his head off tryin' to land her. Only he'd of said bean instead of head.

Well, Jim's habits and his jokes didn't appeal to Julie and of course he was a married man, so he didn't have no more chance than, well, than a rabbit. That's an expression of Jim's himself. When somebody didn't have no chance to get elected or somethin', Jim would always say they didn't have no more chance than a rabbit.

He didn't make no bones about how he felt. Right in here, more than once, in front of the whole crowd, he said he was stuck on Julie and anybody that could get her for him was welcome to his house and his wife and kids included. But she wouldn't have nothin' to do with him; wouldn't even speak to him on the street. He finally seen he wasn't gettin' nowheres with his usual line so he decided to try the rough stuff. He went right up to her house one evenin' and when she opened the door he forced his way in and grabbed her. But she broke loose and before he could stop her, she run in the next room and locked the door and phoned to Joe Barnes. Joe's the marshal. Jim could hear who she was phonin' to and he beat it before Joe got there.

Joe was an old friend of Julie's pa. Joe went to Jim the next day and told him what would happen if he ever done it again.

I don't know how the news of this little affair leaked out. Chances is that Joe Barnes told his wife and she told somebody else's wife and they told their husband. Anyways, it did leak out and Hod Meyers had the nerve to kid Jim about it, right here in this shop. Jim didn't deny nothin' and kind of laughed it off and said for us all to wait; that lots of people had tried to make a monkey out of him, but he always got even.

Meanw'ile everybody in town was wise to Julie's bein' wild mad over the Doc. I don't suppose she had any idear how her face changed when him and her was together; of course she couldn't of, or she'd of kept away from him. And she didn't know that we was all noticin' how many times she made excuses to go up to his office or pass it on the other side of the street and look up in his window to see if he was there. I felt sorry for her and so did most other people.

Hod Meyers kept rubbin' it into Jim about how the Doc had cut him out. Jim didn't pay no attention to the kiddin' and you could see he was plannin' one of his jokes.

One trick Jim had was the knack of changin' his voice. He could make you think he was a girl talkin' and he could mimic any man's voice. To show you how good he was along this line, I'll tell you the joke he played on me once.

You know, in most towns of any size, when a man is dead and needs a shave, why the barber that shaves him soaks him five dollars for the job; that is, he don't soak *him*, but whoever ordered the shave. I just charge three dollars because personally I don't mind much shavin' a dead person. They lay a whole lot stiller than live customers. The only thing is that you don't feel like talkin' to them and you get kind of lonesome.

Well, about the coldest day we ever had here, two years ago last winter, the phone rung at the house w'ile I was home to dinner and I answered the phone and it was a woman's voice and she said she was Mrs. John Scott and her husband was dead and would I come out and shave him.

Old John had always been a good customer of mine. But they live seven miles out in the country, on the Streeter road. Still I didn't see how I could say no.

So I said I would be there, but would have to come in a jitney and it might cost three or four dollars besides the price of the shave. So she, or the voice, it said that was all right, so I got Frank Abbott to drive me out to the place and when I got there, who should open the door but old John himself! He wasn't no more dead than, well, than a rabbit.

It didn't take no private detective to figure out who had played me this little joke. Nobody could of thought it up but Jim Kendall. He certainly was a card!

I tell you this incident just to show you how he could disguise his voice and make you believe it was somebody else talkin'. I'd of swore it was Mrs. Scott had called me. Anyways, some woman.

Well, Jim waited till he had Doc Stair's voice down pat; then he went after revenge.

He called Julie up on the night when he knew Doc was over in Carterville. She never questioned but what it was Doc's voice. Jim said he must see her that night; he couldn't wait no longer to tell her somethin'. She was all excited and told him to come to the house. But he said he was expectin' an important long distance call and wouldn't she please forget her manners for once and come to his office. He said they couldn't nothin' hurt her and nobody would see her and he just *must* talk to her a little w'ile. Well, poor Julie fell for it.

Doc always keeps a night light in his office, so it looked to Julie like they was somebody there.

Meanw'ile Jim Kendall had went to Wright's poolroom, where they was a whole gang amusin' themselves. The most of them had drank plenty of gin, and they was a rough bunch even when sober. They was always strong for Jim's jokes and when he told them to come with him and see some fun they give up their card games and pool games and followed along.

Doc's office is on the second floor. Right outside his door they's a flight of stairs leadin' to the floor above. Jim and his gang hid in the dark behind these stairs.

Well, Julie come up to Doc's door and rung the bell and they was nothin' doin'. She rung it again and she rung it seven or eight times. Then she tried the door and found it locked. Then Jim made some kind of a noise and she heard it and waited a minute, and then she says, "Is that you, Ralph?" Ralph is Doc's first name.

They was no answer and it must of came to her all of a sudden that she'd been bunked. She pretty near fell downstairs and the whole gang after her. They chased her all the way home, hollerin', "Is that you, Ralph?" and "Oh, Ralphie, dear, is that you?" Jim says he couldn't holler it himself, as he was laughin' too hard.

Poor Julie! She didn't show up here on Main Street for a long, long time afterward.

And of course Jim and his gang told everybody in town, everybody but Doc Stair. They was scared to tell him, and he might of never knowed only for Paul Dickson. The poor cuckoo, as Jim called him, he was here in the shop one night when Jim was still gloatin' yet over what he'd done to Julie. And Paul took in as much of it as he could understand and he run to Doc with the story.

It's a cinch Doc went up in the air and swore he'd make Jim suffer. But it was a kind of a delicate thing, because if it got out that he had beat Jim up, Julie was bound to hear of it and then she'd know that Doc knew and of course knowin' that he knew would make it worse for her than ever. He was goin' to do somethin', but it took a lot of figurin'.

Well, it was a couple days later when Jim was here in the shop again, and so was the cuckoo. Jim was goin' duck-shootin' the next day and had came in lookin' for Hod Meyers to go with him. I happened to know that Hod had went over to Carterville and wouldn't be home till the end of the week. So Jim said he hated to go alone and he guessed he would call it off. Then poor Paul spoke up and said if Jim would take him he would go along. Jim thought a w'ile and then he said, well, he guessed a half-wit was better than nothin'.

I suppose he was plottin' to get Paul out in the boat and play some joke on him, like pushin' him in the water. Anyways, he said Paul could go. He asked him had he ever shot a duck and Paul said no, he'd never even had a gun in his hands. So Jim said he could set in the boat and watch him and if he behaved himself, he might lend him his gun for a couple of shots. They made a date to meet in the mornin' and that's the last I seen of Jim alive.

Next mornin', I hadn't been open more than ten minutes when Doc Stair come in. He looked kind of nervous. He asked me had I seen Paul Dickson. I said no, but I knew where he was, out duck-shootin' with Jim Kendall. So Doc says that's what he had heard, and he couldn't understand it because Paul had told him he wouldn't never have no more to do with Jim as long as he lived.

He said Paul had told him about the joke Jim had played on Julie. He said Paul had asked him what he thought of the joke and the Doc had told him that anybody that would do a thing like that ought not to be let live.

I said it had been a kind of a raw thing, but Jim just couldn't resist no kind of a joke, no matter how raw. I said I thought he was all right at heart, but just bubblin' over with mischief. Doc turned and walked out.

At noon he got a phone call from old John Scott. The lake where Jim and Paul had went shootin' is on John's place. Paul had came runnin' up to the house a few minutes before and said they'd been an accident. Jim had shot a few ducks and then give the gun to Paul and told him to try his luck. Paul hadn't never handled a gun and he was nervous. He was shakin' so hard that he couldn't control the gun. He let fire and Jim sunk back in the boat, dead.

Doc Stair, bein' the coroner, jumped in Frank Abbott's flivver and rushed out to Scott's farm. Paul and old John was down on the shore of the lake. Paul had rowed the boat to shore, but they'd left the body in it, waitin' for Doc to come.

Doc examined the body and said they might as well fetch it back to town. They was no use leavin' it there or callin' a jury, as it was a plain case of accidental shootin'.

Personally I wouldn't never leave a person shoot a gun in the same boat I was in unless I was sure they knew somethin' about guns. Jim was a sucker to leave a new beginner have his gun, let alone a half-wit. It probably served Jim right, what he got. But still we miss him round here. He certainly was a card!

Comb it wet or dry?

Discussion of "Haircut"

Ringgold Wilmer Lardner (1885-1933), usually known as Ring Lardner, rose to fame during the 1920's as an American sports columnist and short-story writer with a keen ear for the slangy vernacular of everyday speech and a penchant for satire that amuses while it stings. Much of what he wrote has already been forgotten on the dust-shelves of history, but the best of his stories seem assured of a permanent place in American fiction.

"Haircut," his most famous story, is included here for two reasons: first, simply because it is such an excellent story; and second, because it shows how fun can become evil if it is had at the expense of other people. Although the story is written very cleverly, providing amusement all the way through, most readers will realize that underneath the entertainment the author has a serious purpose: to show how twisted and cruel humor can be when it causes other people to suffer.

One reason "Haircut" is such an excellent story is that in it dramatic irony is sustained so brilliantly from beginning to end. As a general term applied to language, "irony" is saying one thing but meaning the opposite, as in Shakespeare's *Julius Caesar* when Mark Antony repeatedly calls Brutus an "honorable" man but means that he is dishonorable. Dramatic irony is that special kind of irony when words are spoken ironically by accident or ignorance rather than by intent, as in Shakespeare's *Othello* when Othello repeatedly refers to Iago as "honest Iago." Othello really believes that Iago is honest. The audience, however, clearly realizes that Iago is as cunningly dishonest as a villain can be. The phrase "honest Iago" is completely ironic even though Othello does not perceive the irony of what he is saying. This is dramatic irony.

And so it is with the barber who narrates the story in "Haircut." He tells incident after incident about Jim Kendall and his "jokes" while whacking away at the visitor's hair, but is too stupid, insensitive, and imperceptive to realize that Jim's humor, instead of being funny, is really twisted, cruel, perverted, and "sick." In fact, the barber is even too stupid to realize how Jim actually died. This is surely one of the finest things about the story as a work of art: that it is written with such skill that the barber tells a story he doesn't understand in such a way that the reader fully understands.

Thoughts and Questions for Further Discussion:

(1) Point out details in the story which show that Jim Kendall does have a perverted, cruel sense of humor. Note, among other things, the anonymous postal cards he mails signed "A Friend," the jokes he plays on Paul Dickson, and the trap he sets for Julie Gregg.

(2) Are Jim's friends much better than Jim himself? Note the poolroom gang that jeers at Julie Gregg outside of Dr. Stair's office.

(3) Point out details which show that the narrator (the barber) also has a perverted sense of humor and is rather stupid in addition. Does the very fact that he laughs at Jim's jokes and finds Jim so funny show that his own sense of humor is questionable? Does the narrator's language reveal a good deal about him? Note not only his extensive use of slang but also such silly comments (silly in their repetitiousness, that is) as "Well, last year, our coroner died, died of the flu. Ken Beatty, that was his name. He was the coroner." What does such language reveal about a person who talks this way?

(4) The barber says, "But I guess that I shouldn't ought to be gossipin'." Does he really feel guilty about gossiping? Should he?

(5) At the end of the story the barber says, regarding Jim's death, "It was a plain case of accidental shootin'." Apparently the barber actually believes this. Does the reader? Does Dr. Stair?

(6) Did Dr. Stair intend for Paul to kill Jim? What quali-

ties in Dr. Stair's character make us confident that he did not—that, in fact, he would never have deliberately maneuvered to have Paul kill Jim? Nevertheless, is there some evidence that Dr. Stair was unwittingly and unintentionally responsible for Paul's actions?

(7) As a final point before we leave this story we want to re-emphasize that one reason for including it in this section on entertainment is to show that humor is never really humor and fun is never really fun if they must be had at the cost of ridicule or injury to someone else. As our children learn in Primary, "Fun is not fun unless it's fun for everyone." And in adult words, "Entertainment that is not uplifting can turn thoughtless indulgence into real degradation."

Baker's Blue-Jay Yarn

by Mark Twain

One afternoon I got lost in the woods about a mile from the hotel, and presently fell into a train of dreamy thought about animals which talk, and kobolds, and enchanted folk, and the rest of the pleasant legendary stuff; and so, by stimulating my fancy, I finally got to imagining I glimpsed small flitting shapes here and there down the columned aisles of the forest. It was a place which was peculiarly meet for the occasion. It was a pine wood, with so thick and soft a carpet of brown needles that one's footfall made no more sound than if he were treading on wool; the tree-trunks were as round and straight and smooth as pillars, and stood close together; they were bare of branches to a point about twenty-five feet above ground, and from there upward so thick with boughs that not a ray of sunlight could pierce through. The world was bright with sunshine outside, but a deep and mellow twilight reigned in there, and also a silence so profound that I seemed to hear my own breathings.

When I had stood ten minutes, thinking and imagining, and getting my spirit in tune with the place, and in the right mood to enjoy the supernatural, a raven suddenly uttered a hoarse croak over my head. It made me start; and I was angry because I started. I looked up, and the creature was sitting on a limb right over me, looking down at me. I felt something of the same sense of humiliation and injury which one feels when he finds that a human stranger has been clandestinely inspecting him in his privacy and mentally commenting upon him. I eyed the raven, and the raven eyed me. Nothing was said during some seconds. Then the bird stepped a little way along his limb to get a better point of observation, lifted his wings, stuck his head far down below his shoulders toward me, and croaked again—a croak with a distinctly insulting expression about it. If he had spoken in English he could not have said any more plainly than he did say in raven, "Well, what do *you* want here?" I felt as foolish as if I had been caught in some mean act by a responsible being, and reproved for it. However, I made no reply; I would not bandy words with a raven. The adversary waited a while, with his shoulders still lifted, his head thrust down between them, and his keen bright eye fixed on me; then he threw out two or three more insults, which I could not understand, further than that I knew a portion of them consisted of language not used in church.

I still made no reply. Now the adversary raised his head and called. There was an answering croak from a little distance in the wood,— evidently a croak of inquiry. The adversary explained with enthusiasm, and the other raven dropped everything and came. The two sat side by side on the limb and discussed me as freely and offensively as two great

The Place of Entertainment

naturalists might discuss a new kind of bug. The thing became more and more embarrassing. They called in another friend. This was too much. I saw that they had the advantage of me, and so I concluded to get out of the scrape by walking out of it. They enjoyed my defeat as much as any low white people could have done. They craned their necks and laughed at me, (for a raven *can* laugh, just like a man,) they squalled insulting remarks after me as long as they could see me. They were nothing but ravens—I knew that,—what they thought about me could be a matter of no consequence,—and yet when even a raven shouts after you, "What a hat!" "O, pull down your vest!" and that sort of thing, it hurts you and humiliates you, and there is no getting around it with fine reasoning and pretty arguments.

Animals talk to each other, of course. There can be no question about that; but I suppose there are very few people who can understand them. I never knew but one man who could. I knew he could, however, because he told me so himself. He was a middle-aged, simple-hearted miner, who had lived in a lonely corner of California, among the woods and mountains, a good many years, and had studied the ways of his only neighbors, the beasts and the birds, until he believed he could accurately translate any remark which they made. This was Jim Baker. According to Jim Baker, some animals have only a limited education, and use only very simple words, and scarcely ever a comparison or a flowery figure; whereas, certain other animals have a large vocabulary, a fine command of language and a ready and fluent delivery; consequently these latter talk a great deal; they like it; they are conscious of their talent, and they enjoy "showing off." Baker said, that after long and careful observation, he had come to the conclusion that the blue-jays were the best talkers he had found among birds and beasts. Said he:

"There's more *to* a blue-jay than any other creature. He has got more moods and more different kinds of feelings than other creatures; and, mind you, whatever a blue-jay feels, he can put into language. And no mere commonplace language, either, but rattling, out-and-out book-talk—and bristling with metaphor, too—just bristling! And as for command of language—why, *you* never see a blue-jay stuck for a word. No man ever did. They just boil out of him! And another thing: I've noticed a good deal, and there's no bird, or cow, or anything that uses as good grammar as a blue-jay. You may say a cat uses good grammar. Well, a cat does—but you let a cat get excited, once; you let a cat get to pulling fur with another cat on a shed, nights, and you'll hear grammar that will give you the lockjaw. Ignorant people think it's the *noise* which fighting cats make that is so aggravating, but it ain't so; it's the sickening grammar they use. Now I've never heard a jay use bad grammar but very seldom; and when they do, they are as ashamed as a human; they shut right down and leave.

"You may call a jay a bird, Well, so he is, in a measure—because he's got feathers on him, and don't belong to no church, perhaps; but otherwise he is just as much a human as you be. And I'll tell you for why. A jay's gifts, and instincts, and feelings, and interests, cover the whole ground. A jay hasn't got any more principle than a Congressman. A jay will lie, a jay will steal, a jay will deceive, a jay will betray; and four times out of five, a jay will go back on his solemnest promise. The sacredness of an obligation is a thing which you can't cram into no blue-jay's head. Now, on top of all this, there's another thing: a jay can out-swear any gentleman in the mines. You think a cat can swear. Well, a cat can; but you give a blue-jay a subject that calls for his reserve powers, and where is your cat? Don't talk to *me*—I know too much about this thing. And there's yet another thing; in the one little particular of scolding—just good, clean, out-and-out scolding—a blue jay can lay over anything, human or divine. Yes, sir, a jay is everything that a man is. A jay can cry, a jay can laugh, a jay can feel shame, a jay can reason and plan and discuss, a jay likes gossip and scandal, a jay has got a sense of humor, a jay knows when he is an ass just as well as you do—maybe better. If a jay ain't human, he better take in his sign, that's all. Now I'm going to tell you a perfectly true fact about some blue-jays.

"When I first begun to understand jay language correctly, there was a little incident that happened here. Seven years ago, the last man in this region but me moved away. There stands his house—been empty ever since; a log house, with a plank roof—just one big room, and no more; no ceiling—nothing between the rafters and the floor. Well, one Sunday morning I was sitting out here in front of my cabin with my cat, taking the sun, and looking at the blue hills, and listening to the leaves rustling so lonely in the trees, and thinking of the home away yonder in the States, that I hadn't heard from in thirteen years, when a blue-jay lit on that house, with an acorn in his mouth, and says, 'Hello, I reckon I've struck something!' When he spoke, the acorn dropped out of his mouth and rolled down the roof, of course, but he didn't care; his mind was all on the thing he had struck. It was a knot-hole in the roof. He cocked his head to one side, shut one eye and put the other one to the hole, like a possum looking down a jug; then he glanced up with his bright eyes, give a wink or two with his wings—which signifies gratification, you understand—and says, 'It looks like a hole, it's located like a hole—blamed if I don't believe it *is* a hole!'

"Then he cocked his head down and took another look; he glances up perfectly joyful this time; winks his wings and his tail both, and says, 'Oh, no, this ain't no fat thing, I reckon! If I ain't in luck!—why it's a perfectly elegant hole!'" So he flew down and got that acorn, and fetched it up and dropped it in, and was just tilting his head back with the heavenliest smile on his face, when all of sudden he was paralyzed into a listen-

The Place of Entertainment 163

ing attitude, and that smile faded gradually out of his countenance like breath off'n a razor, and the queerest look of surprise took its place. Then he says, 'Why I didn't hear it fall!' He cocked his eye at the hole again, and took a long look; raised up and shook his head; stepped around to the other side of the hole, and took another look from that side; shook his head again. He studied a while, then he just went into the *de*tails—walking round and round the hole, and spied into it from every point of the compass. No use. Now he took a thinking attitude on the comb of the roof, and scratched the back of his head with his right foot for a minute, and finally says, 'Well, it's too many for *me*, that's certain; must be a mighty long hole; however, I ain't got no time to fool around here, I got to 'tend to business; I reckon it's all right—chance it, anyway!'

"So he flew off and fetched another acorn and dropped it in, and tried to flirt his eye to the hole quick enough to see what become of it, but he was too late. He held his eye there as much as a minute; then he raised up and sighed, and says, 'Consound it, I don't seem to understand this thing, no way; however, I'll tackle her again.' He fetched another acorn and done his level best to see what become of it, but he couldn't. He says, 'Well, I never struck no such a hole as this before; I'm of the opinion it's a totally new kind of hole.' Then he begun to get mad. He held in for a spell, walking up and down the comb of the roof, and shaking his head and muttering to himself; but his feelings got the upper hand of him presently, and he broke loose and cussed himself black in the face. I never see a bird take on so about a little thing. When he got through he walks to the hole and looks in again for half a minute; then he says, 'Well, you're a long hole, and a deep hole, and a mighty singular hole altogether—but I've started to fill you, and I'm d--d if I *don't* fill you, if it takes a hundred years!'

"And with that, away he went. You never see a bird work so since you was born. He laid into his work like a nigger, and the way he hove acorns into that hole for about two hours and a half was one of the most exciting and astonishing spectacles I ever struck. He never stopped to take a look any more—he just hove 'em in, and went for more. Well, at last he could hardly flop his wings, he was so tuckered out. He comes a-drooping down, once more, sweating like an ice-pitcher, drops his acorn in and says, '*Now* I guess I've got the bulge on you by this time!' So he bent down for a look. If you'll believe me, when his head come up again he was just pale with rage. He says, 'I've shoveled acorns enough in there to keep the family thirty years, and if I can see a sign of one of 'em, I wish I may land in a museum with a belly full of sawdust in two minutes!'

"He just had strength enough to crawl up on to the comb and lean his back agin the chimbly, and then he collected his impressions and begun to free his mind. I see in a second that what I had mistook for profanity in the mines was only just the rudiments, as you may say.

"Another jay was going by, and heard him doing his devotions, and stops to inquire what was up. The sufferer told him the whole circumstances, and says, 'Now yonder's the hole, and if you don't believe me, go and look for yourself,' So this fellow went and looked, and comes back and says, 'How many did you say you put in there? 'Not any less than two tons,' says the sufferer. The other jay went and looked again. He couldn't seem to make it out, so he raised a yell, and three more jays come. They all examined the hole, they all made the sufferer tell it over again, then they all discussed it, and got off as many leather-headed opinions about it as an average crowd of humans could have done.

"They called in more jays; then more and more, till pretty soon this whole region 'peared to have a blue flush about it. There must have been five thousand of them; and such another jawing and disputing and ripping and cussing you never heard. Every jay in the whole lot put his eye to the hole, and delivered a more chuckle-headed opinion about the mystery than the jay that went there before him. They examined the house all over, too. The door was standing half-open, and at last one old jay happened to go and light on it and look in. Of course, that knocked the mystery galley-west in a second. There lay the acorns, scattered all over the floor. He flopped his wings and raised a whoop. 'Come here!' he says. 'Come here, everybody; hang'd if this fool hasn't been trying to fill up a house with acorns!' They all came a-swooping down like a blue cloud, and as each fellow lit on the door and took a glance, the whole absurdity of the contract that the first jay had tackled hit him home and he fell over backwards suffocating with laughter, and the next jay took his place and done the same.

"Well, sir, they roosted around here on the house-top and the trees for an hour, and guffawed over that thing like human beings. It ain't no use to tell me a blue-jay hasn't got a sense of humor, because I know better. And memory too. They brought jays here from all over the United States to look down that hole, every summer for three years. Other birds too. And they could all see the point, except an owl that came from Nova Scotia to visit the Yo Semite, and he took this thing in on his way back. He said he couldn't see anything funny in it. But then, he was a good deal disappointed about Yo Semite, too."

Discussion of "Baker's Blue-jay Yarn"

One of the great humorists of all time was Samuel Langhorne Clemens (1835-1910), better know as Mark Twain.

Probably his greatest work is *The Adventures of Huckleberry Finn*, which, on top of being a book filled with rich humor, is a truly great novel for all levels of readers, from youth to full maturity. In addition, he wrote many other novels, stories, and essays that continue to attract readers all over the world, including *The Adventures of Tom Sawyer*, "The Celebrated Jumping Frog of Calaveras County," *The Innocents Abroad, Roughing It, A Tramp Abroad, Life on the Mississippi, The Prince and the Pauper, A Connecticut Yankee in King Arthur's Court, Pudd'nhead Wilson, Tom Sawyer Abroad, Tom Sawyer Detective*, "The Awful German Language," "The Man That Corrupted Hadleyburg," and "The Mysterious Stranger." Although pessimism and bitterness color some of his later writings, most of his works are characterized by vividly accurate description, high-spirited humor, and a keen ear for the colloquial speech of frontier people.

Perhaps the most hilarious of Mark Twain's tales is "The Invalid's Story"—a rollicking account of a man who thought he was escorting a coffin on a railroad trip but instead was escorting by mistake a heavy box of guns and a package of limburger cheese.

Less hilarious, but still rich with humor, and more representative of Twain's wonderful ability to combine delightful exaggeration with accurate details, is "Baker's Blue-jay Yarn," excerpted here from its place in Chapters II and III of *A Tramp Abroad*.

Charles Lamb and the Informal Essay

Although space does not permit the printing of a complete essay by him, it would be unfair to end this section on entertainment without making at least a few comments on the writer who, all things considered, is probably the most delightful essayist English letters has ever produced—Charles Lamb (1775-1834). Even if we do not have space to print his essays here, perhaps we can awaken a sufficient interest in him to send readers to the library, where the essays are easily available in many editions. For all who will take the time to discover Lamb with his inimitable style and ineffable charm, hours of leisurely, delightful reading are guaranteed.

Basically there are two kinds of essays—the formal or expository essay, whose main purpose is to instruct, explain, or persuade, and the informal essay (also called the personal or familiar essay), whose main purpose is to entertain. If clarity is the key to the formal essay, then charm is the key to the informal essay.

In spite of a good deal of tragedy in his personal life, and of drudgery in his professional life, Lamb had a sense of humor that bubbled up in all that he said and wrote. The story is told that Lamb's boss at the East India House, where Lamb worked for years as a clerk, reprimanded Lamb for arriving late several mornings in succession. "I observe, Mr. Lamb," said the boss, "that you habitually come to work late." "Yes," retorted Lamb, "but I always leave early." Reportedly the boss was so taken aback that he said nothing further on the matter.

On the side, while affectionately taking care of a beloved sister who suffered from periods of violent insanity, Lamb found time to write several dozen of the most delightful essays ever published—"Modern Gallantry," "The Two Races of Men," "Mrs. Battle's Opinions on Whist," "A Chapter on Ears," "All Fools' Day," "A Quaker's Meeting," "Imperfect Sympathies," "Grace before Meat," "Dream Children,"

The Place of Entertainment

"A Dissertation upon Roast Pig," "Poor Relations," "The Superannuated Man," "Old China," etc. As he plays up and down the whole scale of humor, we feel his humanity, his genial warmth, the endless charm of his prose style, and the range of his keen, curious mind.

Although he has a great deal to say on a wonderful variety of subjects, his chief aim is to entertain, not to instruct or persuade. And entertain he surely does, captivating readers with the magic charm of his matchless style in almost every paragraph that he wrote.

Sometimes in his essays he is serious. For example, in "Dream Children" he lovingly talks about the children he yearns for but never had. In "Old China," one of the loveliest of his essays, he reminisces about his youth, when possessions were scanty but joys were spontaneous and dreams were free. And in "Modern Gallantry" he regrets that men tend to be more gallant with young or pretty or wealthy women than with women who are homely or poor or old. Men should treat *all* women with the same gallantry, he feels—just because they are women, and men are their protectors.

At other times he is less serious, as in "A Dissertation upon Roast Pig," where with great delight he tells how ancient man first discovered the deliciousness of roasted meat —when he accidentally stuck his fingers on a pig that was accidentally burned in an accidental fire. Or as in "The Two Races of Men," where he divides mankind into two classes —the superior race of those who borrow, with their "open, trusting, generous manners," and the inferior race of those who lend, with their "lean and suspicious" looks. Or as in "Poor Relations," where with great tongue-in-cheek delight he laments that we can choose our friends but are stuck with our relatives, no matter how boring they may be, and concludes that there is just one thing worse than a poor relation —and that is a female poor relation.

As brief samples of Lamb's exquisite style, we print the opening lines of "Poor Relations" and of "A Chapter on Ears":

From "Poor Relations"

A poor relation is the most irrelevant thing in nature,—a piece of impertinent correspondency,—an odious approximation,—a haunting conscience,—a preposterous shadow, lengthening in the noontide of your prosperity,—an unwelcome remembrancer,—a perpetually recurring mortification,—a drain on your purse,—a more intolerable dun upon your pride,—a drawback upon success,—a rebuke to your rising,—a stain in your blood,—a blot on your scutcheon,—a rent in your garment,—a death's head at your banquet,—Agathocles' pot,—a Mordecai in your gate,—a Lazarus at your door,—a lion in your path,—a frog in your chamber,—a fly in your ointment,—a mote in your eye,—a triumph to your enemy,—an apology to your friends,—the one thing not needful,—the hail in harvest,—the ounce of sour in a pound of sweet.

From "A Chapter on Ears"

I have no ear.—

Mistake me not reader,—nor imagine that I am by nature destitute of those exterior twin appendages, hanging ornaments, and (architecturally speaking) handsome volutes to the human capital. Better my mother had never borne me. I am, I think, rather delicately than copiously provided with those conduits; and I feel no disposition to envy the mule for his plenty, or the mole for her exactness, in those ingenious labyrinthine inlets—those indispensable side-intelligencers.

Neither have I incurred, or done anything to incur, with Defoe, that hideous disfigurement, which constrained him to draw upon assurance —to feel 'quite unabashed,' and at ease upon that article. I was never, I thank my stars, in the pillory; nor, if I read them aright, is it within the compass of my destiny, that I ever should be.

When therefore I say that I have no ear, you will understand me to mean—*for music.*

If this brief sampling of Lamb has whetted your appetite for more, then go to the library, and you will not be disappointed.

SECTION FIVE

The Necessity of Service

by Robert K. Thomas

"THE BLIND GIRL"
by John Everett Millais (1829-1896) English
Transparency by Three Lions

Commentary by
Floyd E. Breinholt, Chairman, Department of Art
Brigham Young University

John Everett Millais was a precocious child. He was recognized as having great talent at age four. At seven he was drawing amazing likenesses of family and friends. At eleven he was accepted into the Royal Academy as its youngest student and was later elected to membership.

Early in his career as an artist he and several friends formed a group known as Pre-Raphaelites, who set principles of painting somewhat contrary to the accepted manner of painting of the time. They believed art should be based upon and be true to nature and represent sincere expression of sincere beliefs and adhere to the gospel of thoroughness. As a result, Millais' work was full of detail, yet there was nothing harsh. The details were absorbed in the whole truth without detracting from the complete, satisfying beauty of the canvas.

As is so often the case, he was severely criticized by the critics of his time. His most enduring work, "The Blind Girl," has proved to be one for which he was most condemned. One said, "We must protest against sweet, lollipop colours, raw green fields, and lace-up boots ostentatiously large." In Millais' time, he was a revolutionist and it is chiefly because of his revolutionary works that he lives today.

Most creative people seem to have a certain driving force which might be termed a "feeling of destiny"—a conviction that what they are seeking is of worth and importance and they must "get on" with it, which in itself is a service to those who follow. They seem converted to the "rightness" of what they are doing. Perhaps this is what gives the artist direction and a tenacity in spite of obstacles and criticism from others. Anyone out in the forefront runs the risk of being misunderstood. This was true of Millais. If we were to judge his works by present trends in art, he might be considered very conservative, yet during his day he was a revolutionary.

"The Blind Girl" is not difficult to understand. It could be said to be true to nature with an obvious message. Try asking a group of people of any age to look at the painting and tell the story. Abstract the story into one word and see how often it will be "service."

The Necessity of Service

Humblest service done by willing and discerning souls is glory.
—George Eliot

Introductory Comments

For a word that comes easily to many lips, service is the theme of surprisingly few literary efforts. Perhaps the homely, unambiguous combination of compassion, duty, humility, and sympathy which we commonly call service does not lend itself easily to the intensification that is evident in most literature. An account of friendly assistance may be heart-warming, but it is rarely exciting or provocative. "What next?"—that recurring demand of most readers and listeners—seems to suffer some kind of literary letdown when the answer is "She helped finish her neighbor's ironing." Yet it is well to remember that the frictions of family and community might become intolerably abrasive if countless acts of voluntary service were not freely extended and matter-of-factly received.

It may be that we associate service too easily with servility. If our concept of service never frees itself from a connotation of drudgery, we may be unprepared to examine an idea which has unusual significance for the Latter-day Saint woman. At a time when demands upon wives and mothers are greater than ever, it is easy to speak again Martha's complaint to the Savior, that she is "to serve alone." The Savior's answer that he found Martha "careful and troubled about many things," but that Mary, who had chosen to serve in another way, was not to be condemned should help us gain additional insights into the meaning of service.

While all service may be acceptable, that which is less than we are able to do is not enough to provide growth for ourselves as well as help for others. Too often, we compromise our efforts by not realizing our own potential. Our opening selection, stanzas from Walt Whitman's "Song of Myself," attempts to expand the reader's self-concept. If he verges on the bombastic occasionally, and exaggerates often, Whitman gives exhilarating extension to human capacity. He insists that you move with him in a breathless catalog of identification. For those imprisoned by narrow interests and overly modest vision, Whitman is a liberating force.

Emily Dickinson's fine poem on one of the most profound ways in which a person must learn to serve himself if he is to be prepared to serve others provides a good transition to the selfless effort that is the theme of "A Wreath for Miss Totten." This story may have a school setting, but it is not so much a story of education as it is a revelation of that capacity and determination to help young people grow that distinguishes those who truly teach, whether in the school or in the home. Note that the child most obviously aided in the story may not have been the one most profoundly served. The grown woman who unexpectedly remembers Miss Totten has now come to the realization of how lasting and important the attitude behind an action can be.

Ralph Waldo Emerson's "Concord Hymn" also attempts to inculcate an attitude. Although this poem has been so widely reprinted that its opening stanza is one of the best known in American poetry, its final lines are almost forgotten. Not seeing this poem as a whole makes it little more than a work written to fit an occasion. It is surely this, but unlike most occasional verse, it also attempts to provide a context which will help those who read it understand why the farmers at Lexington were willing to fight and die.

After reading of the Concord soldiers' service to those who have followed them we are prepared to understand the letter that a Royal Air Force pilot wrote to his mother before his death. Those who can remember World War II will have little trouble in identifying with the spirit of this letter. For those to whom this war is only a historical fact rather than an intensely memorable experience, this letter will speak that belief in principle which is beginning to have an old-fashioned sound. The idealism of the young pilot is neither vague nor simplistic. He does not choose the way in which to serve his country, but he sees clearly that the best way to serve those dearest to him is to act the part given him with his whole heart. The force of duty in service has seldom been so well stated.

While Zona Gale's "The Woman," from Volume II of *Out of the Best Books,* offers an unsurpassed and wholly convincing picture of how a wife can serve her husband, in the short article "Mother of Comptons," in which Otelia Compton provides direction for her famous children, we meet a totally positive influence which should be an inspiration to all mothers.

A final, especially touching account of service is found in the story of Jephthah's daughter from the eleventh chapter of Judges. There is the inevitability of Greek tragedy here, but something far more significant than effective literary form. The serenity which is a hallmark of those who serve without guile, who are prepared to find their lives in losing them, burns away the final dross from our concept of service; we begin to recognize how truly our effort in behalf of others is the measure of our service to the Lord.

Song of Myself
by Walt Whitman

1

I celebrate myself;
And what I assume you shall assume;
For every atom belonging to me, as good belongs to you.

I loafe and invite my Soul;
I lean and loafe at my ease, observing a spear of summer
    grass.

2

The smoke of my own breath;
Echoes, ripplies, buzz'd whispers, love-root, silk-thread
    crotch and vine;
My respiration and inspiration, the beating of my heart,
    the passing of blood and air through my lungs;
The sniff of green leaves and dry leaves, and of the
    shore, and dark color'd sea-rocks, and of hay in the
    barn;
The sound of the belch'd words of my voice, words
    loos'd to the eddies of the wind;
A few light kisses, a few embraces, a reaching around of
    arms;
The play of shine and shade on the trees as the supple
    boughs wag;
The delight alone, or in the rush of the streets, or along
    the fields and hill-sides;
The feeling of health, the full-noon trill, the song of me
    rising from bed and meeting the sun.

Have you reckon'd a thousand acres much? have you
    reckon'd the earth much?
Have you practis'd so long to learn to read?
Have you felt so proud to get at the meaning of poems?

Stop this day and night with me, and you shall possess
    the origin of all poems;
You shall possess the good of the earth and sun—(there
    are millions of suns left;)
You shall no longer take things at second or third hand,
    Not look through the eyes of the dead, nor feed on
    the spectres in books;
You shall not look through my eyes either, nor take
    things from me:
You shall listen to all sides, and filter them from yourself.

4

Trippers and askers surround me;
People I meet—the effect upon me of my early life, or the ward and city I live in, or the nation,
The latest dates, discoveries, inventions, societies, authors old and new,
My dinner, dress, associates, looks, compliments, dues,
The real or fancied indifference of some man or woman I love,
The sickness of one of my folks, or of myself, or ill-doing or loss or lack of money, or depressions or exaltations;
Battles, the horrors of fratricidal war, the fever of doubtful news, the fitful events;
These come to me days and nights, and go from me again,
But they are not the Me myself.

Apart from the pulling and hauling stands what I am;
Stands amused, complacent, compassioning, idle, unitary;
Looks down, is erect, or bends an arm on an impalpable certain rest,
Looking with side-curved head, curious what will come next;
Both in and out of the game, and watching and wondering at it.
Backward I see in my own days where I sweated through fog with linguists and contenders;
I have no mockings or arguments—I witness and wait.

6

A child said, What is the grass? fetching it to me with full hands;
How could I answer the child? I do not know what it is, any more than he.
I guess it must be the flag of my disposition, out of hopeful green stuff woven.

Or I guess it is the handkerchief of the Lord,
A scented gift and remembrancer, designedly dropt,
Bearing the owner's name someway in the corners, that we may see and remark, and say, Whose?

Or I guess the grass is itself a child, the produced babe
    of the vegetation.

Or I guess it is a uniform hieroglyphic;
And it means, Sprouting alike in broad zones and narrow
    zones,
Growing among black folks as among white;
Kanuck, Tuckahoe, Congressman, Cuff, I give them the
    same, I receive them the same.

And now it seems to me the beautiful uncut hair of
    graves.

Tenderly will I use you, curling grass;
It may be you transpire from the breasts of young men;
It may be if I had known them I would have loved them;
It may be if you are from old people, and from women, and
    from offspring taken soon out of their mothers' laps;
And here you are the mothers' laps.

The grass is very dark to be from the white heads of old
    mothers;
Darker than the colorless beards of old men;
Dark to come from under the faint red roofs of mouths.
O I perceive after all so many uttering tongues'.
And I perceive they do not come from the roofs of
    mouths for nothing.

I wish I could translate the hints about the dead young
    men and women,
And the hints about old men and mothers, and the off-
    spring taken soon out of their laps.
What do you think has become of the young and old
    men?
And what do you think has become of the women and
    children?

They are alive and well somewhere;
The smallest sprout shows there is really no death;
And if ever there was, it led forward life, and does not
    wait at the end to arrest it,
And ceas'd the moment life appear'd.

All goes onward and outward—nothing collapses;
And to die is different from what any one supposed, and
    luckier.

17

These are really the thoughts of all men in all ages and lands—
  they are not original with me;
If they are not yours as much as mine, they are nothing,
  or next to nothing;
If they are not the riddle, and the untying of the riddle,
  they are nothing;
If they are not just as close as they are distant, they are
  nothing.
This is the grass that grows wherever the land is, and
  the water is,
This is the common air that bathes the globe.

Discussion of "Song of Myself"

In Volume II of *Out of the Best Books* we presented two poems by Walt Whitman and a brief biographical sketch. The stanzas which we include in this section are from the work which is most characteristic of him. In fact, at one time it was entitled simply "Walt Whitman."

It would be a mistake, however, to find in this poem simply autobiography. While it is unmistakably a free-flowing recapitulation of the process by which a man of many roles becomes a poet, it is just as clearly an account of how a poet—or any man—reaches his Godlike potential. Although there has been much critical discussion of the structure, or lack of it, in this work, probably Whitman intended "Song of Myself" to have as many structures as there were readers. For he aimed not simply to create a poet and raise him to his divine possibilities, but to assist at the creation of the poetic and Godlike in every reader.

Whitman's most astute critics suggest that "Song of Myself" is an American epic. If so, however, it is an epic of a peculiar and modern sort. It does not celebrate a hero and action of ancient days; it evokes a hero of future days, thereby trusting to summon the heroism implicit in each individual.

From the very beginning, there is an assertive, dramatic tone to "Song of Myself." We are being called to celebrate our health and our identity as brothers. If Whitman often seems preoccupied with the physical, he is determined to have us appreciate our senses. His language is occasionally informal to the point of being mildly tasteless, but there is such a zest for participation that we are inclined to indulge his lapses.

What Whitman has to say to most of us is not to be afraid to enjoy life and to expand that capacity to its fullness. He is aware that this is not a new message; the opening line of section 17 identifies what he is asserting with the "thoughts of all men in all ages and lands." But each man must create his own wholeness. The catalogs Whitman is so fond of are just the raw material out of which each may construct the poem that epitomizes his life.

The importance of such an expansive view of human potential for those who would serve significantly can hardly be overstressed. In our sincerest effort to help we may be hampered by such a low opinion of ourselves that our attempts are mean and superficial. Similarily, our view of the world surrounding us may be so myopic that we become insensitive to the exciting possibilities that are inherent in the most unpromising circumstances, if we are completely alive to our environment.

Failure to appreciate different and possibly better ways to serve is memorably documented in the sixth chapter of Acts. Apparently the Greeks could understand only that service which relieved physical wants, and they complained that the Hebrews were neglecting their widows. The comment of the Twelve is significant: "It is not reason that we should leave the word of God and serve tables." Whitman's secular exhortation to magnify our callings meshes beautifully with the scriptural injunction to perfect ourselves.

To Fight Aloud

by Emily Dickinson

To fight aloud is very brave,
But gallanter, I know,
Who charge within the bosom,
The cavalry of woe.

Who win, and nations do not see,
Who fall, and none observe,
Whose dying eyes no country
Regards with patriot love.

We trust, in plumed procession,
For such the angels go,
Rank after rank, with even feet
And uniforms of snow.

Discussion of "To Fight Aloud"

There seems to be something intensely personal about this poem of Emily Dickinson's. It is almost as if we are being confided in. Yet what appeals to us most in these brief lines is not their subjective quality, but their general relevance. Who hasn't felt a twinge of disappointment in not having someone to share a triumph with, and, even more disheartening, who hasn't felt an added burden in having to accept failure alone?

It is only when we look at this poem more closely that we see how much deeper than this Miss Dickinson is probing. Note the word "aloud" in the opening line. Not only may we have to forgo the satisfaction of action; we may not even be able to talk about it. Many of us might be tempted to indulge in passive resignation at this point, and it is to these that Miss Dickinson suggests a "gallanter" choice: take the offensive against woes that are so personal that they can't be shared or so overwhelming that a direct attack seems only to invite disaster.

Under such circumstances one thing we can do is trust ourselves enough to carry on. If we are dependent upon the plaudits of men, we may well be denied them. We must rise above the egoism that demands attention to ourselves, and join those who have earned their right to divine approbation through self-discipline. To do anything short of this is to ask that we be indulged. Note that the military image that threads through this poem implies subordinating one's own personality to that of the group.

Our trust is finally in those who lead us, and Miss Dickinson suggests that the distinguishing characteristic of the angelic host is such trust in God that they have purified themselves of self-concern. Such a concept is a necessary corrective to the expansive mood of "Song of Myself," for it is hard to remain humble and submissive under Whitman's assertive prodding. If "Song of Myself" prepares us to serve by insisting that we realize our full potential, "To Fight Aloud" reminds us that we must identify with the group if we are to serve the group.

A Wreath for Miss Totten
by Hortense Calisher

Children growing up in the country take their images of integrity from the land. The land with its changes is always about them, a pervasive truth, and their midget foregrounds are crisscrossed with minute dramas which are the animalcules of a larger vision. But children who grow in a city where there is nothing greater than the people brimming up out of subways, rivuleting in the streets—these children must take their archetypes where and if they find them.

In P.S. 146, between periods, when the upper grades were shunted through the halls in that important procedure known as "departmental," most of the teachers stood about chatting relievedly in couples; Miss Totten, however, always stood at the door of her "home room," watching us straightforwardly, alone. As straggling and muffled, we lined past other teachers, we often caught snatches of upstairs gossip which we later perverted and enlarged; passing before Miss Totten we deflected only that austere look, bent solely on us.

Perhaps with the teachers, as with us, she was neither admired nor loathed but simply ignored. Certainly none of us ever fawned on her as we did on the harshly blonde and blue-eyed Miss Steele, who never wooed us with a smile but slanged us delightfully in the gym, giving out the exercises in a voice like scuffed gravel. Neither did she obsess us in a way of the Misses Comstock, two liverish, stunted women who could have had nothing so vivid about them as our hatred for them. And though all of us had a raffish hunger for metaphor, we never dubbed Miss Totten with a nickname.

Miss Totten's figure, as she sat tall at her desk or strode angularly in front of us rolling down the long maps over the blackboard, had that instantaneous clarity, one metallic step removed from the real, of the daguerreotype. Her clothes partook of this period too—long, saturnine waists and skirts of a stuff identical with that in a good family umbrella. There was one like it in the umbrella stand at home—a high black one with a seamed ivory head. The waists enclosed a vestee of fine but steadfast lace; the skirts grazed narrow boots of that etiolated black leather, venerable with creases, which I knew to be a sign of both respectability and foot trouble. But except for the vestee, all of Miss Totten, too, folded neatly to the dark point of her shoes, and separated from these by her truly extraordinary length, her face presided above, a lined, ocher ellipse. Sometimes, on drowsy afternoons, her face floated away altogether and came to rest on the stand at home. Perhaps it was because of this guilty image that I was the only one who noticed Miss Totten's strange preoccupation with Mooley Davis.

Most of us in Miss Totten's room had been together as a group since first grade, but we had not seen Mooley since down in second grade, under the elder and more frightening of the two Comstocks. I had forgotten Mooley completely but when she reappeared I remembered clearly the incident which had given her her name.

That morning, very early in the new term, back in Miss Comstock's, we had lined up on two sides of the classroom for a spelling bee. These were usually a relief to good and bad spellers alike, since they were the only part of our work which resembled a game, and even when one had to miss and sit down there was a kind of dreamy catharsis in watching the tenseness of those still standing. Miss Comstock always rose for these occasions and came forward between the two lines, standing there in an oppressive close-up in which we could watch the terrifying action of the cords in her spindling gray neck and her slight smile as someone was spelled down. As the number of those standing was reduced, the smile grew, exposing the oversize slabs of her teeth, through which the words issued in a voice increasingly unctuous and soft.

On this day the forty of us still shone with the first fall neatness of new clothes, still basked in that delightful anonymity in which neither our names nor our capacities were already part of the dreary foreknowledge of the teacher. The smart and quick had yet to assert themselves with their flying, staccato hands; the uneasy dull, not yet forced into recitations which would make their status clear, still preserved in the small, sinking corners of their hearts a lorn, factitious hope. Both teams were still intact when the word "mule" fell to the lot of a thin colored girl across the room from me, in clothes perky only with starch, her rusty fuzz of hair drawn back in braids so tightly sectioned that her eyes seemed permanently widened.

"Mule," said Miss Comstock, giving out the word. The ranks were still full. She had not yet begun to smile.

The girl looked back at Miss Comstock, soundlessly. All her face seemed drawn backward from the silent, working mouth, as if a strong, pulling hand had taken hold of the braids.

My turn, I calculated, was next. The procedure was to say the word, spell it out and say it again. I repeated it in my mind: Mule. M-u-l-e. Mule.

Miss Comstock waited quite a long time. Then she looked around the class, as if asking them to mark well and early her handling of this first malfeasance.

"What's your name?" she said.

"Ull-ee." The word came out in a glottal, molasses voice, hardly articulate, the *l*'s scarcely pronounced.

"Lilly?"
The girl nodded.
"Lilly what?"
"Duh--avis."
"Oh, Lilly Davis. Mmmm. Well, spell 'mule,' Lilly." Miss Comstock thrilled out the name beautifully.

The tense brown bladder of the girl's face swelled desperately, then broke at the mouth. "Mool," she said, and stopped. "Mmmm--ooo--"

The room tittered. Miss Comstock stepped closer.

"Mule!"

The girl struggled again. "Mool."

This time we were too near Miss Comstock to dare laughter.

Miss Comstock turned to our side. "Who's next?"

I half raised my hand.

"Go on." She wheeled around on Lilly, who was sinking into her seat. "No. Don't sit down."

I lowered my eyelids, hiding Lilly from my sight. "Mule," I said. "M-u-l-e. Mule."

The game continued, words crossing the room uneventfully. Some children survived. Others settled, abashed, into their seats, craning around to watch us. Again the turn came around to Lilly.

Miss Comstock cleared her throat. She had begun to smile.

"Spell it now, Lilly," she said. "Mule."

The long-chinned brown face swung from side to side in an odd writhing movement. Lilly's eyeballs rolled. Then the thick sound from her mouth was lost in the hooting, uncontrollable laughter of the whole class. For there was no doubt about it: the long, coffee-colored face, the whitish glint of the eyeballs, the bucking motion of the head suggested it to us all—a small brown quadruped, horse or mule, crazily stubborn or at bay.

"Quiet!" said Miss Comstock. And we hushed, although she had not spoken loudly. For the word had smirked out from a wide, flat smile and on the stringy neck beneath there was a creeping, pleasurable flush which made it pink as a young girl's.

That was how Mooley Davis got her name, although we had a chance to use it for only a few weeks, in a taunting singsong when she hung up her coat in the morning or as she flicked past the little dustbin of a store where we shed our pennies for nigger babies and tasteless, mottoed hearts. For after a few weeks, when it became clear that her cringing, mucoused talk was getting worse, she was transferred to the "ungraded" class. This group, made up of the mute, the shambling and the oddly tall, some of whom were delivered by bus, was housed in a basement, with a separate entrance which was forbidden us not only by rule but by a lurking distaste of our own.

The year Mooley reappeared in Miss Totten's room, a dispute in the school system had disbanded all the ungraded classes in the city. Here and there in the back seat of a class now there would be some grown-size boy who read haltingly from a primer, fingering the stubble on his slack jaw. Down in 4-A there was a shiny, petted doll of a girl, all crackling hair bow and nimble wheel chair, over whom the teachers shook their heads feelingly saying, "Bright as a dollar! Imagine!" as if there were something sinister in the fact that useless legs had not impaired the musculature of a mind. And in our class, in harshly clean, faded dresses which were always a little too infantile for her, her spraying ginger hair cut short now and held by a round comb which circled the back of her head like a snaggle-toothed tiara which had slipped, there was this bony, bug-eyed wraith of a girl who raised her hand instead of saying "present!" when Miss Totten said "Lilly Davis?" at roll call, and never spoke at all.

It was Juliet Hoffman who spoke Mooley's nickname first. A jeweler's daughter, Juliet had achieved an eminence even beyond that due her curly profile, embroidered dresses and prancing, leading-lady ways when, the Christmas before, she had brought as her present to teacher a real diamond ring. It had been a modest diamond, to be sure, but undoubtedly real, and set in real gold. Juliet had heralded it for weeks before and we had all seen it—it and the peculiar look on the face of the teacher, a young substitute whom we hardly knew, when she had lifted it from the pile of hankies and fancy note paper on her desk. The teacher, over the syrupy protests of Mrs. Hoffman, had returned the ring, but its sparkle lingered on, iridescent around Juliet's head.

On our way out at three o'clock that first day with Miss Totten, Juliet nudged at me to wait. Obediently, I waited behind her. Twiddling her bunny muff, she minced over to the clothes closet and confronted the new girl.

"I know you," she said, "Mooley Davis, that's who you are!" A couple of the other children hung back to watch.

"Aren't you? Aren't you Mooley Davis?"

I remember just how Mooley stood there because of the coat she wore. She just stood there holding her coat against her stomach with both hands. It was a coat of some pale, vague tweed, cut the same length as mine. But it wrapped the wrong way over for a girl and the revers, wide ones, came all the way down and ended way below the pressing hands.

"Where you been?" Juliet flipped us all a knowing grin. "You been in ungraded?"

One of Mooley's shoulders inched up so that it almost touched her ear, but beyond that she did not seem able to move. Her eyes looked at us, wide and fixed. I had the feeling that all of her had retreated far, far back behind the eyes, which large and purposefully empty, had been forced to stay.

My back was to the room but on the suddenly wooden faces of the others I saw Miss Totten's shadow. Then she loomed thinly over Juliet, her arms, which were crossed at her chest, hiding the one V of white in her garments so that she looked like an umbrella tightly furled.

"What's your name?" she asked, addressing not so much Juliet as the white muff, which, I noticed now, was slightly soiled.

"Jooly-ette."

"Hmm. Oh, yes. Juliet Hoffman."

"Jooly-ette, it is." She pouted creamily up at Miss Totten, her glance narrow with the assurance of finger rings to come.

Something flickered in the nexus of yellow wrinkles around Miss Totten's lips. Poling out a bony forefinger, she held it against the muff. "You tell your mother," she said slowly, "that the way she spells it, it's Juliet."

Then she dismissed the rest of us but put a delaying hand on Mooley. Turning back to look, I saw that she had knelt down painfully, her skirt hem graying in the floor dust, and, staring absently over Mooley's head, she was buttoning up the wrongly shaped coat.

After a short, avid flurry of speculation we soon lost interest in Mooley and in the routine Miss Totten devised for her. At first, during any kind of oral work, Mooley took her place at the blackboard and wrote down her answers, but later Miss Totten sat her in the front row and gave her a small slate. She grew very quick at answering, particularly in "mental arithmetic" and in the card drills when Miss Totten held up large manila cards with significant locations and dates inscribed in her Palmer script, and we went down the rows, snapping back the answers.

Also, Mooley had acquired a protector in Ruby Green, the other Negro girl in the class—a huge, black girl with an arm-flailing, hee-haw way of talking and a rich contralto singing voice which we had often heard in solo at Assembly. Ruby, boasting of her singing in night clubs on Saturday nights, of a father who had done time, cowed us all with these pungent inklings of the world on the other side of the dividing line of Amsterdam Avenue, that deep, velvet murk of Harlem which she lit for us with the flash of razors, the honky-tonk beat of the "numbahs," and the plangent wails of the mugged. Once, hearing David Hecker, a doctor's son, declare, "Mooley has a cleft palate, that's what," Ruby wheeled and put a large hand on his shoulder in menacing caress.

"She ain' got no cleff palate, see? She talk sometime, roun' home." She glared at us each in turn with such a pug scowl that we flinched thinking she was going to spit. Ruby giggled. "She got no cause to talk, roun' here. She just don' need to bother." She lifted her hand from David, spinning him backward, and joined arms with the silent Mooley. "Me neither!" she added, and walked Mooley away, flinging back to us her gaudy, syncopated laugh.

Then one day, lolloping home after three, I suddenly remembered my books and tam and above all my homework assignment, left in the pocket of my desk at school. I raced back there. The janitor, grumbling, unlocked the side door at which he had been sweeping and let me in. In the mauve, settling light the long maw of the gym held a rank, uneasy stillness. I walked up the spiral metal stairs feeling that I thieved on some part of the school's existence not intended for me. Outside the ambushed quiet of Miss Totten's room I stopped, gathering breath. I heard voices, one surely Miss Totten's dark firm tones, the other no more than an arrested gurgle and pause.

I opened the door slowly. Miss Totten and Mooley raised their heads. It was odd, but although Miss Totten sat as usual at her desk, her hands clasped to one side of her hat, lunch box and the crinkly boa she wore all spring, and although Mooley was at her own desk in front of a spread copy of our thick reader, I felt the distinct, startled guilt of someone who interrupts an embrace.

"Yes?" said Miss Totten. Her eyes had the drugged look of eyes raised suddenly from close work. I fancied that she reddened slightly, like someone accursed.

"I left my books."

Miss Totten nodded and sat waiting. I walked down the row to my desk and bent over, fumbling for my things, my haunches awkward under the watchfulness behind me. At the door, with my arms full, I stopped, parroting the formula of dismissal. "Good afternoon, Miss Totten."

"Good afternoon."

I walked home slowly. Miss Totten, when I spoke, had seemed to be watching my mouth, almost with enmity. And in front of Mooley there had been no slate.

In class the next morning, as I collected the homework in my capacity as monitor, I lingered a minute at Mooley's desk, expecting some change, perhaps in her notice of me, but there was none. Her paper was the same as usual, written in a neat script quite legible in itself but in a spidery backhand that just faintly silvered the page, like a communique issued out of necessity but begrudged.

The Necessity of Service

Once more I had a glimpse of Miss Totten and Mooley together, on a day when I had joined the slangy, athletic Miss Steele, who was striding capably along in her Ground Grippers on the route I usually took home. Almost at once I had known I was unwelcome, but I trotted desperately in her wake, not knowing how to relieve her of my company. At last a stitch in my side forced me to stop, in front of a corner fishmonger's.

"Folks who want to walk home with me have to step on it!" said Miss Steele. She allotted me one measuring, stone-blue glance and moved on.

Disposed on the bald white window stall of the fish store there was a rigidly mounted eel that looked as if only its stuffing prevented it from growing onward, sinuously, from either impersonal end. Beside it were several tawny shells. A finger would have to avoid the spines on them before being able to touch their rosy, pursed throats. As the pain in my side lessened, I raised my head and saw my own face in the window, egg-shaped and sad. I turned away. Miss Totten and Mooley stood on the corner, their backs to me, waiting to cross. A trolley clanged by, then the street was clear, and Miss Totten, looking down, nodded gently into the black boa and took Mooley by the hand.

As they passed down the hill to St. Nicholas Avenue and disappeared, Mooley's face, smoothed out and grave, seemed to me, enviably, like the serene, guided faces of children seen walking securely under the restful duennaship of nuns.

Then came the first day of Visiting Week, during which, according to convention, the normal school day would be on display but for which we had actually been fortified with rapid-fire recitations which were supposed to erupt from us in sequence—like the somersaults which climax acrobatic acts. On this morning, just before we were called to order, Dr. Piatt, the principal, walked in. He was a gentle man, keeping to his office like a snail, and we had never succeeded in making a bogey of him, although we tried. Today he shepherded a group of mothers and two men, officiously dignified, all of whom he seated on some chairs up front at Miss Totten's left. Then he sat down too, looking upon us benignly, his head cocked a little to one side in a way he had, as if he hearkened to some unseen arbiter who whispered constantly to him of how bad children could be but he benevolently, insistently continued to disagree.

Miss Totten, alone among the teachers, was usually immune to visitors, but today she strode restlessly in front of us, and as she pulled down the maps one of them slipped from her hand and snapped back up with a loud, flapping roar. Fumbling for the roll book, she sat down and began to call the roll, something she usually did without looking at the book, favoring each of us with a warming nod instead.

"Arnold Ames?"
"Pres-unt!"
"Mary Bates?"
"Pres-unt!"
"Wanda Becovic?"
"Pres-unt!"
"Sidney Cohen?"
"Pres-unt!"
"L-Lilly Davis?"

It took us a minute to realize that Mooley had not raised her hand. A light, impatient groan rippled over the class. But Mooley, her face uplifted in its blank, cataleptic stare, was looking at Miss Totten. Miss Totten's own lips moved. There seemed to be a cord between her lips and Mooley's. Mooley's lips moved, opened.

"Pres-unt!" said Mooley.

The class caught its breath, then righted itself under the sweet absent smile of the visitors. With flushed, lowered lids but in a rich full voice, Miss Totten finished calling the roll. Then she rose and came forward with the manila cards. Each time, she held up the name of a State and we answered with its capital city.

Pennsylvania.

"Harrisburgh!" said Arnold Ames.

Illinois.

"Springfield!" said Mary Bates.

Arkansas.

"Little Rock!" said Wanda Becovic.

North Dakota.

"Bismark!" said Sidney Cohen.

Idaho.

We were afraid to turn our heads.

"Buh . . . Boise!" said Mooley Davis. After this we could hardly wait for the turn to come around to Mooley again. When Miss Totten, using a pointer against the map, indicated that Mooley was to "bound" the state of North Carolina, we focused with such attention that the visitors, grinning at each other, shook their heads at such zest. But Dr. Piatt was looking straight at Miss Totten, his lips parted, his head no longer to one side.

"N-North Cal . . . Callina." Just as the deaf gaze at the speaking, Mooley's eyes never let Miss Totten's. Her voice issued, burred here, choked there, but unmistakably a voice. "Bounded by Virginia on the north . . . Tennessee on the west . . . South Callina on the south and on the east . . . and on the east . . ." She bend her head and gripped her desk with her hands. I gripped my own desk, until I saw that she suffered only from the common failing—she had forgotten. She raised her head.

"And on the east," she said joyously, "and on the east by the Atlannic Ocean."

Later that term Miss Totten died. She had been forty years in the school system, we heard in the eulogy at Assembly. There was no immediate family, and any of us who cared to might pay our respects at the chapel. After this, Mr. Moloney, who usually chose "Whispering" for the dismissal march, played something slow and thrumming which forced us to drag our feet until we reached the door.

Of course none of us went to the chapel, nor did we bother to wonder whether Mooley went. Probably she did not. For now that the girl withdrawn for so long behind those rigidly empty eyes had stepped forward into them, they flicked about quite normally, as captious as anyone's.

Once or twice in the days that followed we mentioned Miss Totten, but it was really death that we honored, clicking our tongues like our elders. Passing the umbrella stand at home I sometimes thought of Miss Totten, furled forever in her coffin. Then I forgot her too, along with the rest of the class. After all, this was only reasonable in a class which had achieved Miss Steele.

But memory, after a time, dispenses its own emphasis, making a feuilleton of what we once thought most ponderable, laying its wreath on what we never thought to recall. In the country, the children stumble upon the griffin mask of the mangled pheasant and they learn; they come upon the murderous topknot of the mantis and they surmise. But in the city, although no man looms very large against the sky, he is silhouetted all the more sharply against his fellows. And sometimes the children there, who know so little about the natural world, stumble still upon that unsolicited good which is perhaps only a dislocation in the insensitive rhythm of the natural world. And if they are lucky, memory holds it in waiting. For what they have stumbled upon is their own humanity—their aberration and their glory. That is why I find myself wanting to say aloud to someone: "I remember . . . a Miss Elizabeth Totten."

Discussion of "A Wreath for Miss Totten"

Hortense Calisher (1911-) has been the recipient of a Guggenheim Fellowship and a teacher and lecturer in several universities. Although known for several novels, she has been unusually successful as a short story writer. Her work is characterized by a dramatic simplicity that succeeds in investing apparently common incidents with uncommon significance.

In this story, for instance, note how matter-of-factly—almost cruelly—we are introduced to Miss Totten. Miss Calisher manages to recreate the thoughtless inhumanity of elementary school with pitiless accuracy, but her recollection is that of a grown woman who can now sift the significant from the trivial. Part of the effectiveness of this story is that childish candor and adult identification are skillfully interwoven into a growing experience that we are allowed to share.

We soon begin to understand, along with the teller of this story, that it may be less Miss Totten's skill as a teacher than her caring as a person that is effecting a change in Mooley Davis. This is not lost on Dr. Piatt, the principal; in fact, the climax of the story may well be at that point when he realizes what Miss Totten has been able to do.

We are given some hints that should prepare us to know the heart under Miss Totten's drab exterior. She is immediately sensitive to Mooley's plight on the first day of school and does something to show it. Her help is not confined to school hours—when it is her duty to serve—but includes seeing Mooley home.

What Miss Calisher calls "unsolicited good" is her descriptive phrase for both Miss Totten's concern and her activity in support of that concern. Our hearts may seem to be right, but unless we translate our desire to help into positive, committed, unqualified action, we will never understand how completely service can be its own reward.

Concord Hymn

by Ralph Waldo Emerson

By the rude bridge that arched the flood,
    Their flag to April's breeze unfurled,
Here once the embattled farmers stood
    And fired the shot heard round the world.

The foe long since in silence slept;
    Alike the conqueror silent sleeps;
And Time the ruined bridge has swept
    Down the dark stream which seaward creeps.

On this green bank, by this soft stream,
    We set today a votive stone;
That memory may their deed redeem,
    When, like our sires, our sons are gone.

Spirit, that made those heroes dare
    To die, and leave their children free,
Bid Time and Nature gently spare
    The shaft we raise to them and thee.

Discussion of "Concord Hymn"

A monument to the Minute Men who fought the British troops at Concord in 1775 was set up in the middle 1830's on a piece of land which had been presented to the town by one of Ralph Waldo Emerson's forebears. Although Emerson himself could not be present for the dedication of the monument on the Fourth of July, 1837, the hymn he had composed for the event was sung by a choir to the tune of "Old Hundred."

The title of this famous poem helps set a tone of reverence that is appropriate for lines which attempt to inculcate a spiritual attitude. Other images, the "bridge" between the event and its religious significance, the "votive" stone, and the redeeming (with its echoes of Judgment Day) which memory is to provide for us, reinforce the focus upon the sacred which underlies this work. For, as the opening lines of the second stanza suggest, the battle itself was only significant for what it *symbolized* to those who participated in it and, especially, for what it stands for to later generations.

If we try to emphasize the deed itself, we cannot keep Time from eroding all the details which establish our picture. If we concentrate on the *attitude* out of which the action took place, this can have meaning for untold generations. Despite the poet's plea for Time and Nature to spare the memorial which has been erected, the imposing shaft is only a little more lasting than the bridge which has long since been swept away.

The desire to keep their children free, however, transcends all material limitations and gives the "embattled farmers" the literary immortality they deserve. While there may have been some self-serving in the resistance shown at Lexington Bridge, it is the descendants of the Minute Men who have reaped the continuing benefits of freedom, and it is to these that Emerson is addressing himself.

The shot was not "heard round the world" because a few loosely organized men engaged in a skirmish with those they thought of as oppressors. History is full of defiant deeds in support of causes, and the Colonists in America appear to have been under the mildest of yokes. But the fact that they felt there were principles involved for which a man would willingly die provides an example for all who will heed it. Emerson's concluding lines are a prayer that we will understand the forces which prompted our ancestors to take their stand for freedom and, by implication, that we will be equally ready to serve.

An Airman's Letter
Anonymous

Among the personal belongings of a young R.A.F. pilot in a Bomber Squadron who was recently reported "missing, believed killed," was a letter to his mother—to be sent to her if he were killed.

"This letter was perhaps the most amazing one I have ever read; simple and direct in its wording but splendid and uplifting in its outlook," says the young officer's station commander. "It was inevitable that I should read it—in fact he must have intended this, for it was left open in order that I might be certain that no prohibited information was disclosed.

"I sent the letter to the bereaved mother, and asked her whether I might publish it anonymously, as I feel its contents may bring comfort to other mothers, and that every one in our country may feel proud to read of the sentiments which support 'an average airman' in the execution of his present arduous duties. I have received the mother's permission, and I hope this letter may be read by the greatest possible number of our countrymen at home and abroad."

Dearest Mother,—Though I feel no premonition at all, events are moving rapidly, and I have instructed that this letter be forwarded to you should I fail to return from one of the raids which we shall shortly be called upon to undertake. You must hope on for a month, but at the end of that time you must accept the fact that I have handed my task over to the extremely capable hands of my comrades of the Royal Air Force, as so many splendid fellows have already done.

First, it will comfort you to know that my role in this war has been of the greatest importance. Our patrols far out over the North Sea have helped to keep the trade routes clear for our convoys and supply ships, and on one occasion our information was instrumental in saving the lives of the men in a crippled lighthouse relief ship. Though it will be difficult for you, you will disappoint me if you do not at least try to accept the facts dispassionately, for I shall have done my duty to the utmost of my ability. No man can do more, and no one calling himself a man could do less.

I have always admired your amazing courage in the face of continual setbacks; in the way you have given me as good an education and background as anyone in the country, and always kept up appearances without ever losing faith in the future. My death would not mean that your stuggle has been in vain. Far from it. It means that your sacrifice is as great as mine. Those who serve England must expect nothing from her; we debase ourselves if we regard our country as merely a place in which to eat and sleep.

History resounds with illustrious names who have given all, yet their sacrifice has resulted in the British Empire, where there is a measure of peace, justice, and freedom for all, and where a higher standard of civilization has evolved, and is still evolving, than anywhere else. But this is not only concerning our own land. Today we are faced with the greatest organized challenge to Christianity and civilization that the world has ever seen, and I count myself lucky and honoured to be the right age and fully trained to throw my full weight into the scale. For this I have to thank you. Yet there is more work for you to do. The home front will still have to stand united for years after the war is won. For all that can be said against it, I still maintain that this war is a very good thing; every individual is having the chance to give and dare all for his principle like the martyrs of old. However long the time may be, one thing can never be altered—I shall have lived and died an Englishman. Nothing else matters one jot nor can anything ever change it.

You must not grieve for me, for if you really believe in religion and all that it entails that would be hypocrisy. I have no fear of death; only a queer elation . . . I would have it no other way. The universe is so vast and so ageless that the life of one man can only be justified by the measure of his sacrifice. We are sent to this world to acquire a personality and a character to take with us that can never be taken from us. Those who just eat and sleep, prosper and procreate, are no better than animals if all their lives they are at peace.

I firmly and absolutely believe that all evil things are sent into the world to try us; they are sent deliberately by our Creator to test our mettle because He knows what is good for us. The Bible is full of cases where the easy way out has been discarded for moral principles.

I count myself fortunate in that I have seen the whole country and known men of every calling. But with the final test of war I consider my character fully developed. Thus at my early age my earthly mission is already fulfilled and I am prepared to die with just one regret, and only one that I could not devote myself to making your declining years more happy by being with you; but you will live in peace and freedom and I shall have directly contributed to that, so here again my life will not have been in vain.

Your loving Son . . .

The Necessity of Service

Discussion of "An Airman's Letter"

As the opening paragraphs of the selection indicate, the writer of this letter remains anonymous. For a work with such a universal message this seems especially appropriate. We do not try to see the writer so much as we try to see ourselves in his place.

The fact that the armed forces of a nation are often called "the service" testifies to the basic nature of our relationship to them. The rewards for the time spent in defense of one's country are never simply monetary, and they resist being stated in any terms which do not go beyond the material. Sacrifice must be assumed and devotion taken for granted.

At a time when clamorous voices are being raised against the draft of young men to serve their country, the clear, committed voice of this British airman is reassuring. We have not misremembered how many young men and women felt who faced and accepted death in wartime. The writer of this letter does not appear to be insensitive to the dangers he faces or simply caught up in the excitement of battle. He is not afraid to accept the implication of his beliefs, and in so doing he must also accept the responsibilities inherent in them. In his assertion that "the life of one man can only be justified by the measure of his sacrifice," he has written a fitting epitaph for all who consecrate their country by their blood.

Mother of Comptons
by Milton S. Mayer

Honorary degrees are supposed to signify achievement. Sometimes they signify the achievement of the recipient in science or the arts. Sometimes they signify (though seldom openly) the achievement of the college in wheedling a new dormitory from a prosperous citizen. A few years ago Ohio's historic Western College for Women bestowed a doctorate of laws for neither of these reasons. The recipient, whose bearing denied that a woman is old at 74, was awarded the LL.D. "for outstanding achievement as wife and mother of Comptons."

Having received this recognition of her contribution to American life, the new doctor hurried back to the welcome obscurity of an old frame house on a quiet street in the little college town of Wooster, Ohio. Otelia Compton doesn't want to be famous, and she isn't. Four of the men to whom she is wife or mother occupy a whole page in "Who's Who in America," but the larger achievement of a middle western farm girl is unrecorded.

Those who extol the virtues of heredity may examine with profit the Compton family tree. For the ancestors of the first family of science were common farmers and unskilled mechanics, and the only one of them associated with scholarship was a carpenter who helped nail together the early buildings of Princeton. True, Elias Compton and Otelia Augspurger both taught school to help support the farms on which they were born, but so had farmers' sons and daughters before them. And there was no reason to predict that the union of two country school teachers would produce a page in "Who's Who."

Nor could the naked eye distinguish in the simple Compton household a special genius in the practice of domestic wisdom. Still, the genius must have been there, for of the four children born to Elias and Otelia Compton, Karl, the oldest, is a distinguished physicist, now (1938) president of the great institution, Massachusetts Institute of Technology; Mary, the second, is principal of a missionary school in India and wife of the president of Allahabad Christian College there; Wilson, the third, is a noted economist and general manager of the U. S. Lumber Manufacturers' Association, and Arthur, the "baby," is, at forty-five, one of immortals of science—winner of the Nobel Prize in Physics.

How did it happen? The answer of the four famous Comptons is a nod in the direction of the old frame house in Wooster. In the "sitting room" at Wooster, I found Elias Compton, beloved elder statesman of Ohio education, who died last May at the age of eighty-one. He taught philosophy at Wooster College for forty-five years. But I did not find the answer to my question in the sitting room, for the father of Comptons explained that he was just one of Otelia's boys and referred me to the kitchen, where the mother of Comptons, at the age of 79, manages the home that gave America one of its most eminent families.

It is characteristic of Otelia Compton's philosophy that she should deny she has a recipe for rearing great men and women. She will admit that her children are "worthy," but what the world calls great has no significance for her. When she heard the news that Arthur had won the world's highest award in science, her first words were, "I hope it doesn't turn his head." In the second place, she refuses to be an expert and has never before permitted herself to be quoted on the secret of successful motherhood. The only way I was able to pry her loose from her reticence was to get her into a good hot argument.

That was the weakness in her armor. For this doctor of laws actually has a set of laws, and to challenge them is to ask for a fight. There is nothing unfair about picking an intellectual quarrel with this woman of almost eighty years; she is more than equal to it. She reads as ardently as any scholar. She thinks as nimbly as any logician. And her youthfulness is such that when, one day this summer, she forgot to take off her wrist-watch before her daily swim, her children kidded her about getting old.

She may disclaim her expertness, but her record is against her. There are her four children, with their total of thirty-one college and university degrees and their memberships in thirty-nine learned societies. They didn't just grow. In addition, there are the hundreds of boys and girls whose lives Otelia Compton shaped during the thirty-five years she spent directing the Presbyterian Church's two homes for the children of its missionaries. Cornered in her kitchen, the mother of Comptons simply had to admit that she knows something about motherhood.

Her recipe is so old it is new, so orthodox it is radical, so commonplace that we have forgotten it and it startles us. "We used the Bible and common sense," she told me. I replied that "the Bible has been misused by knaves and common sense in an attribute every fool imputes to himself." She looked at me hard through her gold-rimmed glasses. Slowly her gray eyes softened. She smiled, and told me to go ahead and tell her what I wanted to know.

The first thing I wanted to know was, "How important is heredity?"

"That depends on what you mean by heredity."

"Well," I said, "let's say 'blue blood.' "

That was easy for the descendant of Alsatian farmers. "If you mean the principle that worth is handed down in the bloodstream, I don't think much of it. Lincoln's 'heredity' was nil. The dissolute kings of history and the worthless sons and daughters of some of the 'best families' in our country are pretty good evidence that blood can run awfully thin. No. I've seen too many extraordinary men and women who were children of the common people to put much stock in heredity.

"Don't misunderstand me. There is a kind of heredity that is all-important. That is the heredity of training. A child isn't likely to learn good habits from his parents unless they learned them from their parents. Call that environment if you want to, or environmental heredity, but it is something that is handed down from generation to generation."

In connection with misplaced faith in heredity, the mother of Comptons has something to say about the notion held by so many today that their children "haven't got a chance." It is a notion, she feels, which is becoming entirely too prevalent. "This denial of the American reality of equal opportunity," she said, "suggests a return to the medieval psychology of a permanently degraded peasant class. Once parents have decided their children haven't got a chance, they are not likely to give them one. And the children, in turn, become imbued with this paralyzing attitude of futility."

Certainly the four young Comptons would never have had a chance had their parents regarded economic hardship as insuperable. Elias Compton was earning $1,400 a year as a professor while his wife was rearing four children and maintaining the status a college community demands of faculty households. The children all had their chores, but household duties—and here is an ingredient of the Compton recipe—were never allowed to interfere either with school work or the recreation that develops healthy bodies and sportsmanship.

If heredity is not the answer, I wanted to know, what is?

"The home."

"That's a pleasant platitude," I said, in an effort to draw my "opponent" into the middle of the ring. I succeeded.

"It's a forgotten platitude," she replied sharply. "The tragedy of American life is that the home is becoming incidental at a time when it is needed as never before. Parents forget that neither school nor the world can reform the finished product of a bad home. They forget that their children are their first responsibility.

"Today servants are hired to take care of children. In my day, no matter how many servants a mother could afford she took care of her children herself.

"The first thing parents must remember is that their children are not likely to be any better than they are themselves. Mothers and fathers who wrangle and dissipate need not be surprised if their observant young ones take after them. The next thing is that parents must obtain the confidence of their children in all things if they do not want to make

The Necessity of Service

strangers of them and have them go to the boy on the street corner for advice. Number three is that parents must explain to the child every action that affects him, even at the early age when parents believe, usually mistakenly, that the child is incapable of understanding. Only thus will the child mature with the sense that justice has been done him and the impulse to be just himself.

"The mother or father who laughs at a youngster's 'foolish' ideas forgets that those ideas are not foolish to the child. When Arthur was 10 years old he wrote an essay taking issue with other experts on why some elephants were three-toed and others five-toed. He brought it to me to read, and I had a hard time keeping from laughing. But I knew how seriously he took his ideas, so I sat down and worked on them with him."

Arthur—he of the Nobel Prize—was listening to our conversation and here he interrupted, "Mother," he said, "if you had laughed at me that day, I think you would have killed my interest in research."

"The reason why many parents laugh at their children," Mrs. Compton went on, "is that they have no interest in the child's affairs. The mother and father cannot retain their influence over their children if their children's life is foreign to them. And it isn't enough to encourage the child; the parents must participate in his interest. They must work with him, and if his interest turns out to be something about which they know nothing it is their business to educate themselves. If they don't the child will discover their ignorance and lose respect for them."

When Karl Compton was twelve he wrote a "book" on Indian fighting. Mary was absorbed in linguistics. Wilson's devotion to the spitball made him the greatest college pitcher in the Middle West. Arthur, too, was a notable athlete, but his first love was astronomy. The combination of Indian fighting, linguistics, the spitball and astronomy might have driven a lesser woman to despair, but Otelia Compton mastered them all as she did their other diversions. For instance, the summer the Compton family caught 1,120 pounds of fish, mother landed her share.

All the toys the young Comptons had could have been bought for a few dollars, but when the four of them were still under ten years of age their mother packed them up, together with a father who had almost died from pneumonia, and took them to the wilds of northern Michigan, where mother and children hewed a clearing and pitched a tent. There these urban-bred children learned simplicity and hard work. There they found that the things which tempt children need not be forbidden them when those things are fishing and woodcraft and the stars. There they imbibed, as the mother of Comptons would have every city child imbibe, of the unity and mystery of nature.

The boys all worked summers and in college, gaining priceless experience; and they all had their own bank accounts, "not," their mother explains, "because we wanted them to glorify money but because we wanted them to learn that money, however much or however little, should never be wasted." Would she put hard work first in her lexicon? Mrs. Compton thought a moment. "Yes," she said, "I would. That is, hard work in the right direction. The child who has acquired the habits of work of the right kind does not need anything else."

And what is the "right kind" of hard work?

"The kind of work that is good in itself."

I baited the trap. "What's wrong with working for money?"

The mother of Comptons exploded. "Everything! To teach a child that money-making for the sake of money is worthy is to teach him that the only thing worth while is what the world calls success. That kind of success has nothing to do either with usefulness or happiness. Parents teach it and the schools teach it, and the result is an age that thinks that money means happiness. The man who lives for money never gets enough, and he thinks that is why he isn't happy. The real reason is that he has had the wrong goal of life set before him."

What did she mean by parents and schools "teaching" that money is happiness?

"I mean all this talk about 'careers' and 'practical' training. Children should be taught how to think, and thinking isn't always practical. Children should be encouraged to develop their natural bents and not forced to choose a 'career.' When our children were still in high school a friend of ours asked Elias what they were going to be. His answer was, 'I haven't asked them.' Some of our neighbors thought we were silly when we bought Arthur a little telescope and let him sit up all night studying the stars. It wasn't 'practical.'" Yet it was his "impractical" love of the stars that brought him the Nobel Prize and something over $20,000; and in order that he might pursue his cosmic ray research, the University of Chicago equipped a $100,000 laboratory for him.

I thought of the four Comptons and the success that has resulted from their early training, and I wondered if "impractical" parents weren't perhaps the most practical. What could be more tangible than the satisfaction and the honors that have come to them because of their far-flung labors?

Discussion of "Mother of Comptons"

The author of this tribute to Otelia Compton does a good reporter's job of effacing himself from that which he is writing. The subject of his article would like to be just as inconspicuous, but her obvious success with her children virtually demands analysis and commendation.

No commentary upon her achievement could be as strikingly simple and convincing as her own recipe for successful motherhood: "We used the Bible and common sense." The examples Mrs. Compton cites in support of this are specific, sensitive, and persuasive. We see children expanding under direction that is as demanding as it is affectionate. As we read this inspiring account it is impossible to think of Mrs. Compton as the woman who merely cooked meals and ironed clothes for her family. Obviously she did much of this, but just as obviously she could serve her husband and children on the level of their needs and was constantly preparing herself to meet those needs.

Perhaps most noteworthy of all in this account is the frank emphasis upon the home as the basis for all achievement. There is no mention of the responsibility which the school had to assume for the intellectual development of the Compton children and no reliance on the church for moral and spiritual training. School and church could only supply what the home had prepared them to receive.

In the refreshing, encouraging picture of an exceptional home which this article displays, we recognize how totally a successful family serves one another and how important the mother can be in setting that tone which makes all service uplifting.

The Story of Jephthah's Daughter

Now Jephthah the Gileadite was a mighty man of valor, and he was the son of an harlot: and Gilead begat Jephthah. And Gilead's wife bare him sons; and his wife's sons grew up, and they thrust out Jephthah, and said unto him, Thou shalt not inherit in our father's house; for thou art the son of a strange woman. Then Jephthah fled from his brethren, and dwelt in the land of Tob; and there were gathered vain men to Jephthah, and went out with him.

And it came to pass in process of time, that the children of Ammon made war against Irsael. And it was so, that when the children of Ammon made war against Israel, the elders of Gilead went to fetch Jephthah out of the land of Tob: and they said unto Jephthah, Come, and be our captain, that we may fight with the children of Ammon. And Jephthah said unto the elders of Gilead, Did not ye hate me, and expel me out of my father's house? and why are ye come unto me now when ye are in distress?

And the elders of Gilead said unto Jephthah, Therefore we turn again to thee now, that thou mayest go with us, and fight against the children of Ammon, and be our head over all the inhabitants of Gilead. And Jephthah said unto the elders of Gilead, If ye bring me home again to fight against the children of Ammon, and the Lord deliver them before me, shall I be your head?

And the elders of Gilead said unto Jephthah, The Lord be witness between us if we do not so according to thy words. Then Jephthah went with the elders of Gilead, and the people made him head and captain over them: and Jephthah uttered all his words before the Lord in Mizpeh. And Jephthah sent messengers unto the king of the children of Ammon, saying, What hast thou to do with me that thou art come against me to fight in my land?

And the king of the children of Ammon answered unto the messengers of Jephthah, Because Israel took away my land, when they came up out of Egypt, from Arnon even unto Jabbok, and unto Jordan: now therefore restore those lands again peaceably.

And Jephthah sent messengers again unto the king of the children of Ammon: and said unto him, Thus saith Jephthah, Israel took not away the land of Moab, nor the land of the children of Ammon: but when Israel came up from Egypt, and walked through the wilderness unto the Red sea, and came to Kadesh; then Israel sent messengers unto the king of Edom saying, Let me, I pray thee, pass through thy land: but the king of Edom would not hearken thereto. And in like manner they sent unto the king of Moab: but he would not consent: and Israel abode in Kadesh.

Then they went along through the wilderness, and compassed the land of Edom, and the land of Moab, and came by the east side of the land of Moab, and pitched on the other side of Arnon, but came not within the border of Moab: for Arnon was the border of Moab. And Israel sent messengers unto Sihon, king of the Amorites, the king of Heshbon; and Israel said unto him, Let us pass, we pray thee, through thy land into my place.

But Sihon trusted not Israel to pass through his coast: but Sihon gathered all his people together, and pitched in Jahaz, and fought against Israel. And the Lord God of Israel delivered Sihon and all his people into the hand of Israel, and they smote them: so Israel possessed all the land of the Amorites, the inhabitants of that country. And they possessed all the coasts of the Amorites, from Arnon even unto Jabbok, and from the wilderness even unto Jordan.

So now the Lord God of Israel hath dispossessed the Amorites from before his people Israel, and shouldest thou possess it? Wilt not thou possess that which Chemosh thy god giveth thee to possess? So whomsoever the Lord God shall drive out from before us, them will we possess. And now art thou any better than Balak the son of Zippor, king of Moab? did he ever strive against Israel, or did he ever fight against them, while Israel dwelt in Heshbon and her towns, and in Aroer and her towns, and in all the cities that be along by the coasts of Arnon, three hundred years? Why therefore did ye not recover them within that time?

Wherefore, I have not sinned against thee, but thou doest me wrong to war against me: the Lord the Judge be judge this day between the children of Israel and the children of Ammon.

Howbeit the king of the children of Ammon hearkened not unto the words of Jephthah which he sent him.

Then the Spirit of the Lord came upon Jephthah, and he passed over Gilead, and Manasseh, and passed over Mizpeh of Gilead, and from Mizpeh of Gilead he passed over unto the children of Ammon. And Jephthah vowed a vow unto the Lord, and said, If thou shalt without fail deliver the children of Ammon into mine hands, then it shall be, that whatsoever cometh forth of the doors of my house to meet me when I return in peace from the children of Ammon, shall surely be the Lord's, and I will offer it up for a burnt offering.

So Jephthah passed over unto the children of Ammon to fight against them; and the Lord delivered them into his hands. And he smote them from Aroer even till he came to Minnith, even twenty cities, and unto the plain of the vineyards, with a very great slaughter. Thus the children of Ammon were subdued before the children of Israel.

And Jephthah came to Mizpeh unto his house, and, behold, his daughter came out to meet him with timbrels and with dances: and she was his only child; beside her he had neither son nor daughter.

And it came to pass, when he saw her, that he rent his clothes, and said, Alas, my daughter! thou hast brought me very low, and thou art one of them that trouble me: for I have opened my mouth unto the Lord, and I cannot go back.

And she said unto him, My father, if thou hast opened thy mouth unto the Lord, do to me according to that which hath proceeded out of thy mouth: forasmuch as the Lord hath taken vengeance for thee of thine enemies, even of the children of Ammon.

And she said unto her father, Let this thing be done for me: let me alone two months, and I may go up and down upon the mountains, and bewail my virginity, I and my fellows. And he said, Go. And he sent her away for two months: and she went with her companions, and bewailed her virginity upon the mountains.

And it came to pass at the end of two months, that she returned unto her father, who did with her according to his vow which he had vowed: and she knew no man. And it was a custom in Israel, that the daughters of Israel went yearly to lament the daughter of Jephthah the Gileadite four years in a year.

Discussion of the Story of Jephthah's Daughter

Although she is given no name in the story of which she is the heroine, the daughter of Jephthah has caught at the heart of generations of readers. She is the subject of a brief exchange between Hamlet and Polonius in Shakespeare's great tragedy and is the source of Charles Lamb's figure in "Mackery End in Hertfordshire."

In the brevity and restraint so typical of Hebraic writing we are left to supply the probable details of this seeming tragedy. We can only surmise how insecure Jephthah may have felt in being driven from his home and how warily he received the offer of the elders to return as king. Our assumptions about him, however, may help us understand the rashness and impetuosity of his promise if the Lord will help him overcome the Ammonites. In the excitement and hope of the moment the most prized animal in his flocks seems little to offer.

The situation is heightened by the continuing simplicity of words and form, but undertones of grief are heard throughout the brief dialogue between father and daughter. We are given little indication of what went on in Jephthah's mind during the two-month stay requested by the young girl who spent her time in bewailing the fact that she would never be a mother in Israel, but we can imagine how poignant his suffering was.

Occasional readers have been so distressed by the circumstances presented here that they have failed to appreciate the lessons which this story may hold for all of us. The utter sacredness of a promise made to the Lord could hardly receive more telling emphasis. Equally important is the example we see of someone whose devotion is so total that life itself is willingly given.

Most of the service we perform for others costs us little more than convenience, and usually we receive such gratitude from those we help that our recompense exceeds our effort. Our attempts to serve the Lord are often equally perfunctory, if not downright grudging. We are not prepared to live for the Lord, much less die for him. Perhaps all service which is not based upon faith in that which we are doing is mildly compromised, but this may not be apparent until some ultimate service is required of us. How will what I do for my neighbor be changed if I truly love my neighbor? It may be that my actions will seem to be the same, but in serving lovingly I prepare myself to understand that love which distinguishes whatever the Lord would ask of me.

SECTION SIX

The Power of Work and the Use of Leisure

by Bruce B. Clark

"SUNDAY AFTERNOON ON THE ISLAND OF LA GRANDE JATTE"
by Georges Seurat (1859-1891) French

Commentary by
Floyd E. Breinholt, Chairman, Department of Art
Brigham Young University

When families are united in their work and play, work becomes more meaningful and leisure more enjoyable.

A casual observer might say that this painting "La Grande Jatte" by Georges Seurat illustrates a popular leisure-time activity—strolling in the park. However, as one looks and reflects, he may find that there is much more to it than that. The reality of the subject has been subjected to stringent refining—not necessarily to improve it—but in order to yield its essence. The unessentials have been dropped away, leaving only images of incisive clarity. A heat haze blurs the detail and gives a static quality. One feels as if he had captured a moment suspended in time, in which order reigns.

Georges Seurat lived at the time Impressionism was at its height. However, he believed that this system of painting was too haphazard, so he developed a systematic method of painting, which was highly intellectual, methodical, and almost scientific in approach. He carefully organized the space on his canvas by using horizontal, vertical, and diagonal lines in perfect balance. Then with careful, almost artificial, precision, he placed the confetti-like, round spots of color next to each other, until his canvas was covered in such a way that the colors, being mixed in the eye of the observer, give a sensation of shimmering vibrancy. He called this method *Divisionism*. Others have called it *Pointillism*. This painting was first shown in 1886, and it marked the painter's arrival at a maturity in the use of the method he invented. His departure from the established way of painting, and from the Impressionism of his time, opened the way for later, so-called "Modern" art.

Seurat must have worked hard to accomplish what he did at such an early age. (He died at the age of 32.) And, as is the case with many highly creative people, he found his recreation in his work. He said, "Art is harmony—harmony comes from placing, side-by-side, contrasting elements and similar elements in tone, in color, and in line."

THE POWER OF WORK AND THE USE OF LEISURE

All true work is sacred; in all true work, were it but true hand-labor, there is something of divineness. —Thomas Carlyle

Without leisure we must live above the surface of things; leisure brings penetration. —Manly Hall

Introductory Comments

As the two preceding quotations from Thomas Carlyle and Manly Hall may suggest, the main point we wish to make in this section is that there should be a happy balance in our lives between work and leisure—perhaps a good deal more work than leisure, but also some time for the rewards that leisure can bring.

That there are abundant values in a lifetime of dedication to honest, constructive work should be self-evident to all thinking people. But perhaps Oscar Wilde also had a point when he once argued that as soon as possible most manual labor should be done by animals or, better still, by machines, so that men and women can be free to enjoy the pleasures and beauties of the world, pursuing the wonders of the spirit and the creative imagination. Probably Wilde was wrong in turning his back so completely on manual labor, yet a person would also be wrong in allowing his life to become so submerged in work and work only that all recreational, aesthetic, and spiritual things are crowded out. Again the need is for a healthy balance.

Some people have a tendency to work too hard; and others, perhaps a greater number, slide through life too easily, never knowing what they might have accomplished if they had really given full effort to their responsibilities. Hardin Craig, famous American educator, once said: "There is nothing commoner than talent among modern men [and women] and nothing rarer than ambition, industry, and faith. . . .The world is simple crazy for men [and women] who will work, so that a conscientious and efficient worker in any line may practically dictate his own terms." Because most people live up to only a fraction of their capabilities, continues Craig, "the improvement of an ordinary mind soon excels the neglect of a better mind."[1]

The selections that now follow are all concerned in one way or another with work and leisure. Some emphasize the values of work, and some the rewards of leisure. Some suggest the balance that is needed between work and leisure, and some the consequences when there is lack of balance.[2]

---

[1] Hardin Craig, from his essay "Imagination to Conceive—Will to Do!"

[2] As examples of lives ennobled by the dignity of work, see "Quality" by John Galsworthy and "Michael" by William Wordsworth in Volume I, "The Revolt of Mother" by Mary E. Wilkins Freeman in Volume II, and "Talk" by John Holmes in Volume IV.

From the Essays of Thomas Carlyle

All work, even cotton-spinning, is noble; work is alone noble: be that here said and asserted once more. And in like manner, too, all dignity is painful; a life of ease is not for any man, nor for any god. . . .

The only happiness a brave man ever troubled himself with asking much about was, happiness enough to get his work done. Not "I can't eat!" but "I can't work!" that was the burden of all wise complaining among men. It is, after all, the one unhappiness of a man. That he cannot work; that he cannot get his destiny as a man fulfilled. Behold, the day is passing swiftly over, our life is passing swiftly over; and the night cometh, wherein no man can work. The night once come, our happiness, our unhappiness,—it is all abolished; vanished, clean gone; a thing that has been: . . . But our work,—behold that is not abolished, that has not vanished: our work, behold, it remains, or the want of it remains;—for endless Times and Eternities, remains; and that is now the sole question with us for evermore! Brief brawling Day, with its noisy phantoms, its poor paper-crowns tinsel-gilt, is gone; and divine everlasting Night, with her star-diadems, with her silences and her veracities, is come! What hast thou done, and how? Happiness, unhappiness: all that was but the *wages* thou hadst; thou hast spent all that, in sustaining thyself hitherward; not a coin of it remains with thee, it is all spent, eaten: and now thy work, where is thy work? Swift, out with it, let us see thy work! . . .

For there is a perennial nobleness, and even sacredness, in Work. Were he never so benighted, forgetful of his high calling, there is always hope in a man that actually and earnestly works; in Idleness alone is there perpetual despair. Work, never so Mammonish, mean, *is* in communication with Nature; the real desire to get Work done will itself lead one more and more to truth, to Nature's appointments and regulations which are truth.

The latest Gospel in this world is, Know thy work and do it. "Know thyself;" long enough has that poor "self" of thine tormented thee; thou wilt never get to "know" it, I believe! Think it not thy business, this of knowing thyself; thou art an unknowable individual: know what thou canst work at; and work at it, like a Hercules! That will be thy better plan.

It has been written, "an endless significance lies in Work"; a man perfects himself by working. Foul jungles are cleared away, fair seed-fields rise instead, and stately cities; and withal the man himself first ceases to be a jungle and foul unwholesome desert thereby. Consider how, even in the meanest sorts of Labour, the whole soul of a man is composed into a kind of real harmony, the instant he sets himself to work! Doubt, Desire, Sorrow, Remorse, Indignation, Despair itself, all these like helldogs lie beleaguering the soul of the poor dayworker, as of every man: but he bends himself with free valour against his task, and all these are stilled, all these shrink murmuring far off into their caves. The man is now a man. The blessed glow of Labour in him, is it not as purifying fire, wherein all poison is burnt up, and of sour smoke itself there is made bright blessed flame! . . .

Blessed is he who has found his work; let him ask no other blessedness. He has a work, a life-purpose; he has found it, and will follow it! How, as a free-flowing channel, dug and torn by noble force through the sour mud-swamp of one's existence, like an ever-deepening river there, it runs and flows;—draining off the sour festering water, gradually from the root of the remotest grass-blade; making, instead of pestilential swamp, a green fruitful meadow with its clear-flowing stream. How blessed for the meadow itself, let the stream and *its* value be great or small! Labour is Life: from the inmost heart of the Worker rises his god-given Force, the sacred Celestial Life-essence breathed into him by Almighty God; from his inmost heart awakens him to all nobleness, —to all knowledge, "self-knowledge" and much else, so soon as Work fitly begins. Knowledge? The knowledge that will hold good in working, cleave thou to that; for Nature herself accredits that, says Yea to that. Properly thou hast no other knowledge but what thou hast got by working: the rest is yet all a hypothesis of knowledge; a thing to be argued of in schools, a thing floating in the clouds, in endless logic-vortices, till we try it and fix it. "Doubt, of whatever kind, can be ended by Action alone.". . .

Work is of a religious nature:—work is of a *brave* nature; which it is the aim of all religion to be. All work of man is as the swimmer's: a waste ocean threatens to devour him; if he front it not bravely, it will keep its word. By incessant wise defiance of it, lusty rebuke and buffet of it, behold how it loyally supports him, bears him as its conqueror along. "It is so," says Goethe, "with all things that man undertakes in this world.". . .

"Religion," I said; for, properly speaking all true Work is Religion: . . . Older than all preached Gospels was this unpreached, inarticulate, but ineradicable, forever-enduring Gospel: Work, and therein have well-being. Man, Son of Earth and of Heaven, lies there not, in the innermost heart of thee, a Spirit of active Method, a Force for Work;—and burns like a painfully smouldering fire, giving thee no rest till thou unfold it, till thou write it down in beneficent Facts around thee! What is immethodic, waste, thou shalt make methodic, regulated, arable; obedient and productive to thee. Wheresoever thou findest Disorder, there is thy eternal enemy; attack him swiftly, subdue him; make Order of him, the subject not of Chaos, but of Intelligence, Divinity and Thee! The thistle that grows in thy path, dig it out, that a blade of useful grass, a drop of nourishing milk, may grow there instead. The waste cotton-shrub, gather its waste white down, spin it, weave it; that, in place of idle litter, there may be folded webs, and the naked skin of man be covered.

But above all, where thou findest Ignorance, Stupidity, Brute-mindedness . . . attack it, I say; smite it wisely, unweariedly, and rest not while thou livest and it lives; but smite, smite, in the name of God! . . .

All true Work is sacred; in all true Work, were it but true hand-labour, there is something of divineness. Labour, wide as the Earth, has its summit in Heaven. Sweat of the brow; and up from that to sweat of the brain, sweat of the heart; which includes all Kepler calculations, Newton meditations, all Sciences, all spoken Epics, all acted Heroisms, Martyrdoms,—up to that "Agony of bloody sweat," which all men have called divine! O brother, if this is not "worship," then I say, the more pity for worship; for this is the noblest thing yet discovered under God's sky. Who art thou that complainest of thy life of toil? Complain not. Look up, my wearied brother; see thy fellow Workmen there, in God's Eternity; surviving there, they alone surviving: sacred Band of the Immortals, celestial Bodyguard of the Empire of Mankind. . . .

And who art thou that braggest of thy life of Idleness; complacently showest thy bright gilt equipages; sumptuous cushions; appliances for folding of the hands to mere sleep? . . . One monster there is in the world: the idle man. . . .

As to the Wages of Work there might innumerable things be said. . . . One thing only I will say here: . . . The "wages" of every noble Work do yet lie in Heaven or else Nowhere. Not in Bank-of-England bills. . . .

My brother, the brave man has to give his Life away. Give it, I advise thee;—thou dost not expect to *sell* thy Life in an adequate manner? What price, for example, would content thee? . . . Thou wilt never sell thy Life, or any part of thy Life, in a satisfactory manner. Give it, like a royal heart; let the price be Nothing: thou *hast* then, in a certain sense, got All for it! The heroic man,—and is not every man, God be thanked, a potential hero?—has to do so, in all times and circumstances. . . .

On the whole, we do entirely agree with those old Monks, *Laborare est Orare*. In a thousand senses, from one end of it to the other, true Work *is* Worship. He that works, whatsoever be his work, he bodies forth the form of Things Unseen; a small Poet every Worker is. . . . No man has worked, or can work, except religiously; not even the poor day-labourer, the weaver of your coat, the sewer of your shoes. All men, if they work not as in a Great Taskmaster's eye, will work wrong, work unhappily for themselves and you. . . .

Be no longer a Chaos, but a World, or even Worldkin. Produce! Produce! Were it but the pitifulest infinitesimal fraction of a Product, produce it, in God's name! 'Tis the utmost thou hast in thee; out with it, then. Up, up! Whatsoever thy hand findeth to do, do it with thy whole might. Work while it is called Today; for the Night cometh, wherein no man can work. . . .

Two men I honor, and no third. First, the toilworn Craftsman that with earth-made Implement laboriously conquers the earth, and makes her man's. Venerable to me is the hard Hand; crooked, coarse. . . . Venerable too is the rugged face, all weather-tanned, besoiled, with its rude intelligence, for it is the face of a Man living manlike. . . .

A second man I honor, and still more highly: Him who is seen toiling for the spiritually indispensable; not daily bread, but the bread of Life. Is not he too in his duty; endeavoring towards inward Harmony; revealing this, by act or by word, through all his outward endeavors, be they high or low? Highest of all, when his outward and his inward endeavor are one: when we can name him Artist; not earthly Craftsman only, but inspired Thinker, who with heaven-made Implement conquers Heaven for us! If the poor and humble toil that we have Food, must not the high and glorious toil for him in return, that he have Light, have Guidance, Freedom, Immortality?—These two, in all their degrees, I honor—all else is chaff and dust, which let the wind blow whither it listeth.

Unspeakably touching is it, however, when I find both dignities united; and he that must toil outwardly for the lowest of man's wants, is also toiling inwardly for the highest. Sublimer in this world know I nothing than a Peasant Saint, could such now anywhere be met with. Such a one will take thee back to Nazareth itself; thou wilt see the splendor of Heaven spring forth from the humblest depths of Earth, like a light shining in great darkness.

Discussion of Excerpts from the Essays of Thomas Carlyle

Out of the Scotch peasantry came Thomas Carlyle (1795-1881) warning the world, like a Biblical prophet, against the evils of materialism, idleness, and all things superficial. Although his writing is rough and even clumsy, he was a courageous, independent thinker concerned above all with human values; and, however clumsy his style, he forces us by vividness of phrase and power of idea to listen to his thoughts. His influence has been felt world-wide, with such men as Emerson and Thoreau acknowledging their indebtedness to him. As a young man Carlyle went through a profound spiritual crisis but found his spiritual footing and thereafter in volume after volume of essays was a vigorous prophet preaching the gospel of work, the worship of heroes, the sacredness of life, the glory of God, and the evil of too much worldliness. He is often opinionated and chaotic in both ideas and style, but he is always forceful—this boisterous, explosive, sincere man of faith.

While studying this section on work and leisure, readers will undoubtedly want to contrast the views of Carlyle and Lin Yutang, who follows next. Surely no one has talked more glowingly of the nobility of work than Carlyle, who even went so far as to call the idle man a monster. At the other extreme, Lin Yutang eloquently defends "the importance of loafing." Before we conclude that the two are completely contradictory, however, we should read carefully what each says. For Carlyle, "all true work is religion" and "all true work is sacred"—but note the emphasis on the word *true* in each statement. For Lin Yutang, "the man who is wisely idle is the most cultured man"—but again note the emphasis on the word *wisely*. These qualifying words make a great difference in what each man is saying and indicate that both are aware of the preciousness of time, whether spent in work or in leisure.

Part of the excerpts printed here from Carlyle were previously printed in Volume II. We are repeating them here —with extensive deletions and additions—because they are the strongest statements we know in literature on the nobility of work, and we will now examine them in a different context than previously, pointing toward a healthy balance between work and leisure in our lives. The excerpts are mostly from Chapters 4, 11, and 12 of *Past and Present*, but the closing four paragraphs are from *Sartor Resartus*.

From "The Importance of Loafing"[3]

Lin Yutang

Culture, as I understand it, is essentially a product of leisure. The art of culture is therefore essentially the art of loafing. From the Chinese point of view, the man who is wisely idle is the most cultured man. For there seems to be a philosophic contradiction between being busy and being wise. Those who are wise won't be busy, and those who are too busy can't be wise. The wisest man is therefore he who loafs most gracefully. Here I shall try to explain, not the technique and varieties of loafing as practised in China, but rather the philosophy which nourishes this divine desire for loafing in China and gives rise to that carefree, idle, happy-go-lucky—and often poetic—temperament in the Chinese scholars, and to a lesser extent, in the Chinese people in general. How did that Chinese temperament—that distrust of achievement and success and that intense love of living as such—arise?

In the first place, the Chinese theory of leisure, as expressed by a comparatively unknown author of the eighteenth century, Shu Paihsiang, who happily achieved oblivion, is as follows: time is useful because it is not being used. "Leisure in time is like unoccupied floor space in a room." Every working girl who rents a small room where every inch of space is fully utilized feels highly uncomfortable because she has no room to move about, and the moment she gets a raise in salary, she moves into a bigger room where there is a little more unused floor space, besides those strictly useful spaces occupied by her single bed, her dressing table and her two-burner gas range. It is that unoccupied space which makes a room habitable, as it is our leisure hours which make life endurable. I understand there is a rich woman living on Park Avenue, who bought up a neighboring lot to prevent anybody from erecting a skyscraper next to her house. She is paying a big sum of money in order to have space fully and perfectly made useless, and it seems to me she never spent her money more wisely.

In this connection, I might mention a personal experience. I could never see the beauty of skyscrapers in New York, and it was not until I went to Chicago that I realized that a skyscraper could be very imposing and very beautiful to look at, if it had good frontage and at least half a mile of unused space around it. Chicago is fortunate in this respect, because it has more space than Manhattan. The tall buildings are better spaced, and there is the possibility of obtaining an unobstructed view of them from a long distance. Figuratively speaking, we, too, are so cramped in our life that we cannot enjoy a free perspective of the beauties of our spiritual life. We lack spiritual frontage. . . .

---

[3] "The Importance of Loafing" is an essay in Lin Yutang's book *The Importance of Living*.

To the Chinese, therefore, with the fine philosophy that "Nothing matters to a man who says nothing matters," Americans offer a strange contrast. Is life really worth all the bother, to the extent of making our soul a slave to the body? The high spirituality of the philosophy of loafing forbids it. The most characteristic advertisement I ever saw was one by an engineering firm with the big words: "Nearly Right Is Not Enough." The desire for one hundred per cent efficiency seems almost obscene. The trouble with Americans is that when a thing is nearly right, they want to make it still better, while for a Chinese, nearly right is good enough.

The three great American vices seem to be efficiency, punctuality and the desire for achievement and success. They are the things that make the Americans so unhappy and so nervous. They steal from them their inalienable right of loafing and cheat them of many a good, idle and beautiful afternoon. One must start out with a belief that there are no catastrophes in this world, and that besides the noble art of getting things done, there is a nobler art of leaving things undone. On the whole, if one answers letters promptly, the result is about as good or as bad as if he had never answered them at all. After all, nothing happens, and while one may have missed a few good appointments, one may have also avoided a few unpleasant ones. Most of the letters are not worth answering, if you keep them in your drawer for three months; reading them three months afterwards, one might realize how utterly futile and what a waste of time it would have been to answer them all. Writing letters really can become a vice. It turns our writers into fine promotion salesmen and our college professors into good efficient business executives. In this sense, I can understand Thoreau's contempt for the American who always goes to the post office.

Our quarrel is not that efficiency gets things done and very well done, too. I always rely on American water-taps, rather than on those made in China, because American water-taps do not leak. That is a consolation. Against the old contention, however, that we must all be useful, be efficient, become officials and have power, the old reply is that there are always enough fools left in the world who are willing to be useful, be busy and enjoy power, and so somehow the business of life can and will be carried on. The only point is who are the wise, the loafers or the hustlers? Our quarrel with efficiency is not that it gets things done, but that it is a thief of time when it leaves us no leisure to enjoy ourselves and that it frays our nerves in trying to get things done perfectly. An American editor worries his hair gray to see that no typographical mistakes appear on the pages of his magazine. The Chinese editor is wiser than that. He wants to leave his readers the supreme satisfaction of discovering a few typographical mistakes for themselves.

More than that, a Chinese magazine can begin printing serial fiction and forget about it halfway. In America it might bring the roof down on the editors, but in China *it doesn't matter, simply because it doesn't matter.* American engineers in building bridges calculate so finely and exactly as to make the two ends come together within one-tenth of an inch. But when two Chinese begin to dig a tunnel from both sides of a mountain, both come out on the other side. The Chinese's firm conviction is that it doesn't matter so long as a tunnel is dug through, and if we have two instead of one, why, we have a double track to boot. Provided you are not in a hurry, two tunnels are as good as one, dug somehow, finished somehow and if the train can get through somehow. And the Chinese are extremely punctual, provided you give them plenty of time to do a thing. They always finish a thing on schedule, provided the schedule is long enough.

The tempo of modern industrial life forbids this kind of glorious and magnificent idling. But worse than that, it imposes upon us a different conception of time as measured by the clock, and eventually turns the human being into a clock himself. This sort of thing is bound to come to China, as is evident for instance in a factory of twenty thousand workers. The luxurious prospect of twenty thousand workers coming in at their own sweet pleasure at all hours is, of course, somewhat terrifying. Nevertheless, this is what makes life so hard and hectic. A man who has to be punctually at a certain place at five o'clock has the whole afternoon from one to five ruined for him already. Every American adult is arranging his time on the pattern of the schoolboy—three o'clock for this, five o'clock for that, six-thirty for change of dress; six-fifty for entering the taxi and seven o'clock for emerging into a hotel room. It just makes life not worth living.

And Americans have now come to such a sad state that they are booked up not only for the following day, or the following week, but even for the following month. An appointment three weeks ahead of time is a thing unknown in China. And when a Chinese receives an invitation card, happily he never has to say whether he is going to be present or not. He can put down on the invitation list "coming" if he accepts, or "thanks" if he declines, but in the majority of cases the invited party merely writes the word "know," which is a statement of fact that he knows of the invitation and not a statement of intention. An American or a European leaving Shanghai can tell me that he is going to attend a committee meeting in Paris on April 19, at three o'clock, and that he will be arriving in Vienna on May 21 by the seven o'clock train. If an afternoon is to be condemned and executed, must we announce its execution so early? Cannot a fellow travel and be lord of himself, arriving when he likes and taking departure when he likes?

Power of Work and Use of Leisure 223

But above all, the American's inability to loaf comes directly from his desire for doing things and in his placing action above being. We should demand that there be character in our lives as we demand there be character in all great art worthy of the name. Unfortunately, character is not a thing which can be manufactured overnight. Like the quality of mellowness in wine, it is acquired by standing still and by the passage of time. The desire of American old men and women for action, trying in this way to gain their self-respect and the respect of the younger generation, is what makes them look so ridiculous to an Oriental. Too much action in an old man is like a broadcast of jazz music from a megaphone on top of an old cathedral. Is it not sufficient that the old people *are* something? Is it necessary that they must be forever *doing* something? The loss of the capacity for loafing is bad enough in men of middle age, but the same loss in old age is a crime committed against human nature.

Character is always associated with something old and takes time to grow, like the beautiful facial lines of a man in middle age, lines that are the steady imprint of the man's evolving character. It is somewhat difficult to see character in a type of life where every man is throwing away his last year's car and trading it in for the new model. As are the things we make, so are we ourselves. . . . We love old cathedrals, old furniture, old silver, old dictionaries and old prints, but we have entirely forgotten about the beauty of old men. I think an appreciation of that kind of beauty is essential to our life, for beauty, it seems to me, is what is old and mellow and well-smoked.

Sometimes a prophetic vision comes to me, a beautiful vision of a millennium when Manhattan will go slow, and when the American "go-getter" will become an Oriental loafer. American gentlemen will float in skirts and slippers and amble on the sidewalks of Broadway with their hands in their pockets, if not with both hands stuck in their sleeves in the Chinese fashion. Policemen will exchange a word of greeting with the slow-devil at the crossings, and the drivers themselves will stop and accost each other and inquire after their grandmothers' health in the midst of traffic. Someone will be brushing his teeth outside his shopfront, talking the while placidly with his neighbors, and once in a while, an absentminded scholar will sail by with a limp volume rolled up and tucked away in his sleeve. Lunch counters will be abolished, and people will be lolling and lounging in soft, low armchairs in an Automat, while others will have learned the art of killing a whole afternoon in some café. A glass of orange juice will last half an hour, and people will learn to sip wine by slow mouthfuls, punctuated by delightful, chatty remarks, instead of swallowing it at a gulp. Registration in a hospital will be abolished, "emergency wards" will be unknown, and patients will exchange their philosophy with their doctors. Fire engines will proceed at a snail's pace, their staff stopping on the way to gaze at and dispute over the number of passing wild geese in the sky. It is too bad that there is no hope of this kind of millennium on Manhattan ever being realized. There might be so many more perfect idle afternoons.

Discussion of "The Importance of Loafing"

Lin Yutang (1895 -   ) can be called genuinely a citizen of the world. Born in China, he received his early education in Shanghai, then studied at Harvard and several German universities. Returning to China, he became a professor of English at Peking, but later fled mainland China when the Communists took over. Since then he has become recognized throughout the world not only as a fluent spokesman for free China but also, since coming to the United States, as a prominent writer in English, especially in his essays. Among his important publications are *My Country and My People, The Importance of Living, A Leaf in the Storm,* and *Between Tears and Laughter.*

"The Importance of Loafing" may well go too far in advocating leisurely living. Everyone knows that efficiency, accuracy, and punctuality are generally virtues, not vices. Work needs to be pushed along with energy, projects and programs need to be completed as expertly as possible, deadlines need to be kept, letters (at least some of them) need to be answered, and fire engines need to hurry to put out fires. But does Lin Yutang have a point? In the rush of twentieth-century living, are we pushed and pressured so constantly from so many sides that we don't have enough time to think, to create, to appreciate the beautiful, or even to experience the spiritual? Do the things we have to do too often get in the way of the things we want to do or, even worse, of the things we ought to do? Do we need to make room in our lives for at least some periods of leisure when the mind can think, the heart can appreciate, and the spirit can commune and grow? Plants are smothered when crowded too tightly in space. Are personalities smothered when crowded too tightly in time?

Lin Yutang is not the only writer who has seen the need for more leisure in the lives of modern men and women. Robert Louis Stevenson almost a century ago made much the same plea in his famous essay "An Apology for Idlers." And many contemporary writers have urged that people must find time to escape from the increasing pressures of the modern world if civilization is to remain healthy. If too much leisure in life is wrong, is it also wrong to have no leisure, or too little? Long ago the Greeks advocated moderation and balance in all things. Is that still the best answer?

Further Thoughts and Questions for Discussion:

(1) What does Lin Yutang mean when in the first paragraph he says, "The man who is wisely idle is the most cultured man"? How important is the word *wisely* in this sentence?

(2) Comment on Lin Yutang's statement in the second paragraph that "It is our leisure hours which make life endurable."

(3) "We lack spiritual frontage," says Lin Yutang at the end of the third paragraph. What does he mean and what does he recommend as a solution?

(4) In the fifth paragraph Lin Yutang says that efficiency, punctuality, and the desire for achievement and success are the three great American vices. Taken in context, again what does he mean and what does he recommend?

(5) In the ninth paragraph he refers to the danger of "placing action above being." What is he getting at by this phrase?

(6) How valid is the argument in the ninth and tenth paragraphs that in America we have not learned to grow old gracefully and do not have proper reverence and appreciation for the beauty of old age.

(7) Most readers will undoubtedly enjoy Lin Yutang's essay whether they agree with it or not because it is written so delightsomely. In your opinion is he fully serious in the essay, partly serious, or not at all serious? Fully right, partly right, or not at all right?

After Apple-Picking

Robert Frost

My long two-pointed ladder's sticking through a tree
Toward heaven still,
And there's a barrel that I didn't fill
Beside it, and there may be two or three
Apples I didn't pick upon some bough.
But I am done with apple-picking now.
Essence of winter sleep is on the night,
The scent of apples: I am drowsing off.
I cannot rub the strangeness from my sight
I got from looking through a pane of glass
I skimmed this morning from the drinking trough
And held against the world of hoary grass.
It melted, and I let it fall and break.
But I was well
Upon my way to sleep before it fell,
And I could tell
What form my dreaming was about to take.
Magnified apples appear and disappear,
Stem-end and blossom-end,
And every fleck of russet showing clear.
My instep arch not only keeps the ache,
It keeps the pressure of a ladder-round.
I feel the ladder sway as the boughs bend.
And I keep hearing from the cellar bin
The rumbling sound
Of load on load of apples coming in.
For I have had too much
Of apple-picking: I am overtired
Of the great harvest I myself desired.
There were ten thousand fruit to touch,
Cherish in hand, lift down, and not let fall.
For all
That struck the earth,
No matter if not bruised or spiked with stubble,
Went surely to the cider-apple heap
As of no worth.
One can see what will trouble
This sleep of mine, whatever sleep it is.
Were he not gone,
The woodchuck could say whether it's like his
Long sleep, as I describe its coming on,
Or just some human sleep.

Discussion of "After Apple-Picking"

Back in Volume II we studied three excellent poems by Robert Frost—"The Death of the Hired Man," "Fire and Ice," and "Home Burial." From that volume we repeat the following biographical paragraph:

Robert Frost (1875 - 1963) is probably the most beloved great poet of modern America (Carl Sandburg being the principal rival for this honor). To an extent far beyond most poets, Frost is both greatly loved by general readers and greatly admired by professional literary critics and teachers. During half a century of writing he has published hundreds of poems with a wholesome yet earthy realism in their substance, a broad wisdom in their thought, and a wonderful variety of people in their characterizations. His volumes of poetry include *A Boy's Will, North of Boston, Mountain Interval, New Hampshire, A Further Range, A Witness Tree, Steeple Bush, A Masque of Reason,* and *A Masque of Mercy.* Spread throughout these volumes are the hundreds of poems that have won their way to the hearts and minds of millions of readers—poems such as "The Tuft of Flowers," "Mending Wall," "Birches," "Brown's Descent," "Two Look at Two," "Stopping by Woods on a Snowy Evening," "Two Tramps in Mud-Time," "After Apple-Picking," "West-Running Brook," "Departmental," and "The Gift Outright."

"After Apple-Picking" is an excellent poem in at least two important ways. For one thing, it is written with extraordinary artistic control, skillfully weaving together accurate realistic details, vivid description, and melodious yet simple loveliness of sound, rhythm, and imagery. It is a simple poem that reaches to the heart of human memory, especially for all who have felt the weariness of harvest work, extending even into one's dreams at night.

For another thing—and our reason for printing it here—it dramatizes what we all have felt: that there is a time for everything, including a time for working and a time for stopping work. As the Bible puts it:

To every thing there is a season, and a time to every purpose under the heaven: A time to be born, and a time to die; a time to plant, and a time to pluck up that which is planted; a time to kill, and a time to heal; a time to break down, and a time to build up; a time to weep, and a time to laugh; a time to mourn, and a time to dance; a time to cast away stones, and a time to gather stones together; a time to embrace, and a time to refrain from embracing; a time to get, and a time to lose; a time to keep, and a time to cast away; a time to rend, and a time to sew; a time to keep silence, and a time to speak; a time to love, and a time to hate; a time of war, and a time of peace. (Ecclesiastes 3:1-8.)

Lives need to be balanced. We need to work, and work hard; but we need also to interrupt working for food, for sleep, for play, for worship, and even occasionally for just doing nothing. Frost says, "I am overtired of the great harvest I myself desired." Have we all felt this way at times? How universal is the experience of this poem?

Life of Ma Parker

Katherine Mansfield

When the literary gentleman, whose flat old Ma Parker cleaned every Tuesday, opened the door to her that morning, he asked after her grandson. Ma Parker stood on the doormat inside the dark little hall, and she stretched out her hand to help her gentleman shut the door before she replied. "We buried 'im yesterday, sir," she said quietly.

"Oh, dear me! I'm sorry to hear that," said the literary gentleman in a shocked tone. He was in the middle of his breakfast. He wore a very shabby dressing-gown and carried a crumpled newspaper in one hand. But he felt awkward. He could hardly go back to the warm sitting-room without saying something—something more. Then because these people set such store by funerals he said kindly, "I hope the funeral went off all right."

"Beg parding, sir?" said old Ma Parker huskily.

Poor old bird! She did look dashed. "I hope the funeral was a—a—success," said he. Ma Parker gave no answer. She bent her head and hobbled off to the kitchen, clasping the old fish bag that held her cleaning things and an apron and a pair of felt shoes. The literary gentleman raised his eyebrows and went back to his breakfast.

"Overcome, I suppose," he said aloud, helping himself to the marmalade.

Ma Parker drew the two jetty spears out of her toque and hung it behind the door. She unhooked her worn jacket and hung that up too. Then she tied her apron and sat down to take off her boots. To take off her boots or to put them on was an agony to her, but it had been an agony for years. In fact, she was so accustomed to the pain that her face was drawn and screwed up ready for the twinge before she'd so much as untied the laces. That over, she sat back with a sigh and softly rubbed her knees. . . .

"Gran! Gran!" Her little grandson stood on her lap in his button boots. He'd just come in from playing in the street.

"Look what a state you've made your gran's skirt into—you wicked boy!"

But he put his arms around her neck and rubbed his cheek against hers.

"Gran, gi' us a penny!" he coaxed.

"Be off with you; Gran ain't got no pennies."

"Yes, you 'ave."

"No, I ain't."

"Yes, you 'ave. Gi' us one!"

Already she was feeling for the old, squashed, black leather purse. "Well, what'll you give your gran?"

He gave a shy little laugh and pressed closer. She felt his eyelid quivering against her cheek. "I ain't got nothing," he murmured. . . .

The old woman sprang up, seized the iron kettle off the gas stove and took it over to the sink. The noise of the water drumming in the kettle deadened her pain, it seemed. She filled the pail, too, and the washing-up bowl.

It would take a whole book to describe the state of that kitchen. During the week the literary gentleman "did" for himself. That is to say, he emptied the tea leaves now and again into a jam jar set aside for that purpose, and if he ran out of clean forks he wiped over one or two on the roller towel. Otherwise, as he explained to his friends, his "system" was quite simple, and he couldn't understand why people make all this fuss about housekeeping.

"You simply dirty everything you've got, get an old woman in once a week to clean up, and the thing's done."

The result looked like a gigantic dustbin. Even the floor was littered with toast crusts, envelopes, cigarette ends. But Ma Parker bore him no grudge. She pitied the poor young gentleman for having no one to look after him. Out of the smudgy little window you could see an immense expanse of sad-looking sky, and whenever there were clouds they looked very worn, old clouds, frayed at the edges, with holes in them, or dark stains like tea.

While the water was heating, Ma Parker began sweeping the floor. "Yes," she thought, as the broom knocked, "what with one thing and another I've had my share. I've had a hard life."

Even the neighbours said that of her. Many a time, hobbling home with her fish bag she heard them, waiting at the corner, or leaning over the area railings, say among themselves, "She's had a hard life, has Ma Parker." And it was so true she wasn't in the least proud of it. It was just as if you were to say she lived in the basement-back at Number 27. A hard life. . . .

At sixteen she'd left Stratford and come up to London as kitching-maid. Yes, she was born in Stratford-on-Avon. Shakespeare, sir? No, people were always arsking her about him. But she'd never heard his name until she saw it on the theatres.

Nothing remained of Stratford except that "sitting in the fireplace of a evening you could see the stars through the chimley," and "Mother always 'ad 'er side of bacon 'anging from the ceiling." And there was something—a bush, there was—at the front door, that smelt ever so nice. But the bush was very vague. She'd only remembered it once or twice in the hospital, when she'd been taken bad.

That was a dreadful place—her first place. She was never allowed out. She never went upstairs except for prayers morning and evening. It was a fair cellar. And the cook was a cruel woman. She used to snatch away her letters from home before she'd read them, and throw them in the range because they made her dreamy. . . . And the beedles! Would you believe it?—until she came to London she'd never seen a black beedle. Here Ma always gave a little laugh, as though—not to have seen a black beedle! Well! It was as if to say you'd never seen your own feet.

When that family was sold up she went as "help" to a doctor's house, and after two years there, on the run from morning till night, she married her husband. He was a baker.

"A baker, Mrs. Parker!" the literary gentleman would say. For occasionally he laid aside his tomes and lent an ear, at least, to this product called Life. "It must be rather nice to be married to a baker!"

Mrs. Parker didn't look so sure.

"Such a clean trade," said the gentleman.

Mrs. Parker didn't look convinced.

"And didn't you like handing the new loaves to the customers?"

"Well, sir," said Mrs. Parker, "I wasn't in the shop above a great deal. We had thirteen little ones and buried seven of them. If it wasn't the 'ospital it was the infirmary, you might say!"

"You might, indeed, Mrs. Parker!" said the gentleman, shuddering, and taking up his pen again.

Yes, seven had gone, and while the six were still small her husband was taken ill with consumption. It was flour on the lungs, the doctor told her at the time. . . . Her husband sat up in bed with his shirt pulled over his head, and the doctor's finger drew a circle on his back.

"Now, if we were to cut him open here, Mrs. Parker," said the doctor, "you'd find his lungs chock-a-block with white powder. Breathe, my good fellow!" And Mrs. Parker never knew for certain whether she saw or whether she fancied she saw a great fan of white dust come out of her poor dead husband's lips. . . .

But the struggle she'd had to bring up those six little children and keep herself to herself. Terrible it had been! Then, just when they were old enough to go to school her husband's sister came to stop with them to help things along, and she hadn't been there more than two months when she fell down a flight of steps and hurt her spine. And for five years Ma Parker had another baby—and such a one for crying!—to look after. Then young Maudie went wrong and took her sister Alice with her; the two boys emigrimated, and young Jim went to India with the army, and Ethel, the youngest, married a good-for-nothing little waiter who died of ulcers the year little Lennie was born. And now little Lennie —my grandson. . . .

The piles of dirty cups, dirty dishes, were washed and dried. The ink-black knives were cleaned with a piece of potato and finished off with a piece of cork. The table was scrubbed, and the dresser and the sink that had sardine tails swimming in it. . . .

He'd never been a strong child—never from the first. He'd been one of those fair babies that everybody took for a girl. Silvery fair curls he had, blue eyes, and a little freckle like a diamond on one side of his nose. The trouble she and Ethel had had to rear that child! The things out of the newspapers they tried him with! Every Sunday morning Ethel would read aloud while Ma Parker did her washing.

"Dear Sir,—Just a line to let you know my little Myrtil was laid out for dead. . . . After four bottils . . . gained 8 lbs. in 9 weeks, and is still putting it on."

And then the egg-cup of ink would come off the dresser and the letter would be written, and Ma would buy a postal order on her way to work next morning. But it was no use. Nothing made little Lennie put it on. Taking him to the cemetery, even, never gave him a colour; a nice shake-up in the bus never improved his appetite.

But he was gran's boy from the first. . . .

"Whose boy are you?" said old Ma Parker, straightening up from the stove and going over to the smudgy window. And a little voice, so warm, so close, it half stifled her—it seemed to be in her breast under her heart—laughed out, and said, "I'm gran's boy!"

At that moment there was a sound of steps, and the literary gentleman appeared, dressed for walking.

"Oh, Mrs. Parker, I'm going out."

"Very good, sir."

"And you'll find your half-crown in the tray of the ink-stand."

"Thank you, sir."

"Oh, by the way, Mrs. Parker," said the literary gentleman quickly, "you didn't throw away any cocoa last time you were here—did you?"

"No, sir."

"Very strange. I could have sworn I left a teaspoonful of cocoa in the tin." He broke off. He said softly and firmly, "You'll always tell me when you throw things away—won't you, Mrs. Parker?" And he walked off very well pleased with himself, convinced, in fact, he'd shown Mrs. Parker that under his apparent carelessness he was as vigilant as a woman.

The door banged. She took her brushes and cloths into the bedroom. But when she began to make the bed, smoothing, tucking, patting, the thought of little Lennie was unbearable. Why did he have to suffer so? That's what she couldn't understand. Why should a little angel child have to arsk for his breath and fight for it? There was no sense in making a child suffer like that.

. . . From Lennie's little box of a chest there came a sound as though something was boiling. There was a great lump of something bubbling in his chest that he couldn't get rid of. When he coughed the sweat sprang out on his head; his eyes bulged, his hands waved, and the great lump bubbled as a potato knocks in a saucepan. But what was more awful than all was when he didn't cough he sat against the pillow and never spoke or answered, or even made as if he heard. Only he looked offended.

"It's not your poor old gran's doing it, my lovey," said old Ma Parker, patting back the damp hair from his little scarlet ears. But Lennie moved his head and edged away. Dreadfully offended with her he looked —and solemn. He bent his head and looked at her sideways as though he couldn't have believed it of his gran.

But at the last. . . . Ma Parker threw the counterpane over the bed. No, she simply couldn't think about it. It was too much—she'd had too much in her life to bear. She'd borne it up till now, she'd kept herself to herself, and never once had she been seen to cry. Never by a living soul. Not even her own children had seen Ma break down. She'd kept a proud face always. But now! Lennie gone—what had she? She had nothing. He was all she'd got from life, and now he was took too. Why must it all have happened to me? she wondered. "What have I done?" said old Ma Parker. "What have I done?"

As she said those words she suddenly let fall her brush. She found herself in the kitchen. Her misery was so terrible that she pinned on her hat, put on her jacket and walked out of the flat like a person in a dream. She did not know what she was doing. She was like a person so dazed by the horror of what has happened that he walks away—anywhere, as though by walking away he could escape. . . .

It was cold in the street. There was a wind like ice. People went flitting by, very fast; the men walked like scissors; the women trod like cats. And nobody knew—nobody cared. Even if she broke down, if at last, after all these years, she were to cry, she'd find herself in the lock-up as like as not.

But at the thought of crying it was as though little Lennie leapt in his gran's arms. Ah, that's what she wants to do, my dove. Gran wants to cry. If she could only cry now, cry for a long time, over everything, beginning with her first place and the cruel cook, going on to the doctor's, and then the seven little ones, death of her husband, the children's leaving her, and all the years of misery that led up to Lennie. But to have a proper cry over all these things would take a long time. All the same, the time for it had come. She must do it. She couldn't put it off any longer; she couldn't wait any more. . . . Where could she go?

"She's had a hard life, has Ma Parker." Yes, a hard life, indeed! Her chin began to tremble; there was no time to lose. But where? Where?

She couldn't go home; Ethel was there. It would frighten Ethel out of her life. She couldn't sit on a bench anywhere; people would come arsking her questions. She couldn't possibly go back to the gentleman's flat; she had no right to cry in strangers' houses. If she sat on some steps a policeman would speak to her.

Oh, wasn't there anywhere where she could hide and keep herself to herself and stay as long as she liked, not disturbing anybody, and nobody worrying her? Wasn't there anywhere in the world where she could have her cry out—at last?

Ma Parker stood, looking up and down. The icy wind blew out her apron into a balloon. And now it began to rain. There was nowhere.

Discussion of "Life of Ma Parker"

Katherine Mansfield (1888-1923) was born and spent her growing-up years in New Zealand, then traveled to England for university study, and later lived in various countries of continental Europe. Immensely talented, she was both a musician and a writer, but achieved her greatest recognition in the short story, in which genre she is universally acclaimed as one of the most gifted of writers. Her stories are plot-thin but character-rich. Atmosphere, mood, impressions, the revelation of a personality—these are the most important ingredients of her writing; and everything is defined with a sharp precision of detail that is matched by few other writers. Although much of her personal life was filled with unhappiness and illness, Katherine Mansfield nevertheless so disciplined her very considerable talents that she unquestionably established herself as one of the most subtly penetrating short-story writers of all time.[4]

Most readers will find "Life of Ma Parker" a very moving story. Miss Mansfield exhibits in it that rare quality, achieved by only the most skillful writers, of combining tender pathos with high literary artistry in such a way that she presents a sentimental story without slipping to sentimentality in the telling of it.

---

[4]For additional comments on the life and writings of Katherine Mansfield, especially three of her stories—"The Fly," "Marriage à la Mode," and "Miss Brill"—see Volume I, pp. 372-379; Volume II, pp. 62-73; and Volume III, pp. 100-102.

The story is printed here to show what can happen to a woman whose life has been so filled with work and sorrow that she knows almost nothing else. Pleasure, relaxation, beauty, happiness, culture, leisure—all these have been crowded out by a life of hard work and disappointment. Sometimes life comes this heavy to people, and when it does we admire the strength of character that enables a man or woman to endure. The danger is, however, that too much work and sorrow, unmixed with joy or beauty or even spiritual understanding, can harden a man or woman to life generally. This is what has happened to Ma Parker. She has been numbed by too much hard work and sorrow—to the point where she can't even find relief in tears.

Thoughts and Questions for Discussion:

(1) As evidence of the artistry of Katherine Mansfield's writing in this story, note such a vivid description as "the men walked like scissors; the women trod like cats." Note also the skill with which Ma Parker's reminiscences are woven into the story.

(2) Point out details which show how deeply Ma Parker loved her little grandson. Why did she have such a special love for him, even greater perhaps than for her own thirteen children?

(3) Does the "literary gentleman" show much genuine sympathy or understanding for Ma Parker? Point out specific evidences which indicate that he does not. Is he, indeed, a little "superior" and callous in his conversations with her?

(4) Carlyle says that all true work is sacred. Would he be pleased with Ma Parker's life or would he desire more purpose, direction, and spiritual uplift in it?

(5) Considering all the hard work and sorrow in Ma Parker's life, what might the "literary gentleman" and others have done to save her from the defeated spirit and numb despair that overtake her at the end of the story?

The Secret Life of Walter Mitty

James Thurber

"We're going through!" The Commander's voice was like thin ice breaking. He wore his full-dress uniform, with the heavily braided white cap pulled down rakishly over one cold gray eye. "We can't make it, sir. It's spoiling for a hurricane, if you ask me." "I'm not asking you, Lieutenant Berg," said the Commander. "Throw on the power lights! Rev her up to 8,500! We're going through!" The pounding of the cylinders increased: ta-pocketa-pocketa-pocketa-pocketa-pocketa. The Commander stared at the ice forming on the pilot window. He walked over and twisted a row of complicated dials. "Switch on No. 8 auxiliary!" he shouted. "Switch on No. 8 auxiliary!" repeated Lieutenant Berg. "Full strength in No. 3 turret!" shouted the Commander. "Full strength in No. 3 turret!" The crew, bending to their various tasks in the huge, hurtling eight-engined Navy hydroplane, looked at each other and grinned. "The Old Man'll get us through," they said to one another. "The Old Man ain't afraid of anything!" . . .

"Not so fast! You're driving too fast!" said Mrs. Mitty. "What are you driving so fast for?"

"Hmm?" said Walter Mitty. He looked at his wife, in the seat beside him, with shocked astonishment. She seemed grossly unfamiliar, like a strange woman who had yelled at him in a crowd. "You were up to fifty-five," she said. "You know I don't like to go more than forty. You were up to fifty-five." Walter Mitty drove on toward Waterbury in silence, the roaring of the SN202 through the worst storm in twenty years of Navy flying fading in the remote, intimate airways of his mind. "You're tensed up again," said Mrs. Mitty. "It's one of your days. I wish you'd let Dr. Renshaw look you over."

Walter Mitty stopped the car in front of the building where his wife went to have her hair done. "Remember to get those overshoes while I'm having my hair done," she said. "I don't need overshoes," said Mitty. She put her mirror back into her bag. "We've been all through that," she said, getting out of the car. "You're not a young man any longer." He raced the engine a little. "Why don't you wear your gloves? Have you lost your gloves?" Walter Mitty reached in a pocket and brought out the gloves. He put them on, but after she had turned and gone into the building and he had driven on to a red light, he took them off again. "Pick it up, brother!" snapped a cop as the light changed, and Mitty hastily pulled on his gloves and lurched ahead. He drove around the streets aimlessly for a time, and then he drove past the hospital on his way to the parking lot.

... "It's the millionaire banker, Wellington McMillan," said the pretty nurse, "Yes?" said Walter Mitty, removing his gloves slowly. "Who has the case?" "Dr. Renshaw and Dr. Benbow, but there are two specialists here, Dr. Remington from New York and Dr. Pritchard-Mitford from London. He flew over." A door opened down a long, cool corridor and Dr. Renshaw came out. He looked distraught and haggard. "Hello, Mitty," he said. "We're having the devil's own time with McMillan, the millionaire banker and close personal friend of Roosevelt. Obstreosis of the ductal tract. Tertiary. Wish you'd take a look at him." "Glad to," said Mitty.

In the operating room there were whispered introductions: "Dr. Remington, Dr. Mitty; Dr. Pritchard-Mitford, Dr. Mitty." "I've read your book on streptothricosis," said Pritchard-Mitford, shaking hands. "A brilliant performance, sir." "Thank you," said Walter Mitty. "Didn't know you were in the States, Mitty," grumbled Remington. "Coals to Newcastle, bringing Mitford and me up here for a tertiary." "You are very kind," said Mitty. A huge, complicated machine, connected to the operating table, with many tubes and wires, began at this moment to go pocketa-pocketa-pocketa. "The new anesthetizer is giving way!" shouted an interne. "There is no one in the East who knows how to fix it!" "Quiet, man!" said Mitty, in a low, cool voice. He sprang to the machine, which was now going pocketa-pocketa-queep-pocketa-queep. He began fingering delicately a row of glistening dials. "Give me a fountain pen!" he snapped. Someone handed him a fountain pen. He pulled a faulty piston out of the machine and inserted the pen in its place. "That will hold for ten minutes," he said. "Get on with the operation." A nurse hurried over and whispered to Renshaw, and Mitty saw the man turn pale. "Coreopsis has set in," said Renshaw nervously. "If you would take over, Mitty?" Mitty looked at him and at the craven figure of Benbow, who drank, and at the grave, uncertain faces of the two great specialists. "If you wish," he said. They slipped a white gown on him; he adjusted a mask and drew on thin gloves; nurses handed him shining. ...

"Back it up, Mac! Look out for that Buick!" Walter Mitty jammed on the brakes. "Wrong lane, Mac," said the parking-lot attendant, looking at Mitty closely. "Gee. Yeh," muttered Mitty. He began cautiously to back out of the lane marked "Exit Only." "Leave her sit there," said the attendant. "I'll put her away." Mitty got out of the car. "Hey, better leave the key." "Oh," said Mitty, handing the man the ignition key. The attendant vaulted into the car, backed it up with insolent skill, and put it where it belonged.

They're so damn cocky, thought Walter Mitty, walking along Main Street; they think they know everything. Once he had tried to take his chains off, outside New Milford, and he had got them wound around the axles. A man had had to come out in a wrecking car and unwind them, a young, grinning garageman. Since then Mrs. Mitty always made him drive to a garage to have the chains taken off. The next time, he thought, I'll wear my right arm in a sling; they won't grin at me then. I'll have my right arm in a sling and they'll see I couldn't possibly take the chains off myself. He kicked at the slush on the sidewalk. "Overshoes," he said to himself, and he began looking for a shoe store.

When he came out into the street again, with the overshoes in a box under his arm, Walter Mitty began to wonder what the other thing was his wife had told him to get. She had told him twice before they set out from their house for Waterbury. In a way he hated these weekly trips to town—he was always getting something wrong. Kleenex, he thought, Squibb's, razor blades? No. Toothpaste, toothbrush, bicarbonate, carborundum, initiative and referendum? He gave it up. But she would remember it. "Where's the what's-its-name?" she would ask. "Don't tell me you forgot the what's-its-name?" A newsboy went by shouting something about the Waterbury trial.

. . . "Perhaps this will refresh your memory." The District Attorney suddenly thrust a heavy automatic at the quiet figure on the witness stand. "Have you ever seen this before?" Walter Mitty took the gun and examined it expertly. "This is my Webley-Vickers 50.80," he said calmly. An excited buzz ran around the courtroom. The Judge rapped for order. "You are a crack shot with any sort of firearms, I believe?" said the District Attorney, insinuatingly. "Objection!" shouted Mitty's attorney. "We have shown that the defendant could not have fired the shot. We have shown that he wore his right arm in a sling on the night of the fourteenth of July." Walter Mitty raised his hand briefly and the bickering attorneys were stilled. "With any known make of gun," he said evenly, "I could have killed Gregory Fitzhurst at three hundred feet with my left hand." Pandemonium broke loose in the courtroom. A woman's scream rose above the bedlam and suddenly a lovely, dark-haired girl was in Walter Mitty's arms. The District Attorney struck at her savagely. Without rising from his chair, Mitty let the man have it on the point of the chin. "You miserable cur!". . .

"Puppy biscuit," said Walter Mitty. He stopped walking and the buildings of Waterbury rose up out of the misty courtroom and surrounded him again. A woman who was passing laughed. "He said 'Puppy biscuit,'" she said to her companion. "That man said 'Puppy biscuit' to himself." Walter Mitty hurried on. He went into an A. & P., not the first one he came to but a smaller one farther up the street. "I want some biscuit for small, young dogs," he said to the clerk. "Any special brand, sir?" The greatest pistol shot in the world thought a moment. "It says 'Puppies bark for it' on the box," said Walter Mitty.

His wife would be through at the hairdresser's in fifteen minutes, Mitty saw in looking at his watch, unless they had trouble drying it; sometimes they had trouble drying it. She didn't like to get to the hotel first; she would want him to be there waiting for her as usual. He found a big leather chair in the lobby, facing a window, and he put the overshoes and the puppy biscuit on the floor beside it. He picked up an old copy of *Liberty* and sank down into the chair. "Can Germany Conquer the World Through the Air?" Walter Mitty looked at the pictures of bombing planes and of ruined streets.

. . . "The cannonading has got the wind up in young Raleigh, sir," said the sergeant. Captain Mitty looked up at him through tousled hair. "Get him to bed," he said wearily, "with the others. I'll fly alone." "But you can't, sir," said the sergeant anxiously. "It takes two men to handle that bomber and the Archies are smashing us in the air. Von Richtman's circus is between here and Saulier." "Somebody's got to get that ammunition dump," said Mitty. "I'm going over. Spot of brandy?" He poured a drink for the sergeant and one for himself. War thundered and whined around the dugout and battered at the door. There was a rending of wood, and splinters flew through the room. "A bit of a near thing," said Captain Mitty carelessly. "The box barrage is closing in," said the sergeant. "We only live once, Sergeant," said Mitty, with his faint, fleeting smile. "Or do we?" He poured another brandy and tossed it off. "I never see a man could hold his brandy like you, sir," said the sergeant. "Begging your pardon, sir." Captain Mitty stood up and strapped on his huge Webley-Vickers automatic. "It's forty kilometres through hell, sir," said the sergeant. Mitty finished one last brandy. "After all," he said softly, "what isn't?" The pounding of the cannon increased; there was the rat-tat-tatting of machine guns, and from somewhere came the menacing pocketa-pocketa-pocketa of the new flame-throwers. Walter Mitty walked to the door of the dugout humming "Auprés de Ma Blonde." He turned and waved to the sergeant. "Cheerio!" he said. . . .

Something struck his shoulder. "I've been looking all over this hotel for you," said Mrs. Mitty. "Why do you have to hide in this old chair? How did you expect me to find you?" "Things close in," said Walter Mitty vaguely. "What?" Mrs. Mitty said. "Did you get the what's-its-name? The puppy biscuit? What's in that box?" "Overshoes," said Mitty. "Couldn't you have put them on in the store?" "I was thinking," said Walter Mitty. "Does it ever occur to you that I am sometimes thinking?" She looked at him. "I'm going to take your temperature when I get you home," she said.

They went out through the revolving doors that made a faintly derisive whistling sound when you pushed them. It was two blocks to the parking lot. At the drugstore on the corner she said, "Wait here for me. I forgot something. I won't be a minute." She was more than a minute. Walter Mitty lighted a cigarette. It began to rain, rain with sleet in it. He stood up against the wall of the drugstore, smoking. . . . He put his shoulders back and his heels together. "To hell with the handkerchief," said Walter Mitty scornfully. He took one last drag on his cigarette and snapped it away. Then, with that faint, fleeting smile playing about his lips, he faced the firing squad; erect and motionless, proud and disdainful, Walter Mitty the Undefeated, inscrutable to the last.

Discussion of "The Secret Life of Walter Mitty"

For forty years, mostly through his writings published in *The New Yorker*, James Grover Thurber (1894 - 1961) has been recognized as a gifted American humorist. In both his cartoons and prose sketches, for which he is equally famous, he has a special penchant for mixing satire, irony, fantasy, and whimsical wit to reveal the complexities and tensions of modern living.

"The Secret Life of Walter Mitty," one of the best of Thurber's sketches, is a delightful portrait of a shy, hen-pecked man who escapes his nagging wife and the other realities of life through daydreams. In the fantasy of his daydreams he emerges as a very masculine hero with a careless bravado in his manner and a masterful courage that is disdainful of danger. The people around him, mostly craven cowards, turn naturally to him for leadership in moments of crisis—and he never fails them. With his cool, gray eyes, his low, cool voice, and a faint, fleeting smile playing about his lips, he can turn disaster into triumph, rewarded from time to time by a lovely, dark-haired girl who falls into his arms. Thus lives Walter Mitty in his world of make-believe—at least until bumped back into reality by a parking-lot attendant, or by his wife tugging at his shoulder.

James Thurber has put the story together with expert cleverness. Note, for example, how the pocketa-pocketa-pocketa sound is woven into several different crises. Obviously Walter Mitty was fond of this particular sound—and also of Webley-Vickers guns. Note, too, how Dr. Renshaw of Mitty's real life becomes the craven Dr. Renshaw in the surgery room of fantasy. Almost any incident in his real life is sufficient to catapult Mitty into the heroic world of fantasy: a newsboy shouting headlines about a trial, an article on war in *Liberty* magazine, the incidental passing of a hospital on his way to a parking lot. Sometimes too the opposite can happen, as when in his daydream he lashes out at a cruel district attorney, calling him a "miserable cur"—and this reminds him that he was supposed to go shopping for some puppy biscuits. Some might call this stream-of-consciousness thinking, but perhaps a better phrase is stream-of-unconsciousness thinking. As Mitty says, "things close in" on him, causing his wife to comment that she must take his temperature again.

Obviously this delightful story is more entertaining than anything else. It also, however, can suggest a few serious thoughts. In real life there undoubtedly is a place for a certain amount of daydreaming and fantasy. When these start to occupy a person's full life, however, even replacing the work that a man or woman ought to be doing, then things have gone too far. Lives need to be balanced with work and leisure; but some men, and more women, have a tendency to replace reality with fantasy—and then there are problems.

From "The Roots of Honor"

John Ruskin

The fact is that people never have had clearly explained to them the true functions of a merchant with respect to other people. I should like the reader to be very clear about this.

Five great intellectual professions, relating to daily necessities of life, have hitherto existed—three exist necessarily, in every civilized nation:
The Soldier's profession is to *defend* it.
The Pastor's, to *teach* it.
The Physician's, to *keep it in health*.
The Lawyer's, to *enforce justice* in it.
The Merchant's, to *provide* for it.
And the duty of all these men is, on due occasion, to *die* for it.
"On due occasion," namely:
The Soldier, rather than leave his post in battle.
The Physician, rather than leave his post in plague.
The Pastor, rather than teach Falsehood.
The Lawyer, rather than countenance Injustice.
The Merchant—What is *his* "due occasion" of death?
It is the main question for the merchant, as for all of us. For, truly, the man who does not know when to die, does not know how to live.

Observe, the merchant's function (or manufacturer's, for in the broad sense in which it is here used the word must be understood to include both) is to provide for the nation. It is no more his function to get profit for himself out of that provision than it is a clergyman's function to get his stipend. The stipend is a due and necessary adjunct, but not the object, of his life, if he be a true clergyman, any more than his fee (or honorarium) is the object of life to a true physician. Neither is his fee the object of life to a true merchant. All three, if true men, have a work to be done irrespective of fee—to be done even at any cost, or for quite the contrary of fee; the pastor's function being to teach, the physician's to heal, and the merchant's, as I have said, to provide. That is to say, he has to understand to their very root the qualities of the thing he deals in, and the means of obtaining or producing it; and he has to apply all his sagacity and energy to the producing or obtaining it in perfect state, and distributing it at the cheapest possible price where it is most needed.

And because the production or obtaining of any commodity involves necessarily the agency of many lives and hands, the merchant becomes in the course of his business the master and governor of large masses of men in a more direct, though less confessed way, than a military officer or pastor; so that on him falls, in great part, the responsibility for the kind of life they lead; and it becomes his duty, not only to be always considering how to produce what he sells in the purest and cheapest forms, but how to make the various employments involved in the production, or transference of it, most beneficial to the men employed.

And as into these two functions, requiring for their right exercise the highest intelligence, as well as patience, kindness, and tact, the merchant is bound to put all his energy, so for their just discharge he is bound, as soldier or physician is bound, to give up, if need be, his life, in such way as it may be demanded of him. Two main points he has in his providing function to maintain: first, his engagements (faithfulness to engagements being the real root of all possibilities in commerce); and, secondly, the perfectness and purity of the thing provided; so that, rather than fail in any engagement, or consent to any deterioration, adulteration, or unjust and exorbitant price of that which he provides, he is bound to meet fearlessly any form of distress, poverty, or labor, which may, through maintenance of these points, come upon him. . . .

And as the captain of a ship is bound to be the last man to leave his ship in case of wreck, and to share his last crust with the sailors in case of famine, so the manufacturer, in any commercial crisis or distress, is bound to take the suffering of it with his men, and even to take more of it for himself than he allows his men to feel; as a father would in a famine, shipwreck, or battle, sacrifice himself for his son.

Discussion of "The Roots of Honor"

Strictly speaking, "The Roots of Honor" by John Ruskin (1819 - 1900)[5] probably does not quite belong in this section because it is not precisely concerned with the relationship between work and leisure. However, its basic thesis—that the first responsibility of any professional man is not to make money but to serve humanity—is so stimulating that we have decided to print it here.

In its old-fashioned emphasis upon service, honor, integrity, and duty, the essay does not, we hope, seem obsolete. If these qualities were needed a hundred years ago when

---

[5]For another essay by Ruskin and for brief comments on his life and writings, see pages 176-178 of Volume IV.

Ruskin wrote the essay, surely they are needed at least as much today. And if they apply to the five professions he names, do they not apply equally to almost any occupation that a man or woman might choose as a life's work?

For all else that the essay says about the ideals and responsibilities of an employer towards his employees and the public he serves, we leave readers to the reading of the essay itself. We especially invite readers to ponder the thought that for every leader there is an ultimate responsibility to give even his own life if necessary rather than betray those he leads and serves.

SECTION SEVEN

The Thrill and Reward of Participation

by Robert K. Thomas

The Thrill and Reward of Participation

Action may not always bring happiness, but there is no happiness without action.—Benjamin Disraeli

Introductory Comments

It is hard not to gauge the significance of our involvement by the size of the project or the length of our effort. Most of us respond positively to that which is imposingly large or notably long. We speak easily of "rising" to occasions, as if all challenges had overtones of physical expansion.

As the two poems which open this section suggest, the real test of meaningful involvement may not depend on either size or extension. In Robert Frost's "Oven Bird," part of the final line—"what to make of a diminished thing"—suggests that we prepare for the diminution we must all face. This is most obvious when our physical powers begin to fail, but probably more disquieting when we begin to have trouble remembering or find it taxing to follow complicated directions.

To begin with, we need to accept the fact of our present situation and that which will inevitably follow. To take drastic measures in order to appear younger than we are is to confess that our concept of meaningful participation is overwhelmingly physical. If we prepare to accept the changes that advancing years present us with, we can experience the unique involvement that is a gift of each stage in our life.

"Life" by George Herbert touches on some of the same things as "Oven Bird," but there is a religious element in

"Life" that is not evident in Frost's poem. "Oven Bird" is set in the world and does not really try to go beyond it. What we must make of a "diminished thing" is strictly a mortal problem. Herbert sees the wilting of plants and flowers as indicators of the transitory nature of all living things, but his thought transcends the earth. There is implication of post-mortal responsibility in "Life's" final stanza.

The importance of a proper mental attitude in keeping ourselves fit for significant participation is the theme of Overstreet's "Keeping Mentally Alive." Action itself is neither positive nor negative, although we are often impressed by the person who seems to be doing things. What Overstreet would have us remember is that we may appear to be thinking vigorously when all we are doing is building defenses against new experiences. This is a particularly appropriate selection for members of a church that is led by a living prophet and that believes in continuous revelation. We must be prepared to adjust ourselves to new ways of doing traditional things and not be afraid to adapt ourselves to directives that chart new courses for us.

The excerpt from *Great Possessions* continues one of the themes from Overstreet's article. The inability of Horace to harvest anything from his land except the obvious hay is an example of the mental stagnation discussed in "Keeping Mentally Alive." But Grayson takes us one step further and lets us share with him the thrill and reward that the simplest sensitive participation in the natural world can provide.

Another poem by Robert Frost, "Stopping by Woods on a Snowy Evening," may now be among the best-known poems ever written in America. It is appealing to both the critics and the public at large, to both children and adults, to those who find most of Frost's poetry appealing and those who select only this poem from his works. Among the meanings which this short lyric suggests is the necessity for discriminating between the pull of that which would take us from the "promises" we have made and the moral commitment that keeps us involved in that which we know we should do.

In our final selection, Hawthorne's "Canterbury Pilgrims," we are presented with an entire spectrum of participation. We meet those who are about to begin their real involvement with the world, and we listen to those who are now retreating from participation that has been too much for them. Although the tone of this story is often gloomy, since most of it is given over to description of "disappointed hopes and unavailing toil, domestic grief and estranged affection," the young couple who are introduced to the world through such somber accounts are not deterred by them and move out into an untried life in realistic confidence.

The Oven Bird

by Robert Frost

There is a singer everyone has heard,
Loud, a mid-summer and a mid-wood bird,
Who makes the solid tree trunks sound again.
He says that leaves are old and that for flowers
Mid-summer is to spring as one to ten.
He says the early petal-fall is past
When pear and cherry bloom went down in showers
On sunny days a moment overcast;
And comes that other fall we name the fall.
He says the highway dust is over all.
The bird would cease and be as other birds
But that he knows in singing not to sing.
The question that he frames in all but words
Is what to make of a diminished thing.

Discussion of "The Oven Bird"

We have reprinted several poems by Robert Frost in earlier volumes of *Out of the Best Books* (see Volume 2 especially), and what may be his most famous lyric is used later in this section. The one we consider now, "Oven Bird," presents a theme which is common in poetry—the impermanence of all living things—but Frost gives it a quite uncommon treatment.

As far back as medieval Latin poetry we come upon the *ubi sunt* (literally "where are") idea. The poet lists a number of things that are no more or that have changed, and he often introduces his list with the question, "Where are . . . ?" Frost's "Oven Bird" is not really following this tradition. He is reflecting less on the transitory nature of life than he is on what we *do* about it.

The oven bird itself, for instance, is first introduced as a "singer" but later is identified as one that "knows in singing not to sing." While there may be some reference to the harsh, almost metallic song of this bird in such a comment, Frost is going beyond saying that this song is different. He is suggesting that the strident call of the oven bird is more than recognition of change and decay; it is invitation to "make" something out of what is left.

In playing on the word "fall" Frost evokes biblical overtones. How did Adam and Eve fare when driven from the garden? If autumn, the fall of the year, is a time of harvest, it is also a time of exhaustion. Even summer is debilitating and in its very intensity prefigures the harsh times to come.

There is a mildly encouraging note to the final line of this poem, however. The question is not *whether* but *what*. It is assumed that we will try, and perhaps the recognition of less to come can prepare us to use what remains more skillfully and imaginatively. If circumstance narrows our interest, it can bring us concentration and focus.

This poem is unusually blunt, however, in recognizing that we cannot hope to recapture spring in the summer, much less the fall. The spontaneity and sprightliness of youth are appropriate to youth. But, advertisements notwithstanding, they seldom become middle age. There comes a day for most of us when "not going"—whatever the occasion —is the happiest of choices, if we are *prepared* to make it.

Life

by George Herbert

I made a posy, while the day ran by:
Here will I smell my remnant out, and tie
    My life within this band.
But Time did beckon to the flowers, and they
By noon most cunningly did steal away,
    And withered in my hand.

My hand was next to them, and then my heart:
I took, without more thinking, in good part
    Time's gentle admonition:
Who did so sweetly death's sad taste convey,
Making my mind to smell my fatal day;
    Yet sugaring the suspicion.

Farewell dear flowers, sweetly your time ye spent,
Fit, while ye lived, for smell or ornament,
    And after death for cures.
I follow straight without complaints or grief,
Since if my scent be good, I care not if
    It be as short as yours.

Discussion of "Life"

George Herbert (1593-1633) occupies a unique place in the history of the religious lyric. More than any other poet he developed this literary type in English. Although he had written some secular verse in his youth, Herbert destroyed it after he became rector of St. Andrew's Church at Bremerton.

While Herbert's poetry shows the influence of John Donne, his verses are more artistically constructed than Donne's. Herbert's work lacks the fire which we associate with much religious poetry, but it lets us see the appealing serenity which a mind and life in accord with Christian principles can produce.

The life of a flower as emblematic of human duration is a standard poetic image. Herbert freshens it by carrying this figure farther than most. He is particularly skillful in using the idea of scent to suggest a number of things: the sensuous delights of life, the ephemeral nature of physical pleasure, the barely apprehended premonition of death, the mildly drug-like effect of sense stimulation, and the offering of his life to the Lord, as incense has so often been a symbol of sacrifice.

He also extends the meaning of flowers beyond their life when he mentions the use of dried flowers in medicinal "cures." In so doing he adds the sacred theme which characterizes his lyrics. Where other poets may be content to imply that the shortness of life justifies spending it in pursuit of physical pleasure, Herbert would have us not forget that our mortal life is only part of our "use"—and probably the least part.

The despair that runs through much of the work of his secular contemporaries is therefore absent in Herbert's poetry. As much as any Cavalier he appreciated the beauties of life, but he was never merely seduced by them. In the midst of earthly delight, he always thought of heaven. The perspective this provided for him is almost as rare today as it was in the turbulent century in which he lived.

"Keeping Mentally Alive"

by H.A. Overstreet

A man goes to his doctor. "No," he replies to the doctor's question: "I haven't any special pain—not that I can notice. Just have lost my zip. Food doesn't taste the way it should. Nothing tastes good. I feel washed out."

The doctor proceeds in the usual manner—tongue, pulse, chest; asks questions. Then:

"How long since you've had an examination of yourself?"

The man looks shamefaced: "Not so long as I can remember."

"Well, how about tomorrow morning?"

"That'll do for me."

"All right, come to the hospital at eight. Don't eat any breakfast, and we'll see what we can do for you."

At eight, the man is at the hospital, ready for what he expects to be a long-drawn-out ordeal of being thumped and probed and made generally conscious of his ailing body. He is told to shed his outer clothes and lie down on a couch.

"Take it easy for a while," says the attendant. "Go to sleep if you want to."

After what seems an endless period of waiting, the attendant comes back, puts clips on the man's nose, and a masklike arrangement over his mouth.

"Just breathe quietly—in and out."

The man does so. A few minutes pass.

"O.K.," says the attendant, and takes off the clips and mask. "That's all."

"All!" says the man. "I thought I was to be examined."

"You have been. Basal metabolism test."

The man gets back into his clothes. "Basal metabolism," he mutters to himself.

"What the devil is that?"

By the time he next sees his doctor, he has mustered up courage enough to ask.

"That test, doctor. They didn't seem to do much to me. What was it all about?"

"Metabolism test. Measures the oxygen you take into your body—measures how much energy is being produced inside you."

Thrill and Reward of Participation

"Oh! What was the report?"

"Showed you're a little below par. Nothing serious, however. It would be a good idea if you took a vacation."

The basal metabolism test is a triumph of medical inventiveness. In spite of its simplicity, it gives us clues to ourselves that are more revealing than the most long-drawn-out series of thumps and probings. Thumps and probings tell us about special parts of ourselves, but the metabolism test tells us about our activity as total beings. With a scratch of a pen on a recording machine, it informs us accurately how well or ill our body produces energy from the food and air we take in.

It would be an equal, perhaps even greater, triumph if we could invent a test that would measure our mental metabolism and inform us how well or ill our minds use what we take into them.

"No, I haven't any phobias or obsessions," says a man to his psychological physician. "But I'm a bore. I bore myself and I bore my friends. They don't tell me so, but I see it in their eyes. What can I do about it?"

Or this other man says: "I've lost my mental pep. Used to have plenty of it. Now I'm just plain dull. My mind won't seem to click any more."

Or another: "I can't get interested in anything. I've reached a point where one thing is as good as another, and nothing is any good."

There are many people who would not even know if anything was wrong with their minds. They are the colorless people, who go through the routines of life, able to get by, neither adding to the wisdom and the gaiety of existence nor subtracting from it—mental ciphers; or smug people, afflicted with what might be called fattening of the brain—satisfied with their place in life, supremely content with themselves, unwilling to face any new experience that might force them to readjust; set people, suffering from what might be called a hardening of the brain—rigid, opinionated, dogmatic, unlistening and unyielding.

It would be a triumph of psychology if we could invent a way of putting such people—and many others who suffer from one or another of the forms of mind-deficiency—through a simple test so that they might know what was wrong with their minds.

The working of the body can be measured accurately. It is very difficult to test the efficiency of a mind because the many and varied forms of human experience are so mingled that we can scarcely separate one from another, or measure them accurately. Besides, there is no one form of experience that shows the efficiency of mind as the use of oxygen tells of the efficiency of the body.

Nevertheless, by watching how minds behave, we can in a general way estimate whether they are getting their proper supplies. It is not difficult, for example, to notice whether a mind is living in a routine of sameness, receiving no new experiences to vitalize its energies, seeing no new people, going to no new places, reading no new books—or old books of the kind that are always new—getting no new ideas. We can lay it down as a rule of the mental life that where there is insufficient intake of fresh experience, there will be symptoms of mental sluggishness, dullness, boredom. The mind will be anemic, listless, weak.

Again, it is not hard to tell whether the supplies taken in by the mind are being properly used and changed into mental energy.

For example, one of the frequent symptoms of mental old age is what might be called "neophobia," the fear of what is new. The mentally old person is afraid of new ideas, new ways of doing things. He insists that the old ways were the better ways, that people are losing the sturdy virtues, the plain common sense they used to have.

We cannot be completely sure just what is wrong with such a mind. But it seems reasonable to believe that what happens is something like this. The old mind has lost the energy to adjust itself to new experiences; it is tired, worn out.

Being a human mind, it does not tell itself that it is worn out, incapable of meeting new experience as new experience should be met. Such a confession would be equal to complete surrender. It would be "giving up the ghost." It would like resigning itself to death.

The mentally old mind has to cling to the illusion that it is still mentally alive. It has to believe, therefore, that its thought-processes are going on as vigorously as ever. Hence, when new experiences come to which it cannot adjust itself, new ways of life, new ideas, new outlooks, all it can do is to build up defenses against them. In building up such defenses, defying the new ideas and denouncing them as evil, it seems to itself to be thinking with vigor and effectiveness, when as a matter of fact it is merely pushing off the experiences it is too worn out to absorb.

This is the pathetic habit of mental old age, to oppose bitterly all that is new, because new things cannot be understood and accepted.

A different and less annoying symptom of mental old age is talking too much about the past. Again, we cannot be completely sure of our diagnosis, but it would seem reasonable to believe that endless and purposeless reminiscing takes place because the mind, being unable to absorb new experiences, is compelled to live upon the stock it has already gathered. It looks back because it has no longer the vigor to look forward. It talks about its past experiences because it has no strength left to be interested in new ones.

Sometimes the symptoms of suspended mental activity take the form of a complete rigidity. They may appear in a person of any age. The mind is fixed in its own opinions. The fixity may be cheerful. "If it was good enough for my father, it's good enough for me." "Yes, stranger, we don't hanker after none of these newfangled ways." Or the fixity may be grim. It might take the form of persecuting those who hold views that are different, breaking up meetings, or casting people into jail.

Mental fixity may easily be a result of too little nourishment taken into the mind; that is, it may be a case of plain ignorance. A metropolitan club of well-to-do people recently turned down a suggested speaker because as the chairman of the program committee said, "one of our members heard her give a lecture on Russian drama, and she praised it. If she likes Russia, she can go there. We don't want her."

Here was plain ignorance of a Russia that had existed many generations before the revolution that they feared and hated, and plain ignorance of the purpose and meaning of creative art.

The mind has to do two essential things if it is to keep its vigor: It has to take in new experience, and it has to transform this experience into fresh thought, emotions, intentions, plans, and activities. When the mind stops taking in, it merely lives along on its past. When it fails to turn its experiences smoothly and effectively into new ways of thinking and doing and acting, it suffers a kind of mental poisoning, such as the body suffers poisoning when intake of food remains undigested. It is under such conditions that the mind becomes suspicious, fearful, opinionated, stubborn, cranky, bitter.

The mind, then, is no exception to the rule of all living things. It must work to keep alive, absorbing its world, transforming that world into its own peculiar energies.

There are more ways than one of dying. Many of us are dead, have been dead many years, before we are buried.
>We die of what we eat and drink,
>But more we die of what we think.

But also, there are more ways than one of keeping alive. The mind that keeps renewing itself with fresh experience remains flexible and young. It has no clogged-up places, no dead areas. It opens its doors to the life stream and turns that stream into its own ever growing wisdom and power.

Discussion of
"Keeping Mentally Alive"

Harry Allen Overstreet (1875 -) was born in San Francisco, educated at the University of California and at Oxford, and is now a professor emeritus and a widely popular lecturer.

Overstreet's books and lectures are notable for simple presentations of difficult subjects. In the foregoing selection, for example, he gains and holds the reader's interest by beginning with a concrete incident, told largely in dialogue, and then makes a skillful transition to his thesis.

At first glance the emphasis of this article would seem to be on reacting positively to that which is new and different. This, however, is only a superficial reading of what Overstreet is trying to convey. We need not accept every change that comes along, but we should be able to evaluate innovations rather than be frightened by them. There are certain basic truths which do not fluctuate, but our capacity to understand and appreciate them should deepen as our experience expands and our minds grow.

To members of a church that is committed to continual revelation, this article is unusually relevant. Under the direction of prophets we move in confidence along new paths, but we are not true to the abilities that the Lord has given us if we do not bring our freshest, most dynamic thinking to the problems that beset us.

The Prophet Joseph said that when taught correct principles the people could govern themselves. This does not license whim but neither does it justify passivity. To be "anxiously engaged" is to be directly involved. No church stresses individual participation more strongly than ours, but we can be *busy* without being truly *active.*

Busyness can easily be mistaken for significant activity, since the physical manifestations may be similar. But the person who is active in the Church is doing more than going through the motions; he is bringing to bear all his belief,

Thrill and Reward of Participation

his skill, and his commitment in support of that which he is trying to live.

The person who is mentally alive is seldom rebellious. Most rebellion is dishearteningly mindless. We have to be mentally awake to catch the spirit as well as the letter, and this keeps us from reacting simplemindedly. No one thinks himself out of the Church. Truth can stand the most rigorous examination. But when we cease to involve ourselves totally, when we no longer follow the precept, it is easy to find fault with the theology.

Overstreet urges us to bring all our mental powers to bear. The first result of such an attempt is always humility. There is so little we know; the most exact sciences are based on unprovable assumptions. The exhilaration of understanding and living the gospel as we prepare ourselves—"by study and by faith"—to receive further light is the most thrilling of spiritual and intellectual pursuits and the only one worthy of our best efforts.

From Great Possessions
by David Grayson

"I am made immortal by apprehending my possession of incorruptible goods."

I have just had one of the pleasant experiences of life. From time to time, these brisk winter days, I like to walk across the fields to Horace's farm. I take a new way each time and make nothing of the snow in the fields or the drifts along the fences.

"Why," asks Harriet, "do you insist on struggling through the snow when there's a good beaten road around?"

"Harriet," I said, "why should anyone take a beaten road when there are new and adventurous ways to travel?"

When I cross the fields, I never know at what moment I may come upon some strange or surprising experience, what new sights I may see, what new sounds I may hear, and I have the further great advantage of appearing unexpectedly at Horace's farm. Sometimes I enter by the cow lane, sometimes by way of the old road through the wood lot, or I appear casually, like a gust of wind, around the corner of the barn, or I let Horace discover me leaning with folded arms upon his cattle fence. I have come to love doing this, for unexpectedness in visitors, as in religion and politics, is disturbing to Horace; and as sand grits in oysters produce pearls, my unexpected appearances have more than once astonished new thoughts in Horace or yielded pearly bits of native humor.

Ever since I have known him, Horace has been rather high-and-mighty with me; but I know he enjoys my visits, for I give him always, I think, a pleasantly renewed sense of his own superiority. When he sees me, his eye lights up with the comfortable knowledge that he can plow so much better than I can, that his corn grows taller than mine, and his hens lay more eggs. He is a wonderfully practical man, is Horace; hard-headed, they call it here. And he never feels so superior, I think, as when he finds me sometimes of a Sunday or an evening walking across the fields where my land joins his, or sitting on a stone fence, or lying on my back in the pasture under a certain friendly thorn-apple tree. This he finds difficult to understand and thinks it highly undisciplined, impractical, no doubt reprehensible.

One incident of this sort I shall never forget. It was on a June day only a year or so after I came here, and before Horace knew me as well as he does now. I had climbed the hill to look off across his own high-field pasture, where the white daisies, the purple fleabane, and the buttercups made a wild tangle of beauty among the tall herd's-grass.

Light airs moved billowing across the field, bobolinks and meadow larks were singing, and all about were the old fences, each with its wild hedgerow of choke cherry, young elms, and black raspberry bushes, and beyond across the miles and miles of sunny green country-side, the mysterious blue of the ever-changing hills. It was a spot I loved then, and have loved more deeply every year since.

Horace found me sitting on the stone fence which there divides our possessions. I think he had been observing me with amusement for some time before I saw him, for when I looked around his face wore a comfortably superior, half-disdainful smile.

"David," said he, "what ye doin' here?"

"Harvesting my crops," I said.

He looked at me sharply to see if I was joking, but I was perfectly sober.

"Harvestin' yer crops?"

"Yes," I said, the fancy growing suddenly upon me, "and just now I've been taking a crop from the field you think you own."

I waved my hand to indicate his high-field pasture.

"Don't I own it?"

"No, Horace, I'm sorry to say, not all of it. To be frank with you, since I came here, I've quietly acquired an undivided interest in that land. I may as well tell you first as last. I'm like you, Horace; I'm reaching out in all directions."

I spoke in as serious as voice as I could command—the tone I use when I sell potatoes. Horace's smile wholly disappeared. A city feller like me was capable of anything!

"How's that?" he exclaimed sharply. "What do you mean? That field came down to me from my Grandfather Jamieson."

I continued to look at Horace with great calmness and gravity.

"Judging from what I now know of your title, Horace," said I, "neither your Grandfather Jamieson nor your father ever owned all of that field. And I've now acquired that part of it, in fee simple, that neither they nor you ever really had."

At this, Horace began to look seriously worried. The idea that anyone could get away from him anything that he possessed, especially without his knowledge, was terrible to him.

"What do you mean, Mr. Grayson?"

He had been calling me David, but he now returned sharply to Mister. In our country when we "Mister" a friend, something serious is about to happen. It's the signal for general mobilization.

I continued to look Horace rather coldly and severely in the eye.

"Yes," said I, "I've acquired a share in that field which I shall not soon surrender."

An unmistakable dogged look came into Horace's face, the look inherited from generations of landowning, home-defending, fighting ancestors. Horace is New England of New England.

"Yes," I said, "I have already had two or three crops from that field."

"Huh!" said Horace. "I've cut the grass and I've cut the rowen every year since you bin here. What's more, I've got the money fer it in the bank."

He tapped his fingers on the top of the wall.

"Nevertheless, Horace," said I, "I've got my crops also from that field, and a steady income too."

"What crops?"

"Well, I've just now been gathering in one of them. What do you think of the value of the fleabane, and the daisies, and the yellow five-finger in that field?"

"Huh!" said Horace.

"I've rarely seen anything more beautiful," I said, "than this field and the view across it. I'm taking that crop now, and later I shall gather in the rowen of goldenrod and aster, and the red and yellow of the maple trees—and store it all away in *my* bank—to live on next winter."

It was some time before either of us spoke again, but I could see from the corner of my eye that mighty things were going on inside of Horace. Suddenly he broke out into a big laugh and clapped his knee with his hand in a way he has.

"Is that all!" said Horace.

I think it only confirmed him in the light esteem in which he held me. Though I showed him unmeasured wealth in his own fields, ungathered crops of new enjoyment, he was unwilling to take them, but was content with hay. It is a strange thing to me, and a sad one, how many of our farmers (and be it said in a whisper, other people too) own their lands without ever really possessing them, and let the most precious crops of the good earth go to waste.

After that, for a long time, Horace loved to joke me about my crops and his. A joke with Horace is a durable possession.

"S'pose you think that's your field," he'd say.

"The best part of it," I'd return; "but you can have all I've taken, and there'll still be enough for both of us."

"You're a queer one!" he'd say, and then add sometimes dryly, "but there's one crop ye don't git, David," and he'd tap his pocket where he carries his fat, worn leather pocketbook. "And as fer feelin's, it can't be beat."

So many people have the curious idea that the only thing the world desires enough to pay its hard money for is that which can be seen or eaten or worn. But there never was a greater mistake. While men will haggle to the penny over the price of hay, or fight for a cent more to the bushel of oats, they will turn out their very pockets for strange, intangible joys, hopes, thoughts, or for a moment of peace in a feverish world—the unknown Great Possessions.

So it was that one day, some months afterward, when we had been thus bantering each other with great good humor, I said to him, "Horace, how much did you get for your hay this year?"

"Off that one little piece." he replied, "I figger fifty-two dollars."

"Well, Horace," said I, "I have beaten you. I got more out of it this year than you did."

"Oh, I know what you mean—"

"No, Horace, you don't. This time I mean just what you do: money, cash, dollars."

"How's that, now?"

"Well, I wrote a little piece about your field, and the wind in the grass, and the hedges along the fences, and the weeds among the timothy, and the fragrance of it all in June, and sold it last week—" I leaned over toward Horace and whispered behind my hand—in just the way he tells me the price he gets for his pigs.

"What!" he exclaimed

Horace had long known that I was "a kind of literary feller," but his face was now a study in astonishment.

"What?"

Horace scratched his head, as he is accustomed to do when puzzled, with one finger just under the rim of his hat.

"Well, I vum!" said he.

Here I have been wandering all around Horace's barn—in the snow—getting at the story I really started to tell, which probably supports Horace's conviction that I am an impractical and unsubstantial person. If I had the true business spirit, I should have gone by the beaten road from my house to Horace's, borrowed the singletree I went for, and hurried straight home. Life is so short when one is after dollars! I should not have wallowed through the snow, nor stopped at the top of the hill to look for a moment across the beautiful wintry earth—gray sky and bare wild trees and frosted farmsteads with homely smoke rising from the chimneys. I should merely have bought home a singletree—and missed the glory of life! As I reflect upon it now, I believe it took me no longer to go by the fields than the road; and I've got the singletree as securely with me as though I had not looked upon the beauty of the eternal hills, nor reflected, as I tramped, upon the strange ways of man.

Oh, my friend, is it the settled rule of life that we are to accept nothing not expensive? It is not so settled for me. That which is freest, cheapest, seems somehow more valuable than anything I pay for; that which is given, better than that which is bought; that which passes between you and me in the glance of an eye, a touch of the hand, is better than minted money!

Discussion of
Great Possessions

David Grayson was the pen name of Ray Stannard Baker (1870-1946). Baker's talents were many. As a journalist he gained the reputation of being America's foremost reporter. As a writer for the periodicals of his day he contributed over two hundred articles to leading magazines —including one on "The Vitality of Mormonism" for *Century Magazine* during 1904. As champion of Woodrow Wilson, he won a Pulitzer Prize for his eight-volume work, *Woodrow Wilson: Life and Letters.*

As David Grayson he wrote a total of nine volumes of "adventures in contentment" which sold more than two million copies. Under this *nom de plume* he debated with himself in public most of the issues that troubled his generation. *Great Possessions* is one of the last of these. It is concerned with an America that is threatened by war on one side and by neglect on the other. Subtitled an "Auction of Antiques," writing it was suggested by the notice of an auction in which one of the pillars of New England has his possessions disposed of after his death.

It occurred to Baker that only the most obvious possessions of a truly great man could come under the auctioneer's hammer, and this book is his attempt to chronicle what constitutes a lasting legacy. The excerpt we reprint here is typical, for the inability of people such as Horace to react to the world in other than material terms is the basic criticism of this work.

Baker's style is informal—even playful—but he is always making a serious point. Horace's participation in life is pointedly focused on things. At this level his involvement is complete and relatively successful. If the characterization of Horace is a bit thin, even stereotyped, he serves as the uncomplicated symbol Baker needs to point up the sterility of a participation that is hopelessly narrow. Baker cannot resist pointing out that so limited a vision is not even totally successful in material terms, for he has received more for writing an article about Horace's field than Horace has from the hay he has harvested there.

Perhaps the most memorable point in this selection is Baker's contention that one can be both practical and aesthetically sensitive. We need not choose one approach to the exclusion of the other. Both mind and body thrive when they are brought into a full, complementary relationship.

Stopping by Woods on a Snowy Evening
by Robert Frost

Whose woods these are I think I know.
His house is in the village though;
He will not see me stopping here
To watch his woods fill up with snow.

My little horse must think it queer
To stop without a farmhouse near
Between the woods and frozen lake
The darkest evening of the year.

He gives his harness bells a shake
To ask if there is some mistake.
The only other sound's the sweep
Of easy wind and downy flake.

The woods are lovely, dark and deep,
But I have promises to keep,
And miles to go before I sleep,
And miles to go before I sleep.

Discussion of
"Stopping by Woods on a Snowy Evening"

We know more about the actual composition of this poem than about most of Robert Frost's work. We even have a facsimile of the last three stanzas as he was working them out. While a detailed analysis of the changes that Frost made in bringing this poem to completion would probably not be of general interest, some of them are very revealing.

To begin with, the actual incident that provided the basis for this work apparently involved two horses, and the original opening line recognizes this: "The steaming horses think it queer." The fact that Frost canceled this line in favor of "My little horse must think it queer" is an excellent example of how a poet turns an actual experience into a poetic truth. If the horse is to be a symbol, it needs to be particularized; and, while the "steaming" is both descriptive and accurate, it tends to keep us thinking of the horse *only* as a horse.

The third line of this stanza is equally interesting. Frost

started with "Between a forest and a lake." In revision, he changed "a forest" to "the woods" and "a lake to "frozen lake." A forest is too big and too vague for this poem. Woods are definite and limited. One knows who owns the woods (note beginning line of poem), but a forest carries overtones of the vast and impersonal—both inappropriate for the intimacy suggested by this account. "A lake" has not the specificity nor the descriptive force of "frozen lake."

The last line of the next stanza has only a single change in the final revision. "Fall of flake" becomes "downy flake." "Downy" not only half chimes with "sounds," but it suggests the ease with which one might yield to forgetting the miles to go and the promises to keep.

The effort it costs to be responsible has rarely been evoked more effectively than in this poem. Frost is not praising the merely habitual. The little horse is quite willing to plod on and is, in fact, impatient to be on his way. The driver, however, is fully aware of a dimension not even sensed by the horse or the type of people he stands for. We need not see in the driver's reactions any "death wish," as some critics have. It is enough that we share with him for a moment the pull of indulgence, the distraction of loveliness, the apparent respite of non-commitment.

It is even more important that we recognize, with Frost, that relaxation before we have earned a rest is not going to satisfy beyond the moment. A truly sensitive person may be susceptible to a range of temptations not shared by everyone, but the fineness of his discriminations is also his best defense. For he can appreciate the sacredness of a promise and the sterility of non-commitment. Much of the thrill of his participation in life stems from his awareness that activity is most rewarding when we are doing what we *ought* to do.

"The Canterbury Pilgrims"
by Nathaniel Hawthorne

The summer moon, which shines in so many a tale, was beaming over a broad extent of uneven country. Some of its brightest rays were flung into a spring of water, where no traveller, toiling, as the writer has, up the hilly road beside which it gushes, ever failed to quench his thirst. The work of neat hands and considerate art was visible about this blessed fountain. An open cistern, hewn and hollowed out of solid stone, was placed above the waters which filled it to the brim, but by some invisible outlet were conveyed away without dripping down its sides. Though the basin had not room for another drop, and the continual gush of water made a tremor on the surface, there was a secret charm that forbade it to overflow. I remember, that when I had slaked my summer thirst, and sat panting by the cistern, it was my fanciful theory that Nature could not afford to lavish so pure a liquid, as she does the waters of all meaner fountains.

While the moon was hanging almost perpendicularly over this spot, two figures appeared on the summit of the hill, and came with noiseless footsteps down towards the spring. They were then in the first freshness of youth; nor is there a wrinkle now on either of their brows, and yet they wore a strange, old-fashioned garb. One, a young man with ruddy cheeks, walked beneath the canopy of a broad-brimmed gray hat; he seemed to have inherited his greatgrandsire's square skirted coat, and a waistcoat that extended its immense flaps to his knees; his brown locks, also, hung down behind, in a mode unknown to our times. By his side was a sweet young damsel, her fair features sheltered by a prim little bonnet, within which appeared the vestal muslin of a cap; her close, long-waisted gown, and indeed her whole attire, might have been worn by some rustic beauty who had faded half a century before. But that there was something too warm and life-like in them, I would here have compared this couple to the ghosts of two young lovers who had died long since in the glow of passion, and now were straying out of their graves, to renew the old vows, and shadow forth the unforgotten kiss of their earthly lips, beside the moonlit spring.

"Thee and I will rest here a moment, Miriam," said the young man, as they drew near the stone cistern, "for there is no fear that the elders know what we have done; and this may be the last time we shall ever taste this water."

Thus speaking, with a little sadness in his face, which was also visible in that of his companion, he made her sit down on a stone, and was about to place himself very close to her side; she, however, repelled him, though not unkindly.

Thrill and Reward of Participation

"Nay, Josiah," said she, giving him a timid push with her maiden hand, "thee must sit farther off, on the other stone, with the spring between us. What would the sisters say, if thee were to sit so close to me?"

"But we are of the world's people now, Miriam," answered Josiah.

The girl persisted in her prudery, nor did the youth, in fact, seem altogether free from a similar sort of shyness; so they sat apart from each other, gazing up the hill, where the moonlight discovered the tops of a group of buildings. While their attention was thus occupied, a party of travellers, who had come wearily up the long ascent, made a halt to refresh themselves at the spring. There were three men, a woman, and a little girl and boy. Their attire was mean, covered with a dust of the summer's day, and damp with the night-dew; they all looked woebegone, as if the cares and sorrows of the world had made their steps heavier as they climbed the hill; even the two little children appeared older in evil days than the young man and maiden who had first approached the spring.

"Good evening to you, young folks," was the salutation of the travellers; and "Good evening, friends," replied the youth and damsel.

"Is that white building the Shaker meeting-house?" asked one of the strangers. "And are those the red roofs of the Shaker village?"

"Friend, it is the Shaker Village," answered Josiah, after some hesitation.

The travellers, who, from the first, had looked suspiciously at the garb of these young people, now taxed them with an intention which all the circumstances, indeed, rendered too obvious to be mistaken.

"It is true, Friends," replied the young man, summoning up his courage. "Miriam and I have a gift to love each other, and we are going among the world's people, to live after their fashion. And ye know that we do not transgress the law of the land; and neither ye, nor the elders themselves, have a right to hinder us."

"Yet you think it expedient to depart without leave-taking," remarked one of the travellers.

"Yes, ye-a," said Josiah, reluctantly, "because father Job is a very awful man to speak with; and being aged himself, he has but little charity for what he calls the iniquities of the flesh."

"Well," said the stranger, "we will neither use force to bring you back to the village, nor will we betray you to the elders. But sit you here awhile, and when you have heard what we shall tell you of the world which we have left, and into which you are going, perhaps you will turn back with us of your own accord. What say you?" added he, turning to his companions. "We have travelled thus far without becoming known to each other. Shall we tell our stories, here by this pleasant spring, for our own pastime, and the benefit of these misguided young lovers?"

In accordance with this proposal, the whole party stationed themselves round the stone cistern; the two children, being very weary, fell asleep upon the damp earth, and the pretty Shaker girl, whose feelings were those of a nun or a Turkish lady, crept as close as possible to the female traveller, and as far as she well could from the unknown men. The same person who had hitherto been the chief spokesman now stood by, waving his hat in his hand, and suffered the moonlight to fall full upon his front.

"In me," said he, with a certain majesty of utterance, "in me, you behold a poet."

Though a lithographic print of this gentleman is extant, it may be well to notice that he was now nearly forty, a thin and stooping figure, in a black coat, out at elbows; notwithstanding the ill condition of his attire, there were about him several tokens of a peculiar sort of foppery, unworthy of a mature man, particularly in the arrangement of his hair, which was so disposed as to give all possible loftiness and breadth to his forehead. However, he had an intelligent eye, and, on the whole, a marked countenance.

"A poet!" repeated the young Shaker, a little puzzled how to understand such a designation, seldom heard in the utilitarian community where he had spent his life. "Oh, ay, Miriam, he means a varse-maker, thee must know."

This remark jarred upon the susceptible nerves of the poet; nor could he help wondering what strange fatality had put into this young man's mouth an epithet, which ill-natured people had affirmed to be more proper to his merit than the one assumed by himself.

"True, I am a verse-maker," he resumed, "but my verse is no more than the material body into which I breathe the celestial soul of thought. Alas! how many a pang has it cost me, this same insensibility to the ethereal essence of poetry, with which you have here tortured me again, at the moment when I am to relinquish my profession forever! O Fate! why hast thou warred with Nature, turning all her higher and more perfect gifts to the ruin of me, their possessor? What is the voice of song, when the world lacks the ear of taste? How can I rejoice in my strength and delicacy of feeling, when they have but made great sorrows out of little ones? Have I dreaded scorn like death, and yearned for fame as others pant for vital air, only to find myself in a middle state between obscurity and infamy? But I have my revenge! I could have given existence to a thousand bright creations. I crush them into my heart, and there let them putrefy! I shake off the dust of my feet against my countrymen! But posterity, tracing my footsteps up this weary hill, will cry shame upon the unworthy age that drove one of the fathers of American song to end his days in a Shaker village!"

During this harangue, the speaker gesticulated with great energy, and, as poetry is the natural language of passion, there appeared reason to apprehend his final explosion into an ode extempore. The reader understands that, for all these bitter words, he was a kind, gentle, harmless, poor fellow enough, whom Nature, tossing her ingredients together without looking at her recipe, had sent into the world with too much of one sort of brain, and hardly any of another.

"Friend," said the young Shaker, in some perplexity, "thee seemest to have met with great troubles; and, doubtless, I should pity them, if—if I could but understand what they were."

"Happy in your ignorance!" replied the poet, with an air of sublime superiority. "To your coarser mind, perhaps, I may seem to speak of more important griefs when I add, what I had well nigh forgotten, that I am out at elbows, and almost starved to death. At any rate, you have the advice and example of one individual to warn you back; for I am come hither, a disappointed man, flinging aside the fragments of my hopes, and seeking shelter in the calm retreat which you are so anxious to leave."

"I thank thee, friend," rejoined the youth, "But I do not mean to be a poet, nor, Heaven be praised! do I think Miriam ever made a varse in her life. So we need not fear thy disappointments. But, Miriam," he added, with real concern, "thee knowest that the elders admit nobody that has not a gift to be useful. Now, what under the sun can they do with this poor varse-maker?"

"Nay, Josiah, do not thee discourage the poor man," said the girl, in all simplicity and kindness. "Our hymns are very rough, and perhaps they may trust him to smooth them."

Without noticing this hint of professional employment, the poet turned away, and gave himself up to a sort of vague reverie, which he called thought. Sometimes he watched the moon, pouring a silvery liquid on the clouds, through which it slowly melted till they became all bright; then he saw the same sweet radiance dancing on the leafy trees which rustled as if to shake it off, or sleeping on the high tops of hills, or hovering down in distant valleys, like the material of unshaped dreams; lastly, he looked into the spring, and there the light was mingling with the water. In its crystal bosom, too, beholding all heaven reflected there, he found an emblem of a pure and tranquil breast. He listened to that most ethereal of all sounds, the song of crickets, coming in full choir upon the wind, and fancied that if moonlight could be heard, it would sound just like that. Finally, he took a draught at the Shaker spring, and, as if it were the true Castalia, was forthwith moved to compose a lyric, a Farewell to his Harp, which he swore should be its closing strain, the last verse that an ungrateful world should have from him. This effusion with two or three other little pieces, subsequently written, he took the first opportunity to send, by one of the Shaker brethren, to Concord, where they were published in the New Hampshire Patriot.

Meantime, another of the Canterbury pilgrims, one so different from the poet that the delicate fancy of the latter could hardly have conceived of him, began to relate his sad experience. He was a small man, of quick, and unquiet gestures, about fifty years old, with a narrow forehead, all wrinkled and drawn together. He held in his hand a pencil, and a card of some commission-merchant in foreign parts, on the back of which, for there was light enough to read or write by, he seemed ready to figure out a calculation.

"Young man," said he, abruptly, "what quantity of land do the Shakers own here, in Canterbury?"

"That is more than I can tell thee, friend," answered Josiah, "but it is a very rich establishment, and for a long way by the roadside thee may guess the land to be ours, by the neatness of the fences."

"And what may be the value of the whole," continued the stranger, "with all the buildings and improvements, pretty nearly, in round numbers?"

"Oh, a monstrous sum, —more than I can reckon," replied the young Shaker.

"Well, sir," said the pilgrim, "there was a day, and not very long ago, neither, when I stood at my counting-room window, and watched the signal flags of three of my own ships entering the harbor, from the East Indies, from Liverpool, and from up the Straits, and I would not have given the invoice of the least of them for the title-deeds of this whole Shaker settlement. You stare. Perhaps, now, you won't believe that I could have put more value on a little piece of paper, no bigger than the palm of your hand, than all these solid acres of grain, grass, and pasture-land would sell for?"

"I don't dispute it, friend," answered Josiah, "but I know I had rather have fifty acres of this good land than a whole sheet of thy paper."

"You may say so now," said the ruined merchant, bitterly, "for my name would not be worth the paper I should write it on. Of course, you must have heard of my failure?"

And the stranger mentioned his name, which, however mighty it might have been in the commercial world, the young Shaker had never heard of among the Canterbury hills.

"Not heard of my failure!" exclaimed the merchant, considerably piqued. "Why, it was spoken of on 'Change in London, and from Boston to New Orleans men trembled in their shoes. At all events, I did fail, and you see me here on my road to the Shaker village, where, doubtless (for the Shakers are a shrewd sect), they will have a due respect for my experience, and give me the management of the trading part of the concern, in which case I think I can pledge myself to double their capital in four or five years. Turn back with me, young man; for though you will never meet with my good luck, you can hardly escape my bad."

"I will not turn back for this," replied Josiah, calmly, "any more than for the advice of the varse-maker, between whom and thee, friend, I see a sort of likeness, though I can't justly say where it lies. But Miriam and I can earn our daily bread among the world's people as well as in the Shaker village. And do we want anything more, Miriam?"

"Nothing more, Josiah," said the girl, quietly.

"Yes, Miriam, and daily bread for some other little mouths, if God send them," observed the simple Shaker lad.

Miriam did not reply, but looked down into the spring, where she encountered the image of her own pretty face, blushing within the prim little bonnet. The third pilgrim now took up the conversation. He was a sunburnt countryman, of tall frame, and bony strength, on whose rude and manly face there appeared a darker, more sullen and obstinate despondency, than on those of either the poet or the merchant.

"Well, now, youngster," he began, "these folks have had their say, so I'll take my turn. My story will cut but a poor figure by the side of theirs; for I never supposed that I could have a right to meat and drink, and great praise besides, only for tagging rhymes together, as it seems this man does; nor ever tried to get the substance of hundreds into my own hands, like the trader there. When I was about of your years, I married me a wife,—just such a neat and pretty young woman as Miriam, if that's her name,—and all I asked of Providence was an ordinary blessing on the sweat of my brow, so that we might be decent and comfortable, and have daily bread for ourselves, and for some other little mouths that we soon had to feed. We had no very great prospects before us; but I never wanted to be idle; and I thought it a matter of course that the Lord would help me, because I was willing to help myself."

"And didn't He help thee, friend?" demanded Josiah, with some eagerness.

"No," said the yeoman, sullenly; "for then you would not have seen me here. I have labored hard for years, and my means have been growing narrower, and my living poorer, and my heart colder and heavier, all the time; till at last I could bear it no longer. I set myself down to calculate whether I had best go on the Oregon expedition, or come here to the Shaker village; but I had not hope enough left in me to begin the world over again; and to make my story short, here I am. And now, youngster, take my advice, and turn back; or else, some few years hence, you'll have to climb this hill, with as heavy a heart as mine."

This simple story had a strong effect on the young fugitives. The misfortunes of the poet and merchant had won little sympathy from their plain good sense and unworldly feelings, qualities which made them such unprejudiced and inflexible judges, that few men would have chosen to take the opinion of this youth and maiden as to the wisdom or folly of their pursuits. But here was one whose simple wishes had resembled their own, and who, after efforts which almost gave him a right to claim success from fate, had failed in accomplishing them.

"But thy wife, friend?" exclaimed the younger man. "What became of the pretty girl, like Miriam? Oh, I am afraid she is dead!"

"Yes, poor man, she must be dead, —she and the children, too," sobbed Miriam.

The female pilgrim had been leaning over the spring, wherein latterly a tear or two might have been seen to fall, and form its little circle on the surface of the water. She now looked up, disclosing features still comely, but which had acquired an expression of fretfulness, in the same long course of evil fortune that had thrown a sullen gloom over the temper of the unprosperous yeoman.

"I am his wife," said she, a shade of irritability just perceptible in the sadness of her tone. "These poor little things, asleep on the ground, are two of our children. We had two more, but God has provided better for them than we could, by taking them to Himself."

"And what would thee advise Josiah and me to do?" asked Miriam, this being the first question which she had put to either of the strangers.

"Tis a thing almost against nature for a woman to try to part true lovers," answered the yeoman's wife, after a pause: "but I'll speak as truly to you as if these were my dying words. Though my husband told you some of our troubles, he didn't mention the greatest, and that which makes all the rest so hard to bear. If you and your sweetheart marry, you'll be kind and pleasant to each other for a year or two, and while that's the case, you never will repent; but, by and by, he'll grow gloomy, rough, and hard to please, and you'll be peevish, and full of little angry fits, and apt to be complaining by the fireside, when he comes to rest himself from his troubles out of doors; so your love will wear away by little and little, and leave you miserable at last. It has been so with us; and yet my husband and I were true lovers once, if ever two young folks were."

As she ceased, the yeoman and his wife exchanged a glance, in which there was more and warmer affection than they had supposed to have escaped the frost of a wintry fire, in either of their breasts. At that moment, when they stood on the utmost verge of married life, one word fitly spoken, or perhaps one peculiar look, had they had mutual confidence enough to reciprocate it, might have renewed all their old feelings, and sent them back, resolved to sustain each other amid the struggles of the world. But the crisis passed and never came again. Just then, also, the children, roused by their mother's voice, looked up, and added their wailing accents to the testimony borne by all the Canterbury pilgrims against the world from which they fled.

"We are tired and hungry!" cried they. "Is it far to the Shaker village?"

The Shaker youth and maiden looked mournfully into each other's eyes. They had but stepped across the threshold of their homes, when lo! the dark array of cares and sorrows that rose up to warn them back. The varied narratives of the strangers had arranged themselves unto a parable; they seemed not merely instances of woeful fate that had befallen others, but shadowy omens of disappointed hope and unavailing toil, domestic grief and estranged affection, that would cloud the onward path of these poor fugitives. But after one instant's hesitation, they opened their arms, and sealed their resolve with as pure and fond an embrace as ever youthful love had hallowed.

"We will not go back." said they. "The world never can be dark to us, for we will always love one another."

Then the Canterbury pilgrims went up the hill, while the poet chanted a drear and desperate stanza of the Farewell to his Harp, fitting music for that melancholy band. They sought a home where all former ties of nature or society would be sundered, and all old distinctions levelled, and a cold and passionless security be substituted for mortal hope and fear, as in that other refuge of the world's weary outcasts, the grave. The lovers drank at the Shaker spring, and then, with chastened hopes, but more confiding affections, went on to mingle in an untried life.

Discussion of
"The Canterbury Pilgrims"

Many of the themes which he developed at length in later stories and novels can be glimpsed in early form in Nathaniel Hawthorne's "The Canterbury Pilgrims." Here we find hints of guilt, self-contemplation, isolation, and emotional sterility that become dominant ideas in later work. In "The Canterbury Pilgrims," however, they only add to the ambiguity that is basic to this story.

The Shaker village, for instance, is set on a hill, as though symbolizing a lofty ideal, but the only members of the group meeting at the spring who have any idealism left are running away from it. The setting by moonlight seems appropriate for young love but is also suggestive of that falseness—the moonshine—that has led the travellers astray and has precipitated their retreat from life.

The biographies that are related to introduce the young Shaker couple to the world cover a wide spectrum of American life. The artist, adrift in his own ego, is incapable of competing in a world that is not anxious to indulge him. The ruined financier is equally unrealistic, as young Josiah dimly perceives. Having lost all sense of real values in increasingly abstract speculations, he is no more prepared than the artist to change. His failure, in his own eyes, was merely "bad luck." Already he is calculating how he can manipulate the property he is sure the Shakers will want him to manage.

The third traveller, generally personifying labor as the others stand for art and business, is harder to dismiss. Involvement that is essentially selfish may be expected to prove unsatisfying, but the account of the simple laborer is disquietingly prophetic of what the young couple may well experience. All the easy answers are brought into question: apparent love is not an automatic answer to all problems; hard work may not be crowned with material success; the Lord may not help in ways that are expected.

This story does not conclude with the solution to anyone's problems. Those who are renouncing the world for the "cold and passionless security" of the communal Shaker village seem to Hawthorne to be undergoing a kind of death. But the prospects of the young couple are not without clouds. Forbidden by the rules of their group from marrying, they are counting on the depth and purity of their love to sustain them in a totally different world. It is worthy of note that the ending of this story is carefully non-committal. If love propels us to try, it does not guarantee our success.

Thrill and Reward of Participation 277

The one encouraging note in this rather gloomy account is sounded in Hawthorne's description of what might have happened if the older couple, now so disillusioned in their relationship with each other, had been capable even now of "one word fitly spoken, or perhaps one peculiar look, had they had mutual confidence enough to reciprocate it."

Hawthorne seems to suggest that the only real hope lies in love, but love cannot be taken for granted. That this love must finally be focused toward others—and not toward oneself or non-human things—also comes through clearly. Our only hope for success lies in the active love of others. Any involvement short of this will inevitably prove disappointing.

Index of Selections Quoted

"After Apple-Picking," 226-228
"An Airman's Letter," 195-197
"Another April," 76, 79-86
The Autocrat of the Breakfast Table, 76, 87-88
"Baker's Blue-Jay Yarn," 160-165
The Bible, 175, 180, 204-207, 228
The Book of Mormon, 3, 8, 131
"The Bride Comes to Yellow Sky," 3, 16-27
"Can You Get Along With Your In-Laws?" 76, 89-92
"Canterbury Pilgrims," 249, 268-277
"The Challenge of Teaching," 61-67
"A Chapter on Ears," 168
"Cipher in the Snow," 39-41
"Concord Hymn," 174, 193-194
"The Devil and Daniel Webster," 134-147
Dialogues of Plato, 47-52
Doctrine and Covenants, 34
"The Faces of Anger," 60-61
"First Lesson," 54-58
"The Fish, the Man, and the Spirit," 68-69
Great Possessions, 248, 260-265
"A Great Teacher's Method," 42-45
"Haircut," 148-159
"He Ate and Drank the Precious Words," 70
The Hind and the Panther, 3, 5
"The Importance of Loafing," 220-225
"Independence," 12-13
"The Indispensable Opposition," 3, 6-9
"Keeping Mentally Alive," 248, 254-259
"Life," 247, 252-253
"Life of Ma Parker," 229-235
"Mother of Comptons," 175, 198-203
"Neighbor Rosicky," 101-128, 176
"Oven Bird," 247, 250-251
Past and Present, 215-218
"Poor Relations," 168

The Republic, 49-52
"The Roots of Honor," 242-244
Sartor Resartus, 218
"The Secret Heart," 76-78
"The Secret Life of Walter Mitty," 236-241
"Seven Qualities of an Educated Person," 59-60
"The Slave," 14-15
"Song of Myself," 174-180, 182
"Stopping by Woods on a Snowy Evening," 248, 266-267
"Symposium," 47-49
"To Fight Aloud," 181-182
A Tramp Abroad, 160-165
"What Is Liberty?" 9-10
"What Makes a Great Book?" 37-38
"The Woman," 175
"A Wreath for Miss Totten," 174, 183-192

Index of References to Authors

Mortimer Adler, 37-38
Louis Agassiz, 42-45
Aristophanes, 132
Aristotle, 46
Peter Balgha, 36
Stephen Vincent Benét, 134-147
Robert Browning, 36
Hortense Calisher, 183-192
Al Capp, 132
Thomas Carlyle, 213, 215-219, 235
Willa Cather, 76, 101-128
Cicero, 46, 75
Robert P. Tristram Coffin, 77-78
Hardin Craig, 213-214
Stephen Crane, 3, 16-27
René Descartes, 55
Emily Dickinson, 70, 174, 181-182
Benjamin Disraeli, 247
John Donne, 252
John Dryden, 3, 5
Irwin Edman, 53-58
George Eliot, 173
Ralph Waldo Emerson, 174, 193-194, 218
Carl Ewald, 36
Edward D. Fales, Jr., 89-92
William Faulkner, 36
Mary E. Wilkins Freeman, 214
Robert Frost, 226-228, 247, 250-251, 266-267
Richard Fuller, 131
Zona Gale, 175
John Galsworthy, 214
William Gibson, 36
Johann Wolfgang Goethe, 216
David Grayson, 248, 260-265
Manly Hall, 213
Nathaniel Hawthorne, 249, 268-277

George Herbert, 247, 252-253
John Holmes, 214
Oliver Wendell Holmes, 76, 87-88
Mark Hopkins, 46
Leigh Hunt, 68-69
Thomas Henry Huxley, 36
A. E. Johnson, 53
Helen Keller, 36
Charles Lamb, 133, 166-168
Ring Lardner, 148-159
Walter Lippmann, 3, 6-9
Katherine Mansfield, 229-235
Milton S. Mayer, 198-203
David O. McKay, 35-36
Jean E. Mizer, 39-41
John Henry Newman, 36
James Oppenheim, 3, 14-15
Harry A. Overstreet, 248, 254-259
Plato, 46-52, 56
Ezra Pound, 42
John Ruskin, 33, 242-244
Carl Sandburg, 227
Arthur Schopenhauer, 56
Samuel Scudder, 42-45
William Shakespeare, 157, 230
Joseph Smith, 34, 63
T. V. Smith, 53
Socrates, 46-52, 53
Robert Louis Stevenson, 225
Jesse Stuart, 79-85
Henry David Thoreau, 3, 12-13, 218
James Thurber, 132, 236-241
Lionel Trilling, 36
Mark Twain, 36, 38, 76, 93-100, 133, 160-165
Carl Van Doren, 37
Voltaire, 6
Daniel Webster, 134-147
E. B. White, 132
Walt Whitman, 174, 176-180, 182
Oscar Wilde, 213

Index of References to Authors

Woodrow Wilson, 3, 9-11
William Wordsworth, 214
Brigham Young, 34-35
Lin Yutang, 219, 220-225